Concise English Handbook

Instructor's Annotated Edition

Concise English Handbook

[redacted]

James W. Kirkland

East Carolina University

Collett B. Dilworth, Jr.

East Carolina University

D. C. Heath and Company

Lexington, Massachusetts Toronto

Acknowledgments

Amy Lowell, "The Taxi" from *The Complete Poetical Works of Amy Lowell.* Copyright © 1955 by Houghton Mifflin Company. Copyright © 1983 renewed by Houghton Mifflin Company, Brinton P. Roberts, Esq. and G. d'Andelot Belin, Esq. and reprinted by permission of Houghton Mifflin Company.

[redacted]

Published simultaneously in Canada.

Printed in the United States of America.

International Standard Book Number: Student's Edition
0-669-06005-4
Instructor's Edition
0-669-06008-9

Library of Congress Catalog Card Number: 84-81088

For Paula and Colette

To the Instructor

The *Concise English Handbook* is based on the principle that writing is a purposeful process involving discovery, precision in thought and language, and sensitivity to audience.

The *Handbook* offers succinct guidance in the processes of writing and in the features of edited American English. It is more than a grammar book, although it does treat grammatical topics—more than simply a compendium of "rules," although it does survey the conventions of edited American English. Instead, this is a manual emphasizing how writers think and how writing affects readers. For example, the text not only defines and illustrates types of modifiers, it also discusses the contexts in which writers use modifiers and identifies the effects they have on readers; and beyond defining and illustrating common writing errors, it discusses why writers make such errors and identifies their undesirable effects on readers.

The book's organization reflects the essential task confronting writers. Writing occurs in a context that influences the writer throughout the process, from conception of subject to choice of particular words. The *Handbook,* therefore, first addresses the process as a whole and then examines crucial aspects such as determining purpose and perspective, generating ideas, and arranging material. The focus subsequently narrows to the particulars of structuring sentences, choosing the most appropriate words, and punctuating. We then introduce sentence errors in a separate section because we believe that only after students understand the nature of the writing process can they intelligently identify and correct sentence errors in the context of their own writing.

This arrangement also permits the student to read the chapters sequentially to gain a systematic orientation to the processes and technicalities of composition. Chapters 1–6 and 9–17 are especially helpful in explaining writing methods and stylistic options. Chapters 7 and 8 offer background in basic grammatical terminology, terminology useful in thinking about the English sentence. Other topics in the book include spelling, writing for special purposes, and writing the research paper.

The *Handbook* has also been designed for use as a reference. The student may refer to the chart inside the front cover to locate the major topics, which are numbered and organized in eight main parts. The pages in each part are marked with colored tabs visible on the page edges when the book is closed; so, using the labels on the back cover, the student can quickly locate each part and the topic numbers within it.

In addition, the *Concise English Handbook* provides succinct definitions of terms; clear supporting examples, including multiple drafts of selected pieces of student writing; exercises designed to help students understand and practice the principles discussed in each chapter; and a detailed research section based on the 1984 MLA parenthetical documentation style.

Acknowledgements

Many people helped us prepare this book. We express our special appreciation to Phyllis Makuck for her word processing, editorial assistance, and commentary and to Mark Coley for his work on the exercises. We are also most grateful to Ted Simpson, Paul Smith, and Holt Johnson of D. C. Heath for their guidance and encouragement and to Libby Van de Kerkhove, who designed the format.

We thank our many students who provided their writing as examples in the text, especially Sarah Jo Poindexter, Lisa Anne Oughton, Lisa Edwards, Marty Cherry, Joseph Applegate, Richard Hudson, and Amanda Thomas.

We are indebted to the scholars and teachers who reviewed this text in manuscript and gave us invaluable advice: Lynn Beene, The University of New Mexico; Barbara R. Carson, University of Georgia; James P. Davis, University of Illinois at Champaign-Urbana; James Helvey, Davidson County Community College; Kathleen Latimer, Central State University; Timothy P. Martin, University of Pennsylvania; David A. McMurrey, University of Texas—Austin; Elaine M. Miller, Seton Hall University; Terry Miller, Indian River Community College; Allen Ramsey, Central Missouri State University; Thomas N. Salter, Eastern Connecticut State College; Brooks Thorlaksson, California State University, Chico; Evelyn B. Thornton, Texas Southern University; Samuel Watson, Jr., The University of North Carolina at Charlotte; William H. Wiatt, Indiana University; William F. Woods, Wichita State University; and Stephen F. Wozniak, Palomar College.

To the Student

The main goals of the *Concise English Handbook* are to help you become a better writer and to help you find rewards in better writing. Thus, the book treats features of the writing process and elements of sentences and paragraphs not as mechanical parts to be assembled according to rigid formulas, but as options at the disposal of your creativity. As you refine your ability to exercise these options, you will find your consciousness developing in ways unique to writers.

Contents

II Structuring Sentences

IV Punctuating and Following Mechanical Conventions

V Avoiding Common Sentence Errors

1 · Introduction

1a Literacy

Writing, as we use the term in this book, is more than an encoding of speech sounds; it is an act of literacy. Literate people spend important parts of their lives making meaning by reading and writing because, among all the ways of communicating, written texts are uniquely efficient and powerful. For example, consider the text of a note intercepted one Friday by the teacher of an eleventh grade English class:

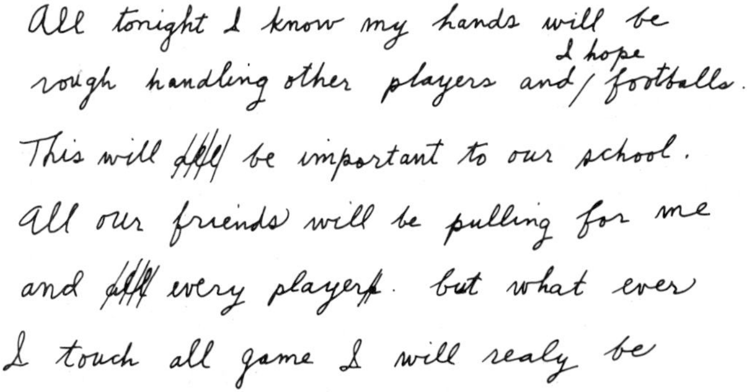
All tonight I know my hands will be
rough handling other players and I hope footballs.
This will be important to our school.
All our friends will be pulling for me
and every player. but what ever
I touch all game I will realy be
trying to touch your heart.

We might dismiss this note as awkward adolescent emoting unless we examine the writing in its context. The writer, a defensive lineman, had a particular audience of one in mind: his girl friend. And he had a particular objective in mind: to communicate certain feelings. Under no conditions was the note meant to be read by anyone else, so the teacher later forwarded it without comment to the young woman. But clearly the young man wanted the message to be read, not heard. He had used writing to compose a special thought based on a figurative contrast particularly meaningful to him. The thought was that his efforts on the football field that night, while important to the entire school, would also be intended especially for his girl friend. The figurative contrast is between physically manhandling other football players and psychologically touching her affections. The writer took some care to revise his work by deleting, adding, and substituting words to make his message more accurate and less redundant.

Obviously his proofreading overlooked errors in capitalization, spelling, and punctuation. Nevertheless the note demonstrates the essential virtue of written composition: it joined the boy and the girl, the writer and the reader, as a community of meaning-makers through a medium that offers an unmatched blend of convenience and power. And if anyone wished, the message could be preserved and reexperienced.

The full benefits of reading and writing, however, occur only for those who adopt the spirit of literacy. This spirit directs people to be alert to life and its possibilities. It encourages them to seek opportunities to originate and discover new ways of living and to share and gain new experiences, new feelings, new knowledge, and new ways of thinking about problems. Those who practice literacy for such purposes assume that people can fundamentally improve themselves and their world. Without this spirit, the means of literacy are useful only in maintaining records; with this spirit, the means insure the growth of consciousness for a lifetime.

1b The practical good of composition

Such benefits are rarely appreciated by people who have either not had or not taken the opportunity to enjoy the fruits of literacy. Students who view writing as merely the imitation of incomprehensible models wonder bitterly why schools require the formal practice of writing. As we have suggested, the basic objective of composition in the curriculum is to help students acquire and strengthen the spirit of literacy. For people without the spirit, practical reasons for developing composition skills are unconvincing. Motivated people, however, are encouraged by the specific practical rationale that writing can help increase the power to think.

When, as a writer, you observe yourself and the world, you are compelled to try to achieve any number of such tasks as these: demonstrating which phenomena are related, establishing what something is, showing how or why something functions, proving the merit of a belief, predicting what will happen, or creating an impression of what took place. This effort helps you to originate thoughts and feelings and give them an enduring presence. Writing to explain or argue or share your feelings helps you to select the crucial features of experience, to manipulate them intellectually and, as a result, to reach conclusions and insights. For example, the high school football player quoted earlier selected aspects of his experience, linked them, made predictions about them, and thus clarified and perhaps strengthened how he felt.

Of course, the social rationale for the study and practice of composition is that it makes for good communication. For a democracy to exist, its citizens must undertake thoughtful, careful discourse, and literate discourse is the means for our most thoughtful, most careful communication in language. The lack of an ability to communicate literately handicaps citizens trying to inform themselves on how best to govern, and if they lose the abilities of self-government, they will lose self-government as well as the rights that go with it. Composition persists throughout the school curriculum, therefore, because citizens in general and educators in particular are convinced that it can help foster the flexible strength of mind required for a full, productive life—the type of life that enriches the individual and our democracy.

1c The writing process

We have defined writing as an act of literacy. This act is commonly understood as a process involving the four functions outlined below.

1. *Prewriting.* As good writers begin their work, they spend time thinking about the task ahead of them. They get an image of their audience and of the reasons they are addressing this audience. They decide on their topic and on how broadly they will treat it. They search their own knowledge and attitudes for relevant information, and they may consult external sources, such as libraries and other knowledgeable people. They make tentative plans for the way their writing will be organized, and they tentatively adopt a "voice," an attitude toward their topic and audience.

2. *Writing.* Initially guided by their prewriting, writers begin putting words on paper (or on the screen of a word processor). They do so, however, ever ready to reassume the prewriting perspective and rethink their intentions. As they write, ideas occur and unanticipated patterns emerge. Good writers are also guided by material they have already written. Prior material determines options for the writing yet to come because it is an avenue of meaning already under construction.

3. *Revising.* "To revise" means to "see again." Periodically, upon completing portions of writing or entire drafts, good writers mentally remove themselves from the intentions they derived in planning and composing, and they consider their work again as if they were reading their text for the first time. Their revision lets them improve the text by substituting, adding, deleting, or moving words, sentences, and paragraphs. Sometimes a writer conceives something that belongs in the essay but does not fit with prior material. Then the prior text must be rewritten to accommodate the new idea; the avenue of meaning must be reconstructed in a new direction.

4. *Editing.* In preparing the final draft, good writers shift their primary concern from the ideas, organization, and flavor of the composition to the mechanics of spelling, usage, and grammar. While they will also have been concerned with these things during composing and revising, they proofread the final working draft with special care to note any language errors, and after the final copy is ready, they proofread it to note any typographical errors or careless omissions.

1d Qualities of effective writing

When thinking about the qualities of composition, you will find it helpful to consider three features: invention, arrangement, and style. *Invention* concerns the writer's ideas. Are they well developed and logical? Is the thesis significant? Are generalizations supported by specifics? Are narrative events worth reporting, and are descriptive details well selected? *Arrangement* concerns the organization of the composition. Do the parts (the sentences and paragraphs, the ideas and images) interrelate so that each part helps every other to give the reader a coherent understanding? *Style* concerns the way words work together in the sentences. Are the best words put in the best places? Are the conventions of written standard English observed? The quality of a composition depends on all of these features. Disorganization or confused language can obscure the most brilliant insights, while even the most rigorous coherence and stylistic conventionality cannot save a paper without significant meaning.

This concise handbook is organized to help guide you in the writing process and to help improve the invention, arrangement, and style that your compositions offer your readers. Part I analyzes the process; Part II describes the basic language resources at your disposal; Part III advises you on using those resources effectively; Part IV describes rules of punctuation and manuscript mechanics; Parts V and VI treat the most common word and sentence errors made by writers; Part VII advises you on writing in certain specialized circumstances; and Part VIII takes you through the process of writing the research paper.

I Composing the Essay

2 · Determining Purpose and Perspective

2a Decide on your reasons for writing.

Our reasons for writing influence fundamentally what and how we write. Students often write in school solely to prove mastery of specific knowledge or skills to a teacher. In such cases, the writer's search for subject matter will be largely confined to course content, and the style of the paper will be governed by the student's understanding of what the teacher expects. Other school compositions, such as reports of original research and essays on ideas original to the writer, are written to give new information. In these cases, the subject matter and style are governed primarily by the student's unique knowledge, feelings, imagination, and sense of audience.

Whatever type of writing we undertake, when we write we construe relationships among four elements that make up the environment of literacy; the elements are a reader, a writer, a text, and the part of the world that we draw on for our subject matter. The quality of a composition will depend in part on how well the writer understands the particular elements in a particular writing task. Different kinds of writing place different relative emphases among the elements. On page 9 is a diagram schematizing these shifting emphases.

1. *Persuading.* As a *persuasive* writer, your objective is to get your reader to do something such as vote for someone, buy a product, participate in an activity, or behave in a particular way. So in determining content and style, you must be primarily guided by an understanding of your audience. What type of people are you trying to persuade? What are their values, fears, hopes, needs? Your choice of subject matter, the way you, the writer, appear in your prose, and the extent to

Continuum of Writing Environments

	(argumentative)			
type of writing:	persuasive	expository	expressive	literary
writer's primary concern:	with reader	with subject	with writer	with text
writer's role:	advocate	teacher	confidant	artist
reader's role:	skeptic	student	confidant	audience

which the writing calls attention to itself should all advance your persuasive objective. Generally, persuasion requires a subject matter directly relevant to your audience's needs, an attractive, trustworthy image of the writer, and a style that does not divert the reader's attention from your appeal.

Dear Roommate,

When we began the semester sharing this dormitory room, we kept our things in order. Recently, though, we have given so much energy to our studies and our social lives that we have neglected our room. Now the dirty and clean clothes, the empty cans and bottles, old newspapers, food-smeared plates, books, and miscellaneous junk are so thick that it's getting downright hard to survive in this place, much less get in and out of it. You've been complaining lately about not being able to bring a date up here and about not even being able to study at your desk. Obviously we need to clean this place and start again our old habit of straightening up a mess as soon as it has been made. With the place we live in back in order, everything else at school should look better too. Let's get together and do it this Thursday!

2. *Explaining.* As an *expository* writer, your objective is to inform your readers about something new to them. Such writing does oblige you to attend to the nature of your

audience: What do they already know? What are their interests? But, as an expositor, you must be primarily guided by your subject matter. Like a good teacher, you should first come to understand your topic well, and then you should word and arrange your message in a way that will most efficiently serve your audience. Your style should reflect enough personality to make the subject matter seem humanly interesting and learnable, but your personality should not supplant the subject at the center of your audience's attention.

Freshmen beginning their residence in a dormitory may anticipate having one of three types of roommates. The invisible roommate reveals his presence as often as twice a month. His few possessions lie unarranged from August to December. During rare appearances, he always seems on his way somewhere else. The ever-present roommate, on the other hand, is only out of the room when he might be of help. He gives no opportunity for solitude. Even when he is not talking, he makes his presence known with barely audible shuffling, tapping, sighing. The most desirable type of roommate is the good friend. He knows when his roommate needs solitude and is able to let his roommate know when he himself needs to be alone. He listens well, gives help when it is needed, and welcomes help when he needs it. The new freshman will find that the best way to get a good friend as a roommate is to be a good friend himself.

3. *Defending arguable propositions.* *Argument* is a type of writing which, like exposition, is meant to inform, yet like persuasion is meant to influence. Unlike persuasion, argument is more concerned with beliefs than with behaviors; and unlike exposition, argument strives more to establish that one proposition is preferable to certain others than to explain the nature of a given reality.

My roommate has confessed to having no interest in any subject matter in any course in college. Nevertheless she believes the money and time she is spending in college are an investment that will guarantee more riches in her future than she could ever expect otherwise. She is wrong. Underemployment and employment out-of-field are what each graduating class expects more than its preceding class. If, instead of spending $40,000 to get a degree, she would invest it in a savings institution, by age 64 she would have earned an amount over twice the difference between what the typical high school graduate and the typical college graduate earn in a career. Since, therefore, the only real benefits she can get in college are intellectual and since she has turned her back on these, she is wasting her time and money.

4. *Sharing personal experience.* *Expressive* writers must assume they can trust their audience to respect the personal information they offer. And since readers of expressive prose approach the text in order to establish a personal acquaintance, the content and style of the writing should be influenced less by the writer's understanding of the audience and of the outside world than by the writer's understanding of herself or himself. Your own feelings, values, hopes, fears, behaviors are the subject matter, and your style of writing should literately and honestly portray your personality.

Unlike most residents of Jones Dorm, I have an attractive view from my room's window. It opens on the thick, deep woods behind the tennis courts. If I stand just a few inches away from the window, I can see only the woods. I am not sure why, but I can stand there looking into the trees for an entire dusk. I'm not interested in spending any time actually in the woods, although I have explored them. I just like being removed from them while I look and think my way into them. Maybe what I'm really doing is looking deep into a quiet, cool place inside myself.

5. *Rendering aesthetic experience.* Writers of *literature* strive to create works of art and so are influenced primarily by the conventions of their particular art form. Writing poetry, fiction, and drama, therefore, requires less allegiance to an audience, to an external reality, or even to the writer's self than to the nature of the art. Note how the student-author of the passage below has used the poetic conventions of line separation and condensed, suggestive language to render an imaginative perception of his roommate.

ROOMMATE

Crusty eyelids stifle a yawn;
Feet steep in fuzzy slippers;
a mouth sags open at the television;
I wave a dim 'bye on my
fast way to the light.

2b Adopt an appropriate tone and stance.

The writer's perspective on the subject and audience is communicated by the tone and the stance evinced in the text. The *tone* of the writing reflects how the author feels about the subject. An objective tone communicates an open mind; an urgent tone communicates emotional commitment; an ironic or satirical tone can suggest disgust; a whimsical tone conveys amusement. *Stance* reflects the author's attitude toward the audience. It may be described in such terms as friendly, aloof, sympathetic, antagonistic, personal, impersonal. We may describe the example of persuasion given above as serious, even urgent, in tone, but friendly in stance. The expository paragraph above suggests the author has approached the topic with a combination of objectivity and amusement; his stance is impersonal but not aloof.

The types of purpose and perspective discussed in this chapter may characterize a piece of writing in general, but they do not necessarily describe all features of a composition. To say, for example, an essay is on the whole expressive is not to say it necessarily lacks expository, literary, or persuasive elements. Note that the expressive paragraph on page 11 begins with an expository description of the writer's dormitory room. On the other hand, an essay might seem expository and still have a strong persuasive effect by objectively describing conditions so intolerable that readers are moved to change them. As you begin the writing process, therefore, your purpose and perspective should guide but not inhibit your thinking, organization, and style.

Exercise

Read each passage below; identify it as persuasive, argumentative, expository, or expressive; and answer the following questions: What is the writer's purpose? Who is the intended audience? What is the writer's tone?

1. Animals are the responsibility of society because we are nature's caretakers. But we often buy a pet without realizing the responsibility that comes with it. One of the most important of these responsibilities is to have our pets spayed or neutered if we do not intend to keep their offspring.

   A persuasive passage written to urge pet owners to desex the pets they do not intend to breed. The tone is one of serious commitment.

2. Strategic deterence is based on a simple idea: neither side will attack the other because an inevitable counterattack would devastate the side that launched first. Effective deterence, therefore, requires each side to know that the other's weaponry is strong enough to survive an attack and still accomplish its destructive mission.

   An expository passage written to explain a concept to a general audience of adults. The tone is objective.

3. I lived adventures every summer of my childhood. My friends and I would trek though the rolling, wooded hills around our homes in search of monsters, hidden treasure, or the simple but dark unknown. At five, I could run though the forest alone, touch snakes, startle rabbits, climb trees, and wade in black glop.

   An expressive account written to share personal memories of childhood with an audience trusted to be appreciative. The tone is one of enjoyment.

4. Sexual harassment is a topic that deserves everyone's attention. For years, women have been frightened and confused about this problem. But does society consider sexual harassment a serious problem? I feel that the answer is no. For although there are agencies that handle sexual harassment complaints and courts that hear sexual

harassment cases, many people continue to tolerate harassers.

An argumentative passage written to establish that the public is indifferent to sexual harassment. The audience is people who are not aware of this indifference, but who are reasonable. The tone is somewhat indignant.

3 · Thinking and Writing

3a Develop strategies for getting started.

One of the crucial questions that every writer must answer is, "How should I begin?" The answer does not always come easily. Even highly skilled authors sometimes find themselves staring in frustration at a blank piece of paper or making one false start after another, so it is not surprising that inexperienced writers often have the same difficulties when they attempt to begin writing. The reasons vary, but several common ones are evident in the following excerpts from the journals of three students who were attempting to describe how they had written a placement essay on the subject, "Discuss the advantages or disadvantages of being the age you are now."

In writing the paper last Tuesday I really had trouble getting started. First I had to organize my thoughts, which was pretty hard to do since my mind wasn't on writing, but on how my feet were hurting from walking to the English building.

When I first saw the topic for the placement essay, I thought I would have little trouble developing it. I started writing immediately, but after a few sentences I found it more and more difficult to get across my feelings. I found it hard to write what I felt because I wasn't sure if the person who would grade it would understand what I meant.

When the topic was given to me, I read it over and over. I realized I was going to have to begin writing immediately if I was ever going to finish. The ideas did not come as readily as I had expected. My heart kept beating with nervousness as I watched everyone else write and write and write.

Distractions (either physical or mental), uncertainties about audience reaction, anxiety induced by the pressure of a deadline—these were serious concerns for this group of writers. For them and for other writers in the same predicament, one solution is to use a strategy for invention, such as the one employed by another student in the same class.

In composing the placement essay in class the other day, I first jotted down the major ideas and feelings I perceived after reading the question. I generally like to brainstorm for a few minutes before I actually start writing. Once I had written down these notes and ideas, I sorted them into categories so I could later formulate paragraphs. This process included first a general separation of thoughts (i.e., advantages opposed to disadvantages) and then I narrowed down further so that I had an adequate number of ideas under each category. I don't like to write an actual outline, but rather I jot down notes and then organize them into related groups.

In the remainder of this chapter, we will examine more specifically some of the techniques skilled writers use to generate ideas and reason logically.

3b Generate free associations.

There are three main techniques for exploiting free association:

1. *Brainstorming*—a process in which the writer lists ideas, impressions, or facts pertaining to the subject as they come to mind, without regard for sequence or coherence.

2. *Free-writing*—in which the objective is to write for a specified amount of time without stopping or lifting pen from

paper, allowing words to flow freely onto the page in a stream-of-consciousness style.

3. *Tree-diagramming*—a more structured form of free association in which the writer starts with a single idea or image and branches out into increasingly more specific clusters of related elements.

The examples below indicate more specifically how these strategies can aid the writer. All three were composed by the same student, who was experimenting with different ways to begin an expressive essay about her childhood experiences in Alaska.

Brainstorming

soft, soggy moss
green fades to gray fades to golden brown to blue
little berries scattered—salmonberries and cranberries
uneven ground, but like walking on a mattress
can see almost 200 miles to range
nippy bite to air, but still relatively warm
soft colors and soft feel to air and soft, almost misty look to the whole place
occasionally clump of willows—but they seem to fade back to flatness
lots of water, the river to one side, small ponds and puddles everywhere

Free-writing

Moss and soft and sitting on it and have a damp spot sink slowly into your jeans and get up but not really dare to sit down again a different way so another damp spot starts forming and eat berries the cranberries taste sour and creamy—not creamy, mealy but the salmonberries shock sour and tart yes tart and are an orange sick color like fish eggs but taste good in ice cream and blackberries, no not blackberries but raspberries I don't know but they taste the best and the sky is whitish grey and the horizon isn't here it just fades back and back even the mountains don't stop the horizon it just never quite meets the tundra goes on forever forever don't stop to think, think, think of water forming in small pools and trickling out to nothing and there are puddles everywhere. . . .

Tree-diagramming

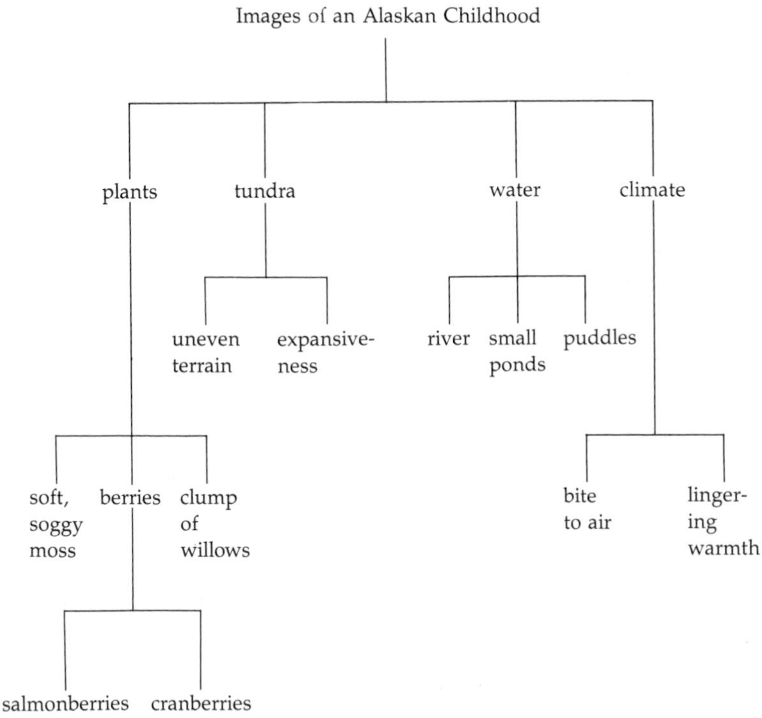

3c Keep and use a journal.

During a normal day new ideas, connections, emotions come regularly but soon fade from our awareness. By keeping a journal we can informally note these thoughts and use them later to stimulate formal composition. Some professional writers report that keeping a journal not only provides them with a record of observations but also causes them to pay closer attention to life and thereby gain insights they would otherwise miss. Note how one college student used journal entries to look beyond the surface of experience.

> One of the guitarists in the band was dressed in the same outrageous punk style as the others, but his posture spoke more than his clothes. He stood, back arched, chin in the air, eyes glazed, moving very little the whole night. He played as he was supposed to, but he never fooled around on stage with the other musicians. He was not of their spirit, so to speak. I sympathized. Sometimes I feel I'm in a group of friends, but not of them. How much do we fool ourselves about where we belong?

> What a fabulous sky! Pure, clear winter blue. If you think about it, the sky really ends at the top of the ground, not somewhere overhead. On a clear day like today, it seems like we are walking around in the sky.

3d Use classical techniques of invention.

In ancient Greece and Rome scholars carefully analyzed the types of thinking their rhetoric required. They so thoroughly classified ways to discover rhetorical points that today writers still find the traditional categories of invention helpful. Although the classical formulas were designed primarily to develop arguments, modern writers use them to discover expository and expressive insights as well. Each inventional category has a set of simple questions from which writers may choose as they inquire systematically into their subject. As the answers develop, so does the content of the essay. The questions outlined below are adapted from rhetorical analyses by Aristotle and Quintilian.

1. *Definition*—What is my topic?
   a. What is its kind? "**Suicide** is a crime against society."
   b. What are its parts? "**The preppie outlook** is a combination of ignorance, egocentricity, and a belief in fashion as the fundamental guide to life."
   c. How does it work? "**Research** proceeds by asking questions, seeking relevant information, guessing answers, and testing answers."
   d. What are some examples of it? "The dog demonstrated **intelligence** when she learned that pawing at the door would get her inside the house."

2. *Comparison*—What does my topic resemble, and from what does it differ?
   a. To what is it analogous? "**The law** is like a dam; in the same way that a dam restrains a wild river and converts its energy to constructive purposes, so the law restrains human drives—thus encouraging positive directions for human energy."
   b. How is it different in kind from a related topic? "**Liberty** is unlike license in that liberty requires the exercise of responsibility but license does not."
   c. How is it different in degree from a related topic? "**A vegetarian diet** is healthier than a meat diet." "**The exercise of liberty** is nobler than the exercise of license."

3. *Causal relationship*—Is my topic a cause or an effect?
   a. What does it cause? "**Her kind heart** makes her vulnerable to exploitation by selfish people."
   b. What causes it? "**A good school system** results from community support and wise professional leadership."

4. *Past and future circumstance*—What is the past or future of my topic?
   a. What happened? "**Cheating** has been common in this school."
   b. What is possible? "Because these students are honest out of school, it is possible to eliminate their **cheating** in school."
   c. What is probable? "The duller the curriculum, the more likely is **misbehavior**."

5. *Testimony*—What do others say about my topic?
   a. What do authorities on my topic say about it? "**Variations in cultures** do not mean that human nature is fundamentally different from one society or era to another; Jean Piaget, the great psychologist, has offered evidence that all children in all societies develop mentally in the same ways."
   b. What is public opinion? "A poll of PTA members in our school system reveals that 84% approve of **the competency testing program**."
   c. What is the statistical evidence? "In the four years since our school system has required **the competency test** for graduation, the average SAT score of high school students has increased three points."
   d. What are the maxims and famous quotations about my topic? "**Beauty** is only skin deep." "**Conceit** in weakest bodies strongest works."—Shakespeare

These strategies for invention provide starting points for your thinking, not completed lines of thought. Statements that define, compare, propose a cause or a possibility, or cite other people's notions all require explanation to demonstrate their validity. For example, having focused your thinking with an analogy about the way the law resembles a hydroelectric dam, you might brainstorm particular similarities that show the extent of the relationship; then you could use a tree diagram to organize the particulars (pp. 15–17). By the time you finish writing, your composition might have no reference to dams, but it would depend on the ideas about the nature of law generated by the analogy.

3e Ask the reporter's questions about your topic.

A fourth strategy is that used by newspaper reporters: asking and answering the questions **who, what, when, where, why,** and **how**. Notice how in the following example the writer uses these questions to focus his thinking. The issue with which he is concerned is a proposed 50% increase in student activity fees to finance construction of a new student center.

Who made this recommendation? Who are its supporters? Who opposes it? Who has the authority to cancel or reduce the amount of the proposed increases?

What are the specific provisions of the policy? What are the alternatives to it?

When was this policy adopted? When will it be implemented? When will the people affected by it have an opportunity to voice their opinion?

Where is the present student center located? Where will the new facility be built? (A related question would be, which location is more convenient for the majority of students?)

Why is there a need for a new student center? Why is such a large increase in fees necessary?

How will the proposed facility differ from the present one? How will the new center benefit currently enrolled students? How will low-income students be affected by the higher fees needed to finance the new center?

3f Use valid logic.

However you derive a proposition, you should examine the quality of its logic. Traditionally scholars identify two types of logic: inductive and deductive. To *induce* is to reach a generalization after considering a number of specific instances; to *deduce* is to reach a conclusion after considering two premises. In daily life induction and deduction link in chains of logic. For example, you might induce from observations of yourself and fellow students that when people repeatedly fail in efforts to learn something, they lose interest and give up. Using that generalization as a first premise, you might deduce that since a friend is failing to learn German (the second premise), he will soon stop studying it (the conclusion).

There are two guidelines to follow when you induce. First, you should base your generalization on enough facts and examples for it to relate to a significantly broad segment of life. Second, your facts and examples should not be biased but should accurately represent the class of cases to which you refer. As an example of invalid induction, consider the generalization "All Republicans are wealthy." To have reached this conclusion, a person must have considered only a few individuals who happened to be both wealthy and Republican; they are obviously not representative of all the party members.

Valid deduction depends on two conditions. First, both premises must be true; second, the conclusion must follow from the premises. Therefore, a deduction using as one premise the previous generalization about Republicans would be invalid because the premise is false. On the other hand, a person might reach an invalid conclusion from true premises: "The Democrats I know would accept inflation in order to reduce unemployment, and since Clara is a Democrat, she must feel that way too." Although the speaker may state the truth about certain Democrats and about Clara being a Democrat, it is illogical to conclude that Clara is necessarily like those Democrats the speaker knows.

In addition to following general principles of reasoning, you should avoid specific logical fallacies. Below are some of the most common.

1. The *post–hoc* ("after that") fallacy consists of proposing that because one event happens after another, the first event caused the second. We are tempted by the post–hoc fallacy because effects always follow causes; but we should resist being hasty in ascribing cause, since precedence itself is not proof. For example, we would be wrong to conclude that because the crime rate has decreased after the imposition of the death penalty, the death penalty has caused the decrease. The new rate might be the result of hidden causes, such as a decrease in the proportion of the population which is in the crime–prone ages of sixteen to twenty-eight.

2. We commit the *ad–hominem* ("to the man") fallacy when we focus on the person who holds a belief rather than on the belief itself: "Because Darwin was agnostic, his ideas on the origins of life have no value." Theories are true or false regardless of who advances them.

3. A statement is *begging the question* when it avoids giving information that the writer seems to promise. For example, a writer might explain a careless act as follows: "He forgot to bring the food basket to the picnic because his memory is so bad." Such an explanation actually states that something is because it is. The explanation "begs" the question, "Yes, but why?" In a more subtle form of this fallacy, a *questionable term* is used: "Abortion is murder, because it is the killing of babies." The term "baby" begs the question, "Is a fetus a baby?"

4. When two propositions which do not relate as premises are nevertheless used in a deduction, the conclusion is called a *non sequitur* (a Latin phrase meaning "it does not follow"). For example, a writer might offer this argument: "Since student government is not benefiting our college and since only fifteen percent of the students vote in campus elections, the quality of student government will improve only when all students are

required to vote." This writer has given no reason to conclude that a low percentage of voters is related to effectiveness of student government; it does not follow, therefore, that requiring students to vote will improve student government.

5. A *false choice* offers the reader only two alternatives when there are actually more: "We must either accept the demands of terrorists or ignore them altogether." Such a proposition ignores other tactics, such as negotiating to save hostages' lives.

6. A writer can sometimes *rely on ignorance* to reach conclusions. To insist on a proposition contradicted by facts is to demonstrate *invincible ignorance*. For example, some people persist in arguing that smoking is not bad for their health despite overwhelming evidence to the contrary. To *argue from ignorance* is to conclude that a proposition is false because it lacks proof. For example, some argue that the theory of evolution is disproved because scientists cannot agree on how it occurs. Such a position depends on a lack of complete knowledge, not on the general merit of the theory in question.

Exercise

Identify the fallacies below as *post hoc, ad hominem*, begging the question, *non sequitur*, false choice, or reliance on ignorance.

1. You should ignore Marvin's candidacy for student body president because he's in a fraternity.

   ad hominen
2. Everytime I wear those red socks to a basketball game, our team wins; so you may be sure I will wear them to the championship game.

   post hoc
3. America: love it or leave it.

   false choice
4. Anyone who doesn't have an academic degree in psychology isn't qualified to give advice on this issue; so we

should disregard the opinions of Mr. Smith, who teaches anthropology.
ad hominem

5. I was confused about some of the questions on the last test because I couldn't understand them.
begging the question
6. Although studies of acid rain have demonstrated its adverse environmental effects, I see no need for antipollution legislation at this time.
reliance on ignorance
7. That candidate cannot have it both ways: Either he is for the Equal Rights Amendment or he is against women's rights.
false choice
8. Student achievement began its decline after the Supreme Court ruled against officially sanctioned prayer in the public schools. Reinstituting formal prayer in the schools will, therefore, reverse academic decline.
post hoc
9. We should elect someone to Congress who is not a professional politician because the professional politicians got us in the mess we are in.
non sequitur
10. People are puzzled by modern art because they cannot figure out what it means.
begging the question

4 · Determining Arrangement

4a Plan your composition.

Understanding why and to whom you are writing and what perspective you will take (Chapter **2**) orients you to the task of arranging your content. Good writers are concerned with arrangement throughout the writing process. In fact, discovering ideas, expressing them, organizing them, and revising them are deeply interrelated. When we analyze the writing process, we separate its aspects artificially. So you should consider the following six–step procedure for determining form not as a stage which you pass through once, but as an activity which you may repeat in part throughout your writing.

1. *Determining a thesis.* Your starting point for gathering and shaping content is an explicit thesis. It might be a persuasive objective ("We should clean this dorm room because the mess is making it hard for us to continue our education"), a proposition requiring argumentative defense ("The main benefit of a college education is intellectual, not monetary"), an expository thesis ("There are three types of roommates"), or an expressive impression ("The view from my window gives me certain feelings").

2. *Discovering material.* Guided by the thesis you should draw on your own knowledge, logic, and memories—and possibly on external sources—for content relevant to your thesis. At this stage, you are doing little to discriminate the value of your points or to group points relevant to each other; you are just gathering such information as your thesis suggests you might later use. The tactics for invention suggested in Chapter **3** can be helpful in this task.

3. *Deciding on a general pattern.* As you accrue enough information to develop your thesis you should look for a pattern in which the material can cohere. Sometimes one of the standard patterns discussed in **4b** will be appropriate for the entire essay. Often, though, the material will require you to modify or combine the standard patterns or to devise a

unique organization. The decisions below illustrate the kinds of judgments made at this stage.

"I will organize my paper to trace effects and causes; I will describe effects first and then suggest certain causes."

"My material fits under three main points, which I will arrange in order of increasing importance."

"My impressions and attitudes seem to fall naturally in a contrasting pattern: those before I met Susan and those afterward."

4. *Relating specific points to the general pattern.* Now is the time to cluster your specific points under the sections of your pattern. For example, you might at this stage separate your specific effects and causes, or you might cluster the details of what you felt before and what you felt after a crucial event.

5. *Filling content voids and eliminating irrelevant material.* After you cluster your points, you may find that the emerging coherence suggests new ideas and reveals that some old ideas do not belong. You should judge each point for how pertinent it is, for how efficiently it helps develop your essay, and for how specific it needs to be. Discard marginally pertinent items, redundant items, and items too vague or general for your thesis. Furthermore, you should judge if your planned composition promises to address your subject completely enough, given your purpose and thesis. If it does not, you will need to develop more material.

6. *Arranging the particulars in a sequence.* Now you should be able to develop an outline that orders the particulars you sorted in the previous stage. You might do this in a formal outline that puts major and subordinate points in order (as for an essay that classifies types of child abuse), or you might simply list particulars in a planned sequence (as for a narrative that traces a personal experience). Techniques for formal outlining are given in **4b**.

Exercise 1

Number the steps given below so they will follow the order of the six–stage process for determining arrangement:

3 You decide on a comparison pattern for your essay.

6 You list in sequence the major points about cars and subordinate the supporting details in order under each major point.

4 You determine the major points and their relevant details.

1 You review in general your past experience with cars, your area of interest, and you realize how much auto styles and buyer attitudes have changed in the last dozen years. You decide to show in your essay how the public's attitude has shifted from a desire for large, powerful cars to a desire for small, efficient, economical cars.

5 You decide you have less content than your purpose requires, so you add a major point and some details.

2 In the library you consult auto magazines published during the last dozen years, looking for particular changes in car designs and specifications. You use this information to supplement your own observations and memories.

4b Prepare an outline.

A formal outline helps you plan the sequence in which you will discuss your points throughout your composition while it also helps you establish subordinate and coordinate relationships among these points.

An outline shows by indentation how points are subordinated. Outlining convention requires that at each level of indentation there must be at least two entries. The conventional numeration and indentation are given below.

I.
A.
1.
a.
1)
2)
b.
2.
B.
II.

This scheme shows main point **I** divided into two subpoints, **A** and **B**; point **A** is subdivided into **1** and **2**; **1** is subdivided into **a** and **b**; and **a** is subdivided into **1**) and **2**).

Be consistent in the way you state the points in your outline. In a topic outline, every heading should be a word or phrase. In a sentence outline, every numbered or lettered heading should be a complete sentence.

Emphasize the coordinate relationship of the main headings and that of the items within each subgroup by stating them in the same grammatical form. For example, if point **I** is a noun, the other Roman numeral headings should also be nouns; if the **A** term in one subgroup is a prepositional phrase, the other capital letter headings in that group should also be prepositional phrases, and so on.

Taking into account the previous information on determining pattern, examine the following example of the entire planning procedure used by a freshman composition student whose purpose was to explain what he believed was wrong with his university's system for dropping and adding courses.

First he listed all points he felt to be relevant to his topic:

1. Frequent computer errors in schedules
2. Impersonality of the whole system
3. Small, cluttered, uncomfortable facilities
4. Physical discomfort due to weather conditions
5. Too many forms to fill out

6. Long lines outside and inside building
7. Anxiety about getting necessary courses and hours
8. Uninformed people at drop and add tables
9. People who ignored students' questions
10. People who were rude to students
11. A few courteous people
12. Not enough people to handle the volume of students needing to drop or add courses

The student then examined all the items more closely, searching for a cluster of related points. What he discovered was that most of the information he had written down (everything except items 1, 2, and 12) could be classified under three broad categories: inefficient procedures, inadequate facilities, and unsatisfactory personnel. After considering these clusters of specific points, he added several more specifics and eliminated some.

Next he developed the following topic outline:

CONFUSION ON CAMPUS: THE STATE COLLEGE DROP/ADD SYSTEM

Thesis: There are three main problems with the drop/add system at State College: the procedures for dropping and adding courses are inefficient, the facilities are inadequate, and the registration staff are, for the most part, incapable of meeting students' needs.

I. Inefficient Procedures
   A. Too many forms to have signed by professors
   B. Too many different lines to stand in
   C. Too few staff members to process change forms
II. Inadequate facilities
   A. Inadequate shelter in the area where students are waiting in line
   B. Poor conditions in the room where drop/add is held
      1. Inadequate space
      2. Inadequate ventilation
      3. Inadequate cooling system

III. Unsatisfactory personnel
    A. Staff members ignorant of necessary information
    B. Staff members indifferent to student questions
    C. Staff members rude to students

The student might have decided to write a sentence outline, in which case, each entry would be a complete sentence. Such an outline would give him a chance to plan his content more thoroughly.

I. Inefficient procedures prolong registration.
    A. There are too many forms to fill out.
    B. There are too many different lines to stand in.
    C. Too few staff members are available to process change forms.
II. The facilities are not large enough.
    A. Long lines of students must stand outside.
        1. In warm weather students swelter.
        2. In cold weather students freeze.
    B. The gym does not accommodate all the people.
        1. People are jammed together from wall to wall.
        2. The lack of ventilation is suffocating.
        3. The air conditioning cannot cope with the heat from the weather and the people.
III. The personnel can't provide adequate service.
    A. Staff members give students incorrect information.
    B. Staff members ignore students' questions.
    C. When staff members do respond, they are rude.

Despite their apparent rigidity, these conventions offer considerable flexibility. For an in-class writing assignment, you might prepare a one-level outline (Roman numeral headings only). For a short out-of-class paper, a two-level outline (Roman numeral headings plus capital letter headings) might be more helpful. And for longer, more complex projects such as research papers, a three or four-level outline might better serve your purposes. You can also vary the number of main headings and subheadings in accordance with your organizational aims and the scope of your paper. Perhaps the most important point to keep in mind when preparing your outline is that it can be changed at any time during the composing process to accommodate new information or insights.

Exercise 2

Arrange the list of topics below in the outline format indicated.

Misbehavior in Our National Parks

Deliberately defacing natural objects
Littering
Interfering with animals
Vandalizing
Throwing trash from vehicles
Behaving destructively
Leaving trash in campsites
Carelessly abusing facilities and environment
Deliberately wrecking park facilities

I. Littering
  A. Leaving trash in campsites
  B. Throwing trash from vehicles
II. Behaving destructively
  A. Carelessly abusing facilities and environment
  B. Vandalizing
    1. Deliberately defacing natural objects
    2. Deliberately wrecking park facilities
III. Interfering with animals

4c Consider adopting a standard pattern.

Sometimes, when the writing process permits, writers choose to fit their compositions to a standard pattern of organization. Such patterns can help focus your search for content and can help you achieve coherence throughout your paper. Blindly following a pattern, however, can handicap you by restraining you from discovering features of your subject that do not fit.

You should, therefore, consider the seven patterns outlined below not as rigid molds into which you pour content, but as recipes that you adapt according to your particular resources and objectives.

1. *Procedure.* The most clear-cut pattern is the specification of the steps in a procedure such as giving a set of directions or tracing a process. Your task is to identify in sequence all steps that make up that procedure. A complex procedure may have clusters of related steps, and you should make these larger stages clear. For example, directions on how to fish for trout with artificial flies might organize all the skills into five main categories: how to prepare the equipment, how to negotiate a stream, how to cast the fly, how to set the hook, and how to net the fish.

   a. If the objective is not clear from the title of your composition, you should orient your reader by briefly describing the objective or result of the procedure.
   b. You next might define any terms and identify any parts the reader may not be familiar with.
   c. To trace the procedure, simply begin with the first step and lead the reader through each subsequent step, using transitional words (**next, second,** etc.) to help the reader keep track.
   d. To conclude, you might describe how the result of a successful procedure looks or works.

Often an audience for a procedure will require only the content mentioned in *c* above. In such cases, simply begin the paper with the first step and end with the last step.

2. *Report and narrative.* A *report* tells what happened first, what followed, and what happened last. The journalist's five questions (see **3e**) can often serve as a guide: tell **who** did **what**; **when**, **where**, and **how** it was done; and, if the reasons are significant, **why** it was done.

Narrative refers to an account that portrays people (or

other creatures) coping with a problem. In this sense, *narrative* and *story* are synonymous. Although "story" suggests literary fiction and drama, nonfiction narratives are useful in all kinds of composition, for true stories can persuade, instruct, and reveal expressively with great power.

To be complete a narrative must have at least one *episode*, which is an account structured in the five stages outlined below:

a. *Setting*—Readers need some sense of place and time in order to envision an episode.
b. *Complication*—Something must happen to upset the equilibrium of the setting. The complication creates a problem or conflict.
c. *Psychological response*—Readers must be able to empathize with the response that the episode's characters have to the complication.
d. *Attempt to cope*—The people act (mentally or physically) to solve the problem or end the conflict.
e. *Results*—There must be an outcome to the attempt.

You can see these stages at work by experimenting with the account below. When you have read it, you will likely find that it fails as a story:

THE VISITOR

One morning when a farmer named Brown was harvesting in the south forty and Mrs. Brown was canning vegetables, there came a knock at their farmhouse door. Mrs. Brown opened the door and was shocked and distressed to see Mr. Smith standing there. He asked to see Mr. Brown. Mrs. Brown, struggling to keep her composure, replied that her husband was not on the farm and that she didn't know when he would be back. Mr. Smith said that he was sorry and that he would return that afternoon.

As soon as he left, Mrs. Brown dashed out the back door and over the fields to her husband. When she reported that Mr. Smith had just been asking for him, the farmer was more shocked and distressed than his wife. At her recommendation, he decided to run away and hide at his brother's house in the town of Blue Springs. So he rushed back to the farmhouse, packed a few things, and left immediately.

That afternoon, Mr. Smith returned and once again asked Mrs. Brown if he might see her husband. She replied that he had left the farm for an extended journey.

Mr. Smith said, "I'm sorry to hear that because I have an appointment with him this evening in Blue Springs."*

This passage does not make sense as a narrative because we cannot tell why the couple react as they do, and we cannot discern a result at the end. If we change one word, however, the story will suddenly pop into focus: instead of *Mr. Smith,* read *Mr. Death.* Now the people's motives and the result are clear, and we can understand the account as a narrative.

3. *Description.* Describing a person, place, or thing requires you to select only those details that will most efficiently create an impression. The four patterns below can help you organize an impression as well as guide you in selecting details.

a. Details may be treated in the order in which they are noted by an observer. The observer either passes through a scene or witnesses details as they appear. The perspective is like that of someone walking down a street or watching things happen in a restaurant.
b. Details may be treated in their order in space. The observer might describe from left to right, from top to bottom, from front to back, or in some other spatial progression.
c. The prominence of a feature can determine its order. The observer might begin with the most outstanding detail and progress to the least noticeable yet still significant detail, or the writer might reverse this order.

*Collett B. Dilworth, "Structuralism, Stories and English Teaching," *English Journal* 72 (January 1983): 82.

d. A detail's significance, in light of the writer's purpose, can also govern arrangement. The observer picks and orders only those details that will give a specific impression. The same used car might be described in terms of its dented fenders and worn tires or conversely in terms of its polished paint and clean interior. Of course, the significance of a detail should always be a consideration for the descriptive writer whatever the pattern.

4. *Comparison.* Your topic may concern two subjects alike in some ways but different in others. Your purpose in comparing such subjects may be simply to inform your audience of their similarities and differences. It could also be to show how one thing is superior to another or to explain something unfamiliar in terms of something familiar.

To organize a comparison you must first determine common areas of similarities and differences. If, for example, you were comparing two political candidates, you would want to treat each in terms of the same general points. If you discuss the economic proposals, the outlook on foreign policy, and the connections to special interests of one candidate, you should discuss these same points for the other.

There are two common patterns for organizing comparisons. In one pattern, you discuss all selected points of comparison for one subject and then all points for the other.

I. Political candidate Jessica Fenster
   A. Economic proposals
   B. Outlook on foreign policy
   C. Connections to special interests
II. Political candidate Phillip Bloom
   A. Economic proposals
   B. Outlook on foreign policy
   C. Connections to special interests

In the other pattern, you discuss each point of comparison in turn:

I. Economic proposals
   A. Jessica Fenster
   B. Phillip Bloom
II. Outlook on foreign policy
   A. Jessica Fenster
   B. Phillip Bloom
III. Connections to special interests
   A. Jessica Fenster
   B. Phillip Bloom

Note that the first pattern focuses on the candidates, whereas the second focuses on the issues. You should pick your pattern according to which aspects of your content you wish to emphasize.

5. *Classification.* Classifying particulars into general categories is a type of thinking essential for making sense of the world. We would have little to talk or think about if we lacked concepts such as **vegetable** and **animal**, **rural** and **urban**, **truth** and **falsehood**. Your purpose in writing a classification is, therefore, to give your readers a new tool for organizing experience. You do so by arranging phenomena according to important shared characteristics.

A classification should be based on a single meaningful principle. A paper on kinds of advertisements would lack a single principle if it discussed the following categories: funny ads, ads for household products, and television ads. To depend on a single principle, the paper would have to classify ads according to their humor and seriousness or according to the type of product or according to the type of medium, but not a combination of these. A paper on television ads that lacked a meaningful classification would be one that grouped them according to length: long, medium, and short. Unless there are substantive differences related to length of time, such an essay could offer little useful information.

Just as your classes should be coherent and meaningful, they should also be mutually exclusive and complete; that is, they should not overlap and should not exclude elements that belong in the classification system. For example, a classification of the media used in political campaigns as electronic, print, and mail is overlapping because mailed materials are a form of print media; the system is also incomplete because it omits personal campaign appearances.

Once your classification system is clear, the pattern of organization for your paper will be obvious. The body of your paper will fall naturally into sections, each treating one of your main classes. The order of your classes should follow some logic such as size (largest to smallest) or importance.

The example paragraph on page 10 illustrates classification.

6. *Persuasion.* Almost any rhetorical form can be turned to persuasive purposes. Certainly in the appropriate contexts, narration, description, comparison, and classification can move people to action. There are also patterns specifically designed for persuasion, and one is outlined below.

a. *Background of the problem*—Trace the history of the present problem. This step can implicitly suggest that if a problem can come into existence, it can go out of existence.
b. *Portrayal of a need*—Describe the problem objectively but vividly. You should convince your audience that conditions are not what they should be.
c. *Portrayal of solution*—Specify what must be done to improve conditions. Stress the feasibility and reasonableness of the recommended course of action.
d. *Visualization*—Describe what conditions will be like after the solution. This description should draw the audience away from the current state toward the improved state.
e. *Call to action*—Conclude with a recommendation on how to begin addressing the problem. Stress the practicality and feasibility of this first step.

The example paragraph on p. 9 illustrates this persuasive pattern.

7. *Argument.* In composition, "argument" does not mean the type of contention occurring when two people in disagreement raise their voices and speak at the same time. Argument is a type of discourse that makes and supports propositions in the light of at least one other contrary proposition. Its objective is to demonstrate that a thesis inevitably follows from a line of logic, and perhaps to convince readers that a thesis represents a superior morality. Argument and the logic that supports it constitute venerable fields of study; since the time of the ancient Greeks, scholars have described and recommended argumentative tactics. The pattern below is a simplified outline of an arrangement advocated by Aristotle and still respected by modern scholars.

a. *Introduction*—The introduction should establish the writer's earnest voice and serious tone and should draw the reader intellectually and perhaps emotionally into the issue. Introductory devices include illustrating a problem with a narrative, a description, or a statement of a paradox.
b. *Background*—The facts behind the issue are stated. The **who, what, when, where, how, why** approach of the report is often useful at this point.
c. *The writer's argument*—Here the writer traces a line of reasoning to show that a particular proposition is valid. All the wisdom, logic, and moral sense of the writer may be brought to bear. The strategies for invention and the rules of logic outlined in Chapter **3** are all useful in developing an argument.
d. *Refutation*—At some point, the opposing argument should be objectively summarized and critically analyzed. The objective here is to reveal illogic or immorality in the opposing argument.
e. *Conclusion*—The conclusion should clinch the writer's argument. A summary might compare the

opposing theses and highlight the point-for-point superiority of the writer's argument. At the end of an argument the reader should feel invited to join a company of enlightened people in opposition to error.

The example paragraph on pages 10–11 illustrates this argumentative pattern.

5 · Writing Effective Paragraphs

5a Understand the function of paragraphs.

One of the simplest but most important conventions of written discourse is the indentation that marks the boundaries between paragraphs. Without the aid of this typographical indicator, readers would face much the same problem they would encounter if there were no spaces between words or no periods between sentences.

Notice, for example, how difficult it is to read the sentence below.

Revengeisakindofwildjustice.

When the words are separated, however, their meaning and the meaning of the sentence as a whole become immediately comprehensible.

Revenge is a kind of wild justice.

Francis Bacon

Likewise, a group of sentences without terminal punctuation and capital letters to signal the beginning of each new sentence would be a confusing jumble of words, as in the following example:

A mohawk of metallic blonde hair adorned Perry's egg-shaped head dangling bravely from his left ear was a silver safety pin in sharp contrast to his unruly hairdo and pierced ear, Perry wore a khaki green army jacket with matching trousers his shoes were a pair of old combat boots that clumped loudly, warning the public to stand at attention dark, horn-rimmed sunglasses sat perched on his pointed ears, even in the darkest of rooms.

Student essay, "Perry the Punker"

If you were to read this paragraph as it was actually written—with a period after **head, pin, trousers,** and **attention**—you would have no difficulty following the author's line of thought or distinguishing one physical detail from the next. This writer was also conscious of the need to subdivide her entire essay into comprehensible units of meaning. Had she not done so, her readers would have been faced with the task of deciphering her intentions from the long, unbroken passage below.

Perry the Punker

Sliding into my desk, I noticed a strange aroma filling my nostrils. I turned to discover its source, an alien-looking creature slouched in the desk next to mine. In an attempt to make conversation, I asked the person his name. "Perry" was the cold, clipped reply. It was obvious from the clothes he wore, the way he smelled, and his strange behavior that Perry was not an ordinary boy.^ A mohawk of metallic blonde hair adorned Perry's egg-shaped head. Dangling bravely from his left ear was a silver safety pin. In sharp contrast to his unruly hairdo and pierced ear, Perry wore a khaki green army jacket with matching trousers. His shoes were a pair of old combat boots that clumped loudly, warning the public to stand at attention. Dark, horn-rimmed sunglasses sat perched on his pointed ears, even in the darkest of rooms.^ Perry emitted an aroma of burnt cheese. I discovered his father owned the local pizzeria, where he worked as a delivery boy. Sometimes the odor was so strong I was forced to hold my breath at specific intervals. This was a difficult task, so I avoided sitting next to him whenever possible.^ One rainy night, my mother decided to order out for supper. Unfortunately, she called the pizza

5 b

place where Perry worked. Within minutes, our doorbell was ringing. I flung open the door to find Perry dripping all over our "pan special." My heart sank as mother invited him inside. He grabbed the money from her hand and bolted out the door into the pouring rain. Slowly shutting the door, my mother remarked that strange boys should not deliver pizzas. ^Whenever I smell the pungent odor of burnt mozzarella, it always reminds me of Perry. I wonder if he is still peddling pizza. I doubt it. He probably is living on a gorgeous estate in California and designing costumes for punk rock bands. ¶

Exercise 1

1. After reading "Perry the Punker," mark the point at which you think each new paragraph should begin. See above.
2. Then notice the sentences enclosed within these boundaries and explain why they constitute a paragraph. Answers will vary.

Of course, writers should do more than arbitrarily mark boundaries in their prose. The material within those boundaries must be unified, coherent, and complete. And the paragraph as a whole must be clearly and logically related to other paragraphs in the same essay.

5b Compose unified paragraphs.

A paragraph is unified if all its parts contribute to the development of its controlling idea or impression. There are two ways to achieve this result in your own writing.

1. State the main point explicitly in a *topic sentence* and add sentences to qualify, explain, illustrate, or in some other way develop it. In this pattern, the topic sentence usually comes at the beginning of the paragraph.

In the spring the sea is filled with migrating fishes, some of them bound for the mouths of great rivers, which they will ascend to deposit their spawn. Such are the spring-run chinooks coming in from the deep Pacific feeding grounds to breast the rolling flood of the Columbia, the shad moving in to the Chesapeake and the Hudson and the Connecticut, the alewives seeking a hundred coastal streams of New England, the salmon feeling their way to the Penobscot and the Kennebec. For months or years these fish have known only the vast spaces of the ocean. Now the spring sea and the maturing of their own bodies lead them back to the rivers of their birth.

Rachel Carson

A topic sentence, however, can also be used in other positions. Note how Loren Eiseley builds up to his topic statement in the final sentence of this paragraph.

Some years ago the old elevated railway in Philadelphia was torn down and replaced by a subway system. This ancient E1 with its barnlike stations containing nut-vending machines and scattered food scraps had, for generations, been the favorite feeding ground of flocks of pigeons, generally one flock to a station along the route of the E1. Hundreds of pigeons were dependent upon the system. They flapped in and out of its stanchions and steel work or gathered in watchful little audiences about the feet of anyone who rattled the peanut-vending machines. They even watched people who jingled change in their hands, and prospected for food under the feet of the crowds who gathered between trains. **Probably very few among the waiting people who tossed a crumb to an eager pigeon realized that this El was like a food-bearing river, and that the life which haunted its banks was dependent upon the running of the trains with their human freight.**

2. Omit the topic sentence and communicate the unifying idea or impression implicitly through word choice, sentence structure, and sentence relationships.

In the passage below, N. Scott Momaday conveys a sense of vastness and mystery through a series of powerful visual images. Note that the opening sentence sets the scene and focuses attention on the houses, but it does not introduce an explicit controlling idea.

Houses are like sentinels in the plain, old keepers of the weather watch. There, in a very little while, wood takes on the appearance of great age. All colors wear soon away in the winds and rain, and then the wood is burned gray and the grain appears and the nails turn red with rust. The windowpanes are black and opaque; you imagine there is nothing within, and indeed there are many ghosts, bones given up to the land. They stand here and there against the sky, and you approach them for a longer time than you expect. They belong in the distance; it is their domain.

5c Compose coherent paragraphs.

A paragraph is coherent when each sentence is clearly related to the next. Conversely, a paragraph lacks coherence if it moves unpredictably from one point to the next. There are many different ways to achieve coherence within a paragraph, but the seven strategies discussed below are among the most effective.

1. *Sequence in time or space.* A technique used extensively in narrative and descriptive writing, this pattern is usually characterized by explicit time markers (**then, later,** etc.) or a movement from one visual reference point to the next.

Never shall I forget the Christmas dances at Taos, twilight, snow, the darkness coming over the great wintry mountains and the lonely pueblo, **then** suddenly, again, like dark calling to dark, the deep Indian cluster—singing around the drum, wild and awful, **suddenly** rousing on the last dusk as the procession starts. And **then** the bonfires leaping suddenly in pure spurts of high flame, columns of sudden flame forming an alley for the procession.

D.H. Lawrence

2. *Logical order.* In this kind of relationship, which is especially common in persuasive or argumentative discourse, one sentence is a proposition and the next is a conclusion or result. Observe that the second sentence in the following passage serves this purpose even though there is no explicit transition word, such as **for.**

All voting is a sort of gaming, like checkers or backgammon, with a slight moral tinge to it, a playing with right and wrong, with moral questions; and betting naturally accompanies it. **The character of the voters is not staked.**

Henry David Thoreau

3. *Amplification and exemplification.* In this pattern, one sentence amplifies an earlier one by defining, qualifying, or illustrating it.

Amplification

Those who believe in the idea of freedom and in the idea of democracy also believe that the truth will set you free, that to have knowledge is to have the chance to understand, perhaps even to cope. **By truth I mean actuality or objective matters capable of discovery.**

Ramsey Clark

Exemplification

The large mammalian brain is the most complicated thing, for its size, known to us. **The human brain weighs three pounds, but in that three pounds are ten billion neurons and a hundred billion smaller cells.**

Isaac Asimov

4. *Accumulation.* In this method, one sentence introduces an idea or example similar to that of a preceding sentence. Often this kind of relationship is signalled by a transition word such as **likewise, also, and, moreover,** or a similar connective.

Even when I was a fairly precocious young man the nothingness of the hopes and strivings which chase most men restlessly through life came to my consciousness with considerable vitality. **Moreover,** I soon discovered the cruelty of the chase, which in those years was much more carefully covered up by hypocrisy and glittering words than is the case today.

Albert Einstein

5 c

5. *Contrast.* Another strategy for achieving coherence is to contrast the idea of one sentence with that of another.

> Of course, it would be a mistake to suppose that there is more blind acceptance of brutal practices in organized football than elsewhere. **On the contrary,** a recent Harvard study has approvingly argued that football's characteristics of "impersonal acceptance of inflicted injury," an overriding "organization goal," the "ability to turn oneself on and off" and being, above all, "out to win" are of "inestimable value" to big corporations.
>
> John McMurtry

6. *Repetition.* In this arrangement, two or more sentences are linked by repetition of key words.

> Then, **he** [Charles II] **loved** the theater, **and** it was thanks to his **patronage** that actors and actresses, hitherto a rather derided race, attained proper respectability. **He loved** horses, **and** the great English racing center of Newmarket owed everything to his **patronage**.
>
> Antonia Fraser

Take care that such repetition does not become an irritation to the reader (see **15b**).

7. *Parallelism.* The passage above is a good example not only of repetition but also of parallelism, the balance achieved by duplicating sentence structures. The sentences that follow are also parallel, but for different reasons. These writers achieve balance by beginning each sentence with the same determiner-adjective-noun pattern and by contrasting such key words as **night—day** and **heavy cover—open spaces**.

> The **thick-set leopard,** heavier by 30 pounds, operates in the shadows of the **night,** relying on **heavy cover,** stealth and close-up ambush tactics. The **trim cheetah** is a creature of the **day** who likes **open spaces** and long vistas.
>
> Emily and Ola d'Aulaire

These seven techniques can be used singly or in various combinations to achieve paragraph coherence. In the first example below, the writer relies almost exclusively on exemplification. In the second paragraph, the author combines the amplification strategy with repetition and parallel structure.

> Euphemisms and palliative phrases are a favorite form of evasive language. "To select out" someone means to dismiss him from a job. People "misspeak" themselves; they never say foolish or deceptive things or (heaven forbid!) lie. Everything from nonsense and propaganda to vicious slanders and incitements to violence is described as "rhetoric." Similarly any falsehood, no matter how malicious, and any indoctrination, no matter how unconscionable, is "consciousness-raising."
>
> Richard Gambino

> If I were to describe my dream university, I would have it organize itself around a central trunk of three disciplines: philosophy, the art studio, and the poetry workshop. Philosophy would be asked to return to the teaching of ontology, epistemology, ethics, and logic in order to remedy the shameful deficiencies of the reasoning now common in the fields of academic specialization. Art education would provide the instruments by which to carry out such thinking. Poetry would make language, our principal medium for communicating thought, fit for thinking in images.
>
> Rudolph Arnheim

For additional information on paragraph structure, see Chapter **4**. It discusses seven commonly used patterns for essay development, all of which can be used as well to achieve paragraph coherence.

5d Develop paragraphs adequately.

Judgments about whether a given paragraph is adequately developed always involve subjective considerations because there are no universal conventions governing paragraph length. In fact, most experienced writers consciously vary the length of their paragraphs just as they vary the length and structure of their sentences. One reason for this practice is that uniformity often translates into monotony. Furthermore, paragraphs varying in importance or purpose should vary in length. Consider the following two paragraphs, both of which are drawn from Roger Verhulst's "Being Prepared in Suburbia."

> Gun legislation is dead for another year. As a result, if statistics are any guide, there's every likelihood that a lot of people now living will also be dead before the year is over.
>
> . . .
>
> Until last fall, I had never owned any weapon more lethal than a water pistol. I opposed guns as esthetically repugnant, noisy, essentially churlish devices whose only practical purpose was to blast holes of various sizes in entities that would thereby be rendered less functional than they would otherwise have been. I didn't object merely to guns that killed people; I also objected to guns that killed animals, or shattered windows, or plinked away at discarded beer bottles. Whenever a gun was put to effective use, I insisted, something broke; and it seemed absurd to go through life breaking things.

Although these paragraphs differ greatly in length, each paragraph is adequately developed for its purpose. By its very brevity and directness, the first paragraph draws the reader's attention to the startling parallel between dead legislation and dead people, setting the stage for the argument that the essay subsequently develops. The second paragraph is much longer and more detailed because it sums up the author's earlier anti-gun sentiments and prepares for a later conflict between these attitudes and the allure of gun ownership.

You are free to exercise those same kinds of options in your own writing, provided that your decisions are based on an understanding of what each paragraph should accomplish and how much information is needed to satisfy your readers' expectations. Here are some specific suggestions to help you make such judgments:

1. Whenever you write a one-or two-sentence paragraph, check to see if its brevity serves some purpose. If not, you have the option of deleting the paragraph, adding supporting sentences, or combining it with the paragraph(s) next to it (if the paragraphs are related).

2. Put yourself in the position of the reader, and ask yourself whether you would be able to understand the point of each paragraph on the basis of the information it provides. If not, add details, using the strategies discussed in **5c.**

5e Use transitions to achieve coherence between paragraphs.

All of the techniques for achieving coherence within paragraphs can be used to establish the same kinds of relationships between paragraphs. Especially useful for this purpose are transitional words or phrases and repetition of key words or their synonyms.

1. To indicate explicitly how one paragraph is related to another, use an appropriate transitional word or expression. A partial list is given below:

Purpose	*Transition Words*
to list	first, second, next, last
to indicate time sequence	before, previously, now, later, meanwhile, then, afterwards,
to establish a spatial relationship	below, above, along, beside, beneath, behind, in front
to amplify	that is, in fact, in other words
to exemplify	for example, for instance

5
e

to establish a logical relationship	therefore, consequently, thus, as a result, for
to add information	and, also, too, in addition, furthermore, moreover
to compare	similarly, likewise
to contrast	but, however, on the other hand, conversely, nevertheless

2. Another effective means of achieving coherence between paragraphs is to repeat key words or synonyms, as in the following series of paragraphs drawn from the body of a student essay entitled "The Second Street War":

Car by car, mower by mower, we waged a neck-to-neck battle with our new neighbors. Each week my father would add a new gadget to his already adequate lawn and garden supplies. He would then proudly strut out on our front yard and demonstrate its many uses. Within minutes, Mr. Jones would charge out his door with the latest weed eater or hedge groomer. The air filled with machine gun blasts of yard warfare. At the climax of the metallic cantata, Mrs. Jones would appear on the horizon modeling the latest addition to her wardrobe. Her outfit hit my father like a low flying torpedo—below the belt. With wallet in hand, he began a desperate search for my mother.

Although material items played a major role in the Second Street War, physical fitness contributed to the battle. Every morning my family assembled on the sidewalk bordering our house. In his most commanding tone, my father hurled exercise instructions into the crisp air. In an effort to even the tug of war, Mr. Jones led his troops on a mile run. Both squads were determined to be the healthiest households on the block. Our den closet became a haven of exercise apparatus. More than once, I was forced to rescue my mother from the clutches of a monstrous muscle toner.

Despite the physical torture of our family feud, the heart of the conflict lay in the social life of our community. My parents had never considered joining the posh Country Club until the Joneses moved in. Piano and dance lessons became necessities for my sister and me (we both agreed this was equivalent to life imprisonment in a concentration camp). Dinner parties, bridge and garden clubs, as well as the Daughters of the American Revolution, invaded our living room each week. Not to be outdone, the Joneses held outdoor barbecues, book club galas, and church circle meetings.

Although there are two explicit transition words (**Although** and **Despite**), the continuity we sense in reading this group of paragraphs results mainly from the sustained metaphor of warfare and the varied synonyms for combat used to keep this neighborhood conflict in focus (e.g., **battle, charge, machine gun blasts of yard warfare, troops, squads, conflict**).

5f Write effective introductions and conclusions.

1. *Introductory paragraph.* In most of the essays you will write in college courses, the first paragraph should do two things: engage the reader's interest and state what you intend to discuss in the body of the essay. There are a number of different techniques for achieving these goals, such as posing and answering a question, stating a problem and offering a solution, telling a story, or describing a setting.

Note in the following paragraph how the author combines a brief narration with a description in her introduction to "The Second Street War." Consider in particular how effectively her account of the arrival of the new neighbors builds up to the thesis statement at the end of the paragraph.

I shall never forget the day the Second Street War started. It was a cold, moist, summer morning. A halo of fog delicately floated above our neighborhood. My sister and I were sitting on our front porch arguing, our favorite pastime. Out of the corner of my eye, I spotted a yellow moving van coming down our street. It pulled into the driveway directly opposite ours. Three enormous men in dirty jumpsuits began unloading its contents. Needless to say, my sister and I had forgotten our disagreement and were staring wide-eyed at the exquisite furniture being carried into the house. A sleek automobile of sparkling burgundy stopped at the curb. I heard a loud gasp behind me and turned to see my mother, who was ghost-white and trembling. "Would you just look at that!"she exclaimed through quivering lips. This phrase was the cannon blast that initiated the financial, physical, and social see-saw of "keeping up with the Joneses."

2. *Concluding paragraph.* The last paragraph in an essay is, in some respects, like the first because it usually returns to the main point. But since this paragraph must also give the reader a sense of closure, it should not simply mirror the introduction. Rather, it should end the essay in some convincing way. It might amplify the thesis statement with a final, dramatic example; it might offer a solution to a problem or question you have posed at the beginning of the paper; it might predict consequences; it might use some other unifying strategy.

Exercise 2

Below is the final paragraph of the student essay "The Second Street War." Identify the tactics the writer uses to achieve unity and coherence.

It was in the middle of two of these simultaneous gatherings that the atomic bomb exploded. Declaring our abstention from the status-seeking games our parents played, Jeremy Jones and I announced our engagement. Our wedding was not only a union of two persons but of two families. I am proud to say Jeremy and I own a solar-heated A-frame home, much nicer than my sister's shabby abode, and my two lovely daughters are enrolled in Madame Goule's secondary ballet class. And, would you just look at that—we have some new neighbors!

Tactics: war metaphors; explicit reference to status-seeking; apparent resolution of conflict through marriage; continuation of the "keeping up with the Joneses" theme through the examples in the next-to-last sentence; completion of cyclical pattern marked by the arrival of the new neighbors

6 · Revising

We have all occasionally wished to go back in time to change something we have said. Perhaps we would like to have made a completely different statement or remained silent or said something in a slightly different way. This feeling derives from a natural urge to communicate; we are naturally distressed when we have not said what we meant or when others misunderstand us. The writing process gives us a chance to exploit this urge, to shape and reshape our communication and so gain confidence that when our readers receive it, they will understand it as we wish. Unless we revise, we lose this chance.

As Chapter **1** states, revision means to "see again," to mentally step back from our writing, assess it, and change it if necessary. Often good writers revise in their heads before they put anything on paper. This activity is called *rehearsal*. It involves mentally putting thoughts into words and testing their suitability for the piece of writing. Rehearsal can take the form of an imagined dialogue between the writer and the intended audience. Most good writers, however, do not depend solely on rehearsal; they also rewrite throughout the writing process.

Revision should be generally guided by the writer's purpose. Changes ought to improve the extent to which a writer fulfills the role of advocate, teacher, confidant, or artist. Exercising good judgment in making such changes requires a special ability to identify with readers. We will call that faculty *writer's empathy*. When you can put yourself in one of the reader's roles and when you can imagine how the words affect a reader in this role, you are exercising writer's empathy. To exploit this perspective fully, you must also consider the effects of revision within the entire context of your composition, not just how the change seems by itself. You must assess how well the words work with what has already been written and how they promise to work with any writing that may be yet to come.

There are four types of revision: adding, deleting, substituting, and reordering what you have already written (or rehearsed). *Add* words, sentences, paragraphs when you realize information is incomplete; *delete* material when you realize information is false, inappropriate, or too repetitive; *substitute* new words for old when simple deletion leaves gaps in the information; *reorder* by moving words, sentences, and paragraphs to improve coherence.

Revision occurs at several levels. Local changes bear little significance outside a single sentence. For example, editorial revision involves correcting spelling and punctuation errors, altering incorrect grammatical forms, and changing usages to conform to standard English. Examples of other local revisions include adding an adjective to make a noun more vivid, substituting one synonym for another to avoid repetition, and moving an adverb from one place to another in the sentence to achieve a different emphasis. Revising a transitional word or phrase can have an effect beyond the sentence level by altering the relationship between sentences and paragraphs. The highest level of revision affects the whole composition. Altering a sequence of sentences or paragraphs, changing a key definition, adding sentences to increase support for a thesis, and even changing the thesis itself are examples of such revision.

The two drafts on the next page illustrate the types and levels of revision.

For the final draft, the writer revised the first sentence from the vague "it is" construction to one with a strong, active main verb ("discourage"). By combining the early draft's second and third sentences, by rearranging their elements and by making changes in their wording, the writer achieved a single, more forcefully ordered second sentence. Likewise, the early draft's last two sentences have been combined and reordered to achieve a tight construction of parallel phrases

Early Draft	*Final Draft*
It is discouraging to try to characterize the Farley Building as a place in which to teach and learn English. Its anti-human design can neutralize even the responses that the study of literature strives to encourage. It is a building architected with an aggressive ill will. It disheartens its inhabitants with every step they take under its vile, filthy ceilings. It mocks with its echoing acoustics and even forces teachers and learners to hike their chins up to high ledges before they are able to see out.	Trying to characterize the Farley Building as a place in which to teach and learn English would discourage anyone. Surely an aggressive ill will is responsible for an architecture so anti-human as to weaken even the responses encouraged by great literature. The building disheartens its inhabitants with every step they take under its vile ceilings, through its mocking acoustics, and before its remote windows, which force teachers and learners to hike their chins to slate ledges before they can gaze out.

that build to a more urgent culmination. Revisions at the local level include deleting "filthy" as repetitive, adding "surely" to qualify an inference, substituting "weaken" for "neutralize" as more accurate, and substituting "gaze" for "see" as more specific.

II Structuring Sentences

7 · Understanding the Parts of Speech

7a The parts of speech

Consider the words below:

and	excitedly	into	stadium	wow	colorful	
football	push	watch	crowd	huge	shuffle	we

Each word by itself can suggest to a reader one or more meanings. **Watch** might be a device for telling time or the act of observing; **into** means from the outside to the inside; **and** suggests coordination of one thing with another.

To communicate, we group words so that one word gains meaning from its place in the group while lending to the group its most appropriate meaning. But only certain types of words go together. **Excitedly stadium** and **push colorful** do not make sense while **colorful crowd** and **football stadium** do.

Obviously there are only certain ways to group words meaningfully in English. For example, you will recognize **colorful crowd** and **football stadium** to be the same type of group as **huge watch**. And you will recognize **we shuffle** and **the crowd pushes** to be the same type of group as **we watch**.

Note that when **watch** comes after **colorful**, it means something different than when it comes after **we**, and it serves a different purpose. After **colorful**, **watch** serves as the name of something; after **we**, it serves to express an action. Before **stadium**, **football** serves as a describer; after **colorful**, it serves as a name. Traditionally we recognize eight different purposes words can serve, and these purposes we identify with the *parts of speech*. If we rearrange the 13 words listed at the first of this chapter and add two determiners, **the** and **a**, we find all eight parts of speech at work. The numbers key these words to each part discussed on the following pages.

3 1 4 2 1 7 1 5 6 4
We watch the colorful crowd shuffle and push excitedly into a huge
4 2 8
football stadium. Wow!

1. Verb
2. Noun
3. Pronoun
4. Adjective
5. Adverb
6. Preposition
7. Conjunction
8. Interjection

7b Verbs

The *verb* is the heart of the sentence. Most verbs tell what happens (**sleep, fly, decide, become**); others express a state of existence (**be, seem, taste**). And certain verbs may be used with other verbs (**have** gone, **is** going). A verb requires a *subject,* which identifies what or who is acting, occurring, existing, or receiving an action. Some verbs also take an *object,* which tells what or who is acted upon. (See **8a** for a full discussion of the verb's role in the sentence.)

The winter **birds** (subject) **sang** (verb of action) all morning.

Their **feeder** (subject) **was** (verb of existence) full.

They (subject) **ate** (verb of action) **every seed** (object) by afternoon.

1. *Regular verbs.* Verbs assume different forms, called *inflections,* to give certain kinds of information in addition to a basic meaning. Three of those forms are the *principal parts*: the *infinitive,* the *past tense,* and the *past participle. Regular verbs* all inflect the principal parts the same way. The infinitive is the basic form which undergoes the inflections. It is the form used just after **to** and is the same form used with **I, we, you,** and **they** when the verb expresses something occurring in the present.

We want **to believe** all our leaders.

I **believe** that politician.

We use a verb's infinitive when we refer to it as a word.

The verb **lie** is rarely used in face-to-face debate.

The infinitive is the form used for listing a verb in a dictionary.

The *past tense* form indicates that the happening or existence is in the past. Regular verbs form the past tense by adding **-d** or **-ed** to the infinitive.

Last year I **believe*d*** that politician, but she **disappointe*d*** me.

The *past participle* form for regular verbs is the same as the past tense form. We indicate an occurrence in the past with the past participle by using **have, has** or **had** before it.

I **have supporte*d*** that politician before, but I am reluctant to support her now.

Past participles can also be used to help describe nouns or pronouns.

Ms. Barton is an **electe*d*** official.

Two other inflections are formed by the addition of **-ing** and **-s** or **-es** to the infinitive. The *present participle* is the **-ing** form. Used with a form of **be**, it can indicate ongoing occurrences; used alone it can modify nouns or pronouns.

I **am prepar*ing*** a political campaign. [an ongoing action]

She lends a **help*ing* hand** to the needy. [modifying a noun]

Whenever we express an occurrence in the present with a singular noun (**7c**) or third person pronoun (**7d**) as subject, we add **-s** or **-es** to the verb.

Her ***manager* holds** the purse strings of her campaign. [singular noun as subject]

***He* argues** with her about her extravagant travel budget. [third person singular personal pronoun as subject]

Everyone* believe*s that politician now. [singular indefinite pronoun as subject]

2. *Irregular verbs.* Some English verbs do not form their past tense or past participle in the regular way. There are four patterns typical of these *irregular verbs*: (1) changing a vowel instead of adding **-ed**; (2) adding an **-n** instead of **-ed**; (3) changing only one form from the infinitive and (4) not changing the infinitive for either past tense or past participle.

	Infinite	*Past Tense*	*Past Participle*
(1) vowel change:	ring	rang	rung
(2) addition of **-n**	arise	arose	arisen
(3) one change	find	found	found
(4) no change	let	let	let

Below is a list of common irregular verbs:

Infinitive	*Past Tense*	*Past Participle*
be	was	been
bite	bit	bitten
blow	blew	blown
break	broke	broken
build	built	built
choose	chose	chosen
come	came	come
deal	dealt	dealt
dig	dug	dug
dive	dived, dove	dived
do	did	done
draw	drew	drawn
drink	drank	drunk
drive	drove	driven
fly	flew	flown
freeze	froze	frozen
get	got	gotten
give	gave	given

7
b

Infinitive	*Past Tense*	*Past Participle*
go	went	gone
have	had	had
know	knew	known
lay (place *or* put)	laid	laid
lead	led	led
lend	lent	lent
lie (recline)	lay	lain
lose	lost	lost
ride	rode	ridden
rise	rose	risen
run	ran	run
see	saw	seen
set	set	set
shine (give light)	shone	shone
shine (polish)	shined	shined
sing	sang	sung
sink	sank, sunk	sunk
sit	sat	sat
steal	stole	stolen
sting	stung	stung
swim	swam	swum
swing	swung	swung
take	took	taken
think	thought	thought
throw	threw	thrown
wear	wore	worn
write	wrote	written

3. *Helping verbs.* Certain verbs are used with other verbs as *helping* or *auxiliary* words to communicate such information as time, type of statement, and the singular or plural nature of the subject. Common auxiliaries are **be, have, do**.

The students **have** finished their work but the period **has** not ended. [**Have** and **has** help to indicate a sequence in time as well as the plurality and singularity of the subjects, **students** and **period**.]

Did she give us an assignment? [**Did** helps to indicate a question as well as past time.]

A number of auxiliaries indicate the *mode* of an occurrence and so are called *modal* auxilaries. *Mode* refers to such indications as ability (**can, could**), possibility (**may, might**), and necessity, duty or willingness (**must, ought, shall, should, would**).

All the pupils in the third grade class **could** do the work, but only a few **would** do it without a threat.

4. *Linking verbs.* *Linking verbs* relate a subject to a word or words that help identify or describe the subject (see **8b**). The way linking verbs serve a clause is similar to the way an equal sign (=) serves an equation.

The artist **was** a vegetarian.

Those mountains **seem** distant.

The pizza **smells** delicious.

5. *Tense.* A verb's *tense* is the feature that communicates time of occurrence. There are three major types of tenses: the *simple tenses*, the *perfect tenses*, and the *progressive tenses*. The simple tenses are the present (using the infinitive form), the past (using the past tense form), and the future (using the infinitive form plus **shall** or **will**).

	Regular	*Irregular*
Present	You ask	She rings
Past	You asked	She rang
Future	You will ask	She will ring

The *perfect tenses* communicate a comparison of times; they express an occurrence at a time before some other time. They are formed with the auxiliary **have** and the *past participle*.

Present Perfect	You have asked	She has rung	[before the present]
Past Perfect	You had asked	She had rung	[before some past time]
Future Perfect	You will have asked	She will have rung	[before some future time]

7
b

The *progressive tenses* communicate a continuing occurrence at a particular time. They are formed with the present participle and the auxiliaries **be** and **have.**

Present	You are asking	She is ringing
Past	You were asking	She was ringing
Future	You will be asking	She will be ringing
Present Perfect	You have been asking	She has been ringing
Past Perfect	You had been asking	She had been ringing
Future Perfect	You will have been asking	She will have been ringing

The usage of **shall** and **will** has changed in this century. Formerly, **shall** was used with the first person (I, we shall) and **will** was used with the second and third persons (you, she, they will). Today **will** has replaced **shall** (I, we will) except in the most formal contexts. To indicate resoluteness or obligation **shall** may be used with second and third persons.

He shall not make that mistake again.

To ask a first-person question requesting an opinion **shall** is sometimes used.

Shall we continue to tolerate these conditions?

6. *Mood.* The *mood* of a verb communicates certain things about the writer's thinking. The *indicative mood* is almost always the mood of normal discourse, for it helps indicate that

the speaker is expressing impressions, facts, or beliefs; and it is the form verbs take in questions. All the sentences used as examples so far in this chapter have verbs in the indicative mood.

Sally **asks** about you every time I see her. [fact or exaggeration]

Does Sally ever **ask** about me? [question]

Sally **needs** more time away from her books. [opinion]

The *imperative mood* is used in giving commands. The imperative verb form is no different from the indicative form used with **you**, but in a command, the subject **you** is omitted.

Ask Billy to the party before someone else does. [**You** as subject of **ask** is deleted.]

Stop! [**You** as subject is deleted.]

The *subjunctive mood* is uncommon even in formal discourse. When used, it helps communicate that the writer is expressing something contrary to fact or that the writer is expressing a request, suggestion, or requirement. Certain verbs followed by **that** require the subjunctive: among these verbs are **ask, insist, recommend, require, request, suggest, urge, wish**. Most of these verbs, whatever their tense, take only the *present subjunctive,* which is the form used with **you** in the present tense.

I recommend [or recommended] that she **reevaluate** her goals from time to time.

The plant manager insisted that each foreman **keep** a daily record of production.

Wish is an exception because it can take the *past subjunctive.* The past subjunctive takes the same form as the past tense.

I wish that she **reevaluated** her goals from time to time.

The plant manager wished that each supervisor **kept** accurate records.

The subjunctive form of **be** is **were** when the verb is in an **if** construction or when it helps express a wish.

If Mary **were** free on the weekends, she would be able to finish writing her novel.

Mary wishes I **were** happier.

In certain constructions, the subjunctive of **be** is **be**.

I require that you **be** on time.

Be it resolved that we will oppose the President's policy.

7. *Voice.* A verb's *voice* is the form it takes to help communicate whether the subject acts or is itself acted upon. The *active voice* makes the subject the actor.

Neil Jones **sold** most of the houses in this development.

The *passive voice* shows that the subject is acted upon.

Most of the houses in this development **were sold** by Neil Jones.

(Active and passive voices are treated more fully in **8c** and Chapter **17**.)

Exercise 1

Circle the main verbs in each of the following sentences, and underline any auxiliary verbs.

1. The mishap would have been a disaster if not for the gymnast's quick recovery.
2. Despite repeated efforts, the frantic parents could find no trace of their missing child.
3. The ceremonies will be starting in an hour.

4. Irritated about my poor performance on the first calculus test, I vowed to study harder for the second exam.

7c Nouns

Nouns are the naming words in English. Whenever we wish to speak of a phenomenon, we can usually choose a noun to represent it. If the phenomenon is new to our culture, we may have to invent a word. **Ship, night,** and **mother** are relatively old nouns in English; **proton, Nevada,** and **astronaut** are relatively new nouns.

Like other parts of speech, nouns are identifiable by their special relationships with other words:

1. *Noun determiners.* Nouns take the special noun-marking *determiners* (also called *articles*) **the** and **a** or **an** immediately before them. **The** and **a/an** always signal the reader that a noun will soon follow:

the stadium, **a** crowd, **an** astronaut.

2. *Noun positions.* Nouns occupy only certain positions such as sentence subject and complement, and phrase object (see Chapter **8**).

subject complement
Ostriches are flightless **birds**.

3. *Noun form changes.* Nouns change their form to convey plurality and possession. Most singular nouns can be made plural by adding a suffix, usually **s** or **es**: several crowd**s**, three astronaut**s**, dozen**s** of dish**es**. Note that some nouns are irregular: two child**ren**, several phenomen**a**. Nouns not ending in **s** add **'s** to show possession: the crowd**'s** anger, the children**'s** courage, the horse**'s** bridle. Singular nouns ending in **s** add **'s**: Mars**'s** orbit, Bill Jones**'s** money. Regular

plural nouns add only an apostrophe to show possession: the astronauts' food, the United Nations' future. (Chapter **29** further explains the apostrophe.)

Words that name general classes (**ship, crowd, anger**) are called *common nouns*. Words that name specific places or people or that act as titles are called *proper nouns* and are capitalized: **Nevada** (place), **Bill Smith** (person), **The Beatles** (title). Some nouns are also said to be *concrete* or *abstract*. We can touch what concrete nouns name: **water, car, skyscraper**. We can only think about what abstract nouns name: **justice, foolishness, democracy**. Three types of nouns refer to quantities. A *collective noun* names a group: **orchestra, pile, committee**. A *count noun* names something that can be counted: **nail, person, inch**. A *mass noun* names something tangible but not usually counted and so not usually found in the plural: **air, water, dirt**.

When a present participle is used as a noun, it is called a *gerund*.

Jogging is a popular recreation.

Lying and **cheating** are violations of the honor code.

Exercise 2

Circle the nouns in the following sentences, and underline any noun determiners.

1. Miles of sea stretched away from the castaways on their tiny isle, making them feel minute and insignificant.
2. The whirlwind romance came to an end when Jan discovered that Mike had three other "steady" girlfriends.

3. The presence of the security chief in the central office indicated to the employees that something was amiss.

4. That painting is not as interesting as its frame.

7d Pronouns

Pronouns do not name in the same way as nouns, but they can serve any role in a sentence that a noun can serve. A pronoun usually stands for a noun, and this noun is called the pronoun's *antecedent*. Compare the two sentences below:

As the people hurried into the stadium, the people craned the people's necks anticipating the excitement in store for the people.

As the people hurried into the stadium, they craned their necks anticipating the excitement in store for them.

The first example is difficult to read because the noun **people** draws our attention so often that it diverts us from the sentence's meaning. The revised example is more understandable because appropriate pronouns are substituted for the antecedent **people**.

1. *Personal pronouns.* The pronouns most often used and the ones with the most *inflections* (different forms) are called *personal pronouns.*

Personal pronouns change their form to reflect three things: *number*, *person*, and *case*. *Singular* pronouns stand for one individual; *plural* pronouns stand for more than one. *First person* pronouns refer to the writer; *second person* pronouns refer to an individual whom the writer is addressing; *third person* pronouns refer to individuals or things about whom someone is writing.

7
d

Personal Pronouns

	Subjective Case	*Objective Case*	*Possessive Case*	*Possessive Case (noun marker)*
First Person				
singular	I	me	mine	my
plural	we	us	ours	our
Second Person				
singular & plural	you	you	yours	your
Third Person				
singular	he	him	his	his
	she	her	hers	her
	it	it	its	its
plural	they	them	theirs	their

The *subjective case* is used when the pronoun is the subject of a clause or phrase or is a complement of a subject:

I have a cat. [subject of clause]

The only victims of the robbery were my sister and **I**. [subject complement]

The *objective case* is used when the pronoun is the object in a clause or phrase.

The cat scratched **me**. [object of verb **scratched**]

I opened a can of food for **her**. [object of preposition **for**]

(Subjects and objects are discussed in **8a** and **8b**.)

Personal pronouns can indicate ownership in the *possessive case* in two ways. As noun markers, they can act like determiners by preceding a noun.

That is **my** cat.

Or they can stand alone.

That cat is **mine**.

The table at left shows that some pronouns do not inflect when others do. For example, **you** has the same form for the subjective and the objective cases. When one pronoun form can serve in more than one role, we must use either the position of the pronoun in the sentence or the context of the statement to tell what the pronoun means.

As **you** know, **I** have high regard for **her**.

Reading the sentence above, we can tell that **you** is the subject of its clause by its position, but we cannot tell whether it is singular or plural without knowing the larger context of the sentence. We know **I** is the subject of the second clause because of its position and its form. (We would not write, "**Me** have high regard for her.") We also know that **I** refers to only one individual, as does **her**, but only the context tells us that **her** is an object and not a possessive preceding a noun (as in, "I have high regard for **her taste**").

In addition to personal pronouns, there are seven other traditional classifications according to the role the pronoun serves.

2. *Reflexive and intensive pronouns.* Personal pronouns with **-self** or **-selves** added can be *reflexive* or *intensive. Reflexive* pronouns refer to the subject of a clause and indicate that the subject receives the action of the verb.

Bill almost killed **himself**.

An *intensive* pronoun stresses a preceding noun or pronoun by in effect repeating it just for emphasis.

Bill sold his house **himself**.

Note that you can delete an intensive pronoun, and the sentence's essential message will remain; but you cannot delete a reflexive pronoun and preserve the sentence's message.

7
d

3. *Demonstrative pronouns.* A writer using *demonstrative pronouns* (**this, that, these, those**) seems to be gesturing or pointing out something.

Those are the cheapest, and **these** are the most expensive.

4. *Indefinite pronouns. Indefinite pronouns* (**all, one, each, either, anyone, something, everybody,** etc.) refer to persons or things generally.

In the United States there is more space where **nobody** is than where **anybody** is.

Gertrude Stein

5. *Relative pronouns.* A *relative pronoun* (**who, which, that, whoever, whichever**) relates words to its antecedent noun or pronoun. Like personal pronouns, the relative pronoun **who** changes form to reflect case: subjective—**who**, possessive—**whose**, objective—**whom**,. **That** does not inflect. **Which** sometimes inflects its possessive as **whose** and sometimes as **of which**.

I know a woman **who** kept over thirty cats. [subject of verb **kept**; antecedent—**woman**]

I know a woman **whose** cats ate over $250.00 worth of food a month. [possessive; antecedent—**woman**]

I know a woman **whom** cats drove crazy. [object of the verb **drove**; antecedent—**woman**]

In the kitchen were four cabinets, the sole use **of which** was to store cat food. [possessive; antecedent—**use**]

6. *Interrogative pronouns. Interrogative pronouns* (**who, which, what**) introduce questions.

Who kept over thirty cats?

Note that a *relative pronoun* relates words after it to a noun before it.

The folklorist interviewed a man **who** claimed to have magical powers. [**Who** refers to **man**.]

Interrogative pronouns, on the other hand, represent an unexpressed noun that is requested as an answer.

Who claimed to have magical powers?

7. *Reciprocal pronouns. Reciprocal pronouns* (**each other, one another, one . . . other**) help communicate a give-and-take relationship between two or more creatures or things.

The armies fought **each other** until darkness separated them.

Exercise 3

Circle the pronouns in the following sentences, and draw a line to their antecedent nouns if an antecedent is present.

1. As Phyllis watched the children playing, she reflected sadly on the differences between their world of childhood and the world of childhood that had been hers.
2. A fan who had spent the entire game yelling at the umpires injured himself when he dropped a bottle of beer on his big toe.
3. Almost every year, someone claims to have discovered new evidence that confirms the existence of UFO's.
4. Whoever knows enough chemistry to understand the ingredients on a box of cake mix should be able to pass the final exam in Chemistry 1100.

7e Adjectives

Adjectives give information about (modify) nouns and pronouns. Adjectives describe by specifying quality or quantity.

We all stopped work to enjoy the **cool** breeze.

A **few** stragglers limped by.

Like nouns, adjectives can appeal to the senses as in the first sentence above or can appeal to abstract thought as in the second sentence.

Linking verbs can be used to link subjects with modifying adjectives. The adjective in such a pattern is called the *subject complement*; it is also called the *predicate adjective*.

The breeze was **cool**.

Certain *pronouns* are traditionally said to serve as adjectives when they precede a noun. The possessive pronouns (**my, our,** etc.), the demonstrative pronouns (**this, that,** etc.), and certain others (**what, which**) can precede nouns and modify them.

Our work discouraged us. [possessive adjective]

That breeze was cool. [demonstrative adjective]

What breeze are you talking about? [interrogative adjective]

Participles can serve as adjectives.

The **discouraging** work exhausted us. [present participle]

A well-**accomplished** job can make workers proud. [past participle]

Nouns can modify other nouns and thereby function as adjectives.

The **football** field was repaired only one hour before the game.

Certain inflections can transform other parts of speech into adjectives. For example, **-y, -al, -ish,** and **-ous** are *adjectival* *suffixes*: **health—healthy, nature—natural, self—selfish, fame—famous**.

Note also that certain adjectives can be inflected to be nouns by adding *nominal suffixes*: **good—goodness; stupid—stupidity.**

Certain adjectives are inflected to communicate *comparative* and *superlative degree*. *Degree* means the extent of the quality communicated by the adjective. The regular comparative suffix is **-er**, and the regular superlative suffix is **-est**.

The breezes are **cooler** today than yesterday. [comparative]

This is the **coolest** day we've had this summer. [superlative]

Some adjectives have irregular inflections for degree: **good, better, best; bad, worse, worst**.

Exercise 4

Circle the adjectives in the following sentences, and draw a line to the words they modify.

1. The engine of the stalled car belched forth thick, black clouds of noxious fumes, causing traffic in the tunnel to come to a complete halt for several hours.
2. The evidence against the political prisoner was fabricated, and the trial itself was a shameful farce.
3. The worst thing about attending a large university is having to stand in long lines to accomplish any official business.

4. Last winter left no visible scars, but the memory of it lay over the people like a dark cloud.

7f Adverbs

7 f

Adverbs can modify verbs, adjectives, and other adverbs as well as groups of words. They usually help communicate how, when, where, or to what extent something occurred or existed.

Victoria listened **carefully**. [**Carefully** modifies the verb **listened**.]

Victoria was **carefully** attentive at the concert. [**Carefully** modifies the adjective **attentive**.]

Victoria listened **very** carefully. [**Very** modifies the adverb **carefully**.]

Most adverbs are formed by adding the suffix **-ly** to an adjective as in sentence #1 above (**careful—carefully**). Note, though, that some adjectives also end in **-ly**.

Victoria was **lovely**, but she did a **cowardly** thing.

Other ways to form adverbs are to add the prefix **a-** to other words (**a**loud, **a**drift, **a**new); to add the suffix **-wise** to certain nouns (length**wise**); to add the suffix **-wards** to certain nouns (back**wards**); to add **some, any, every,** or **no** to certain words (**some**place, **any**way). Several common adverbs are not formed from other words: **always, even, later, now, often, perhaps, seldom, still, then.** Certain other adverbs are called *qualifiers* or *intensifiers*: **very, more, rather**.

Exercise 5

Circle the adverbs in the following sentences, and draw a line to the words they modify.

1. The audience laughed uproariously at the wildly absurd antics of the chimps.
2. Professional umpires seldom lose their composure even before insanely hostile coaches, players, and fans.
3. The orchestra conductor often wondered privately if the musicians would function as well without him as with him.

7g Prepositions

A *preposition* relates a noun, a pronoun, or a group of words acting as a noun to another part of a sentence. The noun or pronoun or word group that follows a preposition is called the *object of the preposition*. The preposition and its object are called a *prepositional phrase*. The relationship that prepositions establish between words is often a matter of sequence in time (**after, until**) or position in space (**in, under**). Common prepositions are listed below:

about	at	considering	like
above	before	despite	near
across	behind	down	of
after	below	during	off
against	beneath	except	on
along	beside	for	onto
amid	between	from	out
among	beyond	in	outside
around	by	inside	over
as	concerning	into	past

regarding
round
since
through
throughout
till
toward
under
unlike
until
unto
up
upon
with
within
without

Bob was very nervous when he was **among** strangers. [The noun **strangers** is object of the preposition **among**; the preposition helps establish the relationship between **he** and **strangers**.]

Several people in the club objected to the discussion **about** who should be denied membership. [The preposition **about** relates its object, **who should be denied membership**, to the word **discussion**.]

Exercise 6

Circle the prepositions in the following sentences, and underline the prepositional phrases.

1. The lawyer was known throughout his career as a man given to theatrics.
2. The scientist studied the photographs sent from the surface of the distant planet by an unmanned probe.
3. The local police chief decided that the case was outside his jurisdiction and called the FBI for assistance.

7h Conjunctions

Conjunctions, like prepositions, relate words and word groups.

1. *Coordinating conjunctions. Coordinating conjunctions* link words or word groups of the same type:

and	for	or	yet
but	nor	so	

Martha **and** Philip have little in common. [two nouns linked]

Martha skydives, **but** Philip is afraid of heights. [two independent clauses linked]

Philip must choose whether to jump **or** to watch. [two infinitives linked]

7 h

2. *Correlative conjunctions. Correlative conjunctions* are word pairs that link words or word groups of the same type:

both . . . and	neither . . . nor
either . . . or	not . . . but
not only . . . but also	

Both Philip **and** Martha play poker but not with each other. [two nouns linked]

They **neither** smile **nor** frown during a game. [two verbs linked]

3. *Subordinating conjunctions. Subordinating conjunctions* link clauses so that one clause is incorporated as a modifying part of another clause. Some common subordinating conjunctions are **although, because, if, unless, while**. (A more extensive list is given in **10b**.)

Martha skydives **although** she is afraid of heights.

The subordinating conjunction **although** makes the clause **she is afraid of heights** subordinate to the clause **Martha skydives**. This *subordinate clause* tells something about the conditions under which Martha does her skydiving. It is actually an adverbial modifier that can be moved within the sentence:

Although Martha is afraid of heights, she skydives.

Note the difference in the ways that coordinating and subordinating conjunctions relate word groups. Coordinating conjunctions are bound between words or word groups of equal significance, so they cannot be moved from their place between the constructions they coordinate. For example, sentence #1 is grammatical, but sentence #2 is not.

Grammatical

1. Martha belongs to several clubs, **but** she hates to attend meetings.

Ungrammatical

2. **But** she hates to attend meetings, Martha belongs to several clubs.

Subordinating conjunctions, on the other hand, precede modifying clauses that can be moved to different places in a sentence. For, example, we can grammatically change sentence #3 to sentence #4.

3. Philip waterskies although he cannot swim.
4. Although he cannot swim, Philip waterskies.

4. *Conjunctive adverbs.* Independent clauses may be linked not only with coordinating conjunctions but also with *conjunctive adverbs.* In linking two independent clauses, a conjunctive adverb modifies the clause following it.

After the speeches, we beat a hasty retreat; **meanwhile**, the audience remained to cheer the speakers. [**Meanwhile** links the two clauses and tells when the audience remained to cheer.]

The flood left ten inches of mud in the hotel. **Nevertheless**, the Optimist Club held its regularly scheduled meeting there.

Note that when conjunctive adverbs occur between two independent clauses they require a semicolon or period immediately before and a comma immediately after.

Common conjunctive adverbs are listed below:

accordingly	furthermore	meanwhile	similarly
also	however	moreover	still
besides	incidentally	nevertheless	then
consequently	instead	now	therefore
finally	likewise	otherwise	thus

These words can also serve as simple adverbs.

She was **finally** gone.

However ugly Fido was, he will remain in our hearts.

Exercise 7

Circle each conjunction in the following sentences, and indicate what kind of conjunction it is.

1. It's up to you to perform this task because you have the proper qualifications and background. **subordinating conjunction**
2. Neither the plaintiff nor the defendant was happy with the court's decision. **correlative conjunction**
3. The kidnapper's father was a reluctant but effective go-between for his son and the multitude of law enforcement officials concerned with the case. **coordinating conjunctions**

7i Interjections

Interjections are expressions that either stand alone or have no grammatical connection with the rest of the sentence in which they appear. They do not work as subjects or verbs or modifiers or words that relate one part of the sentence to another. They are there only to express a writer's exclamation.

Phooey!

Why **in heaven's name** did you do that?

7j Use your understanding of the parts of speech.

Being able to identify the parts of speech is not a skill that in itself will help you write. For your knowledge of the parts of speech to be of help, you must apply it in analyzing your writing. Consider, for example, the passage below:

1. A dress code in the public schools might result in the prevention of competition among students in their dress, but it would be an inhibition to their way of expressing their personalities.

In this sentence, you will find two verbs (counting **result** and its auxiliary **might** as one), ten nouns (counting the gerund **expressing**), two adjectives (including the adjectival noun **dress**), four pronouns, five prepositions, and one conjunction. Now consider sentence #2, which is synonymous with #1 but which has a different distribution of parts of speech.

2. A dress code in the public schools might prevent competition among students in the way they dress, but it would inhibit the way they express their personalities.

Sentence #2 has four verbs, six nouns, three pronouns, two adjectives, four prepositions, and one conjunction. Sentence #2 has twice as many verbs, four fewer nouns, and five fewer total words than sentence #1. Most readers would say that sentence #2 is easier to read, yet some readers and writers might find #1 more impressive and might think that a writer who relies on nouns seems somehow wiser than one who relies on verbs. One reason for such a belief may be that the ability to name things is a characteristic of knowledgeable persons, so the more we translate our knowledge into names rather than actions, the wiser we appear. Unfortunately, in doing so, we often make our message harder for our readers to understand. As you can see from this analysis, an understanding of the parts of speech provides a means for thinking constructively about the language we use.

Exercise 8

Change each of the sentences below as directed.

1. Change the tense of the verb from future to future perfect:

   I will have been talking
   ~~I will talk~~ to their representative Tuesday.

2. Change the tense of the verb from past to present progressive:

   are expecting
   The teachers ~~expected~~ too much from their students.

3. Change the mood of the verb from indicative to imperative. Make any other changes necessary to create a logical and coherent sentence:

   Marsha, help Walt
   ~~Marsha should help Walt~~ with his homework.

4. Change each noun from singular to plural:

   children **papers**
   I told the ~~child~~ to stop throwing the ~~paper~~ everywhere.

5. Change each common noun to a proper noun, deleting noun determiners in the process:

   Wyatt Earp **Billy the Kid**
   ~~The sheriff~~ told ~~the gunslinger~~ to get out of the town.
   [Answers will vary.]

7
j

6. Change each second-person pronoun to third person. Make any necessary changes in the verb forms:

   He/She is **he/she can make his/her**
   ~~You are~~ foolish to believe that ~~you can make your~~ fortune by selling vacuum cleaners door-to-door.

7. Change all modifiers so that the sentence reflects a positive attitude toward the host's remarks:

   flattering **relieved** **pleased**
   The ~~insulting~~ remark by our host left us ~~shocked~~ and ~~disgusted~~. **[Answers will vary.]**

8. Change all modifiers so that the sentence reflects an unfavorable attitude toward the fire fighter.

   cowardly **disgruntled**
   The ~~courageous~~ fire fighter found the ~~appreciative~~ victims. **[Answers will vary.]**

9. Change the meaning of the sentence by substituting different conjunctions:

   and **or**
   The parents ~~or~~ the children will receive a sandwich ~~and~~ a drink at intermission.

10. Change each preposition to create a different meaning:

    inside **after**
    I arrived ~~outside~~ the coliseum ~~before~~ the rock concert had begun. **[Answers will vary.]**

8 · Creating Basic Sentences

8a The basic sentence

8 b

An English sentence has at least these two parts: a *subject* and a verb or verb phrase, or as we will refer to it here, a *predicate*. The subject names a topic for the sentence, and the predicate either asserts something about that topic or specifies action involving it.

Subject	*Predicate*
Running and jogging	are different.
Neil	rode.
All five interior linemen	couldn't protect the aging quarterback.

In this text, what we call a *basic sentence* consists of a subject and a predicate which cannot be made briefer without destroying the sentence's grammatical nature or its fundamental message. **Running and jogging are different** and **Neil rode** are basic sentences; we cannot delete words from the first without destroying its statement, nor can we delete words from the second without destroying it as a sentence. But **All five interior linemen couldn't protect the aging quarterback** is not basic; we can substitute the word **The** for **All five interior**, and we can delete the word **aging** without destroying the essential subject and predicate: **The linemen couldn't protect the quarterback**.

8b Five basic sentence patterns

Basic sentences occur most frequently in five patterns, each of which has a particular kind of predicate.

1. *Linking verbs (see* **7b**) identify a basic sentence's subject directly with a following noun or adjective in the pattern, *noun (or pronoun)—linking verb—noun or adjective*. The word after the linking verb is called the *subject complement* (SC).

N LV N(SC)
1. The boys were pranksters.

N LV ADJ(SC)
2. Harry seems content.

Sometimes the subject complement is omitted from a basic sentence, but the complement remains understood. For example, in a context questioning the identity of some alleged pranksters ("Who were those pranksters?") sentence #1 might be abbreviated to sentence #3.

3. The boys were. (**The pranksters** is omitted but understood.)

Note that sentence #1 is the basic sentence from which sentence #4 is derived:

4. **The** frightened **boys were** utterly inept and harmless **pranksters**.

2. A verb is *intransitive* if it does not require a noun or adjective after it to complete its expression of an action. A basic sentence with an *intransitive verb* has the pattern, *noun—intransitive verb* (IV).

N IV
5. The students doze.

PN IV
6. She has gone.

Note that we would not say **The students doze something**. Note also that sentence #5 is the basic sentence from which sentence #7 is developed:

7. **The students**, in the grip of a smothering boredom, **doze** through interminable announcements.

3. *Transitive verbs* require objects to complete the expression of an action. When the predicate of a basic sentence has a transitive verb in the pattern *noun—transitive verb (TV)—noun,* the noun following the verb is called a *direct object* (DO).

N TV N(DO)
8. The vandals destroyed the books.

N TV N(DO)
9. Jack fooled his sister.

Compare sentences #8 and #9 with sentences #5 and #6. Note that verbs like **doze** and **go** do not invite the reader to ask "what" or "who" but that verbs like **destroy** and **fool** do invite the reader to ask those questions. Many verbs can be both transitive and intransitive depending on their context: **What is Jack doing? He is painting (IV). What is Jack painting? He is painting (TV) the door (DO).**

4. When the transitive verb of a basic sentence requires its direct object to have a *complement,* the pattern is *noun—transitive verb—noun—noun or adjective*. The last noun or adjective in this pattern is called the *object complement* (OC), and it is generated with verbs that promise a name or a describer for the direct object.

N TV N(DO) N(OC)
10. His sister called Jack a fool.

PN TV PN(DO) ADJ(OC)
11. She considered him inept.

5. *Certain transitive verbs, like* **give, send, lend**, and **bring**, specify an act of transference in the pattern *noun—transitive verb—noun—noun*. In this case the noun right after the verb names who or what receives the transfer, and it is called the *indirect object* (IO); the subsequent noun, a direct object, tells what was transferred.

N TV N(IO) N(DO)
12. Mary bought her father a car.

PN TV PN(IO) N(DO)
13. I shall send him the package.

Exercise 1

Circle the subject, write the kind of predicate (transitive, intransitive or linking) over the main verb, and underline any complements or direct objects.

1. The discontented (gathering) quickly became [linking] unruly.
2. The (discovery) of a new type of virus sent [transitive] shock waves through the medical profession.
3. The front (office) sent [transitive] Sheryl a letter of commendation.
4. The heated (debate) between the art critics continued [intransitive] for hours.
5. The (Englishman) thought [transitive] the visiting Texan quite a character.

8c Four alterations to the basic sentence

Basic sentence structures can be changed to meet the special requirements of giving commands and asking questions; and they can be changed to passive and expletive constructions. Those four alterations are described below.

1. *A command* is a sentence with the verb in the present tense and the subject **you** deleted:

Call your sister.

Stop!

2. We can transform a basic sentence into a *question* by moving an auxiliary or linking verb to the first of the sentence: **Were the boys pranksters? Has she gone? Did Jack fool his sister? Shall I send him the package?** Note that questions in this form can be answered *yes* or *no*.

To the beginning of these questions, we can add certain adverbs (**why, when, how**) and so invite extended, detailed answers: **Why did Jack fool his sister? When shall I send him the package?** And we can substitute interrogative pronouns for objects and complements and put them at the first of questions and so require objects or complements as answers: ***What* did the vandals destroy? The vandals destroyed the books** (DO). ***What* did she consider him? She considered him inept** (OC).

We can also make interrogative pronouns the subjects of questions (see **7d**): ***Who* kissed the guitar player? *What* is on the table?**

3. The previous example sentences in this chapter have verbs in the *active voice*. The subjects of these verbs do the behaving or existing proposed in the sentence. In any basic sentence with a direct object, the words may be rearranged and the verb may be converted to the *passive voice* so that the sentence has a subject that receives the action. To express in the passive voice, we do four things:

(1) Either delete the original subject or put it at the end of the sentence with **by** before it.

(2) Transfer the direct object to the subject slot.

(3) Substitute the past participle of the verb in the verb slot.

(4) Add a form of *be* as auxiliary to the past participle.

Active	Jack fooled my sister.
	(2) (4) (3) (1)
Passive	My sister was fooled by Jack.

When the active verb is in the present or future tense, we must add more than one form of **be** before the past participle.

Active	The vandals are destroying the books.
Passive	The books **are being** destroyed by the vandals.
Active	I will send him the package.
Passive	The package **will be** sent to him. (**By me** is deleted here.)

The passive voice is effective only in certain situations (see Chapter **17**).

Exercise 2

Change the following sentences from passive voice to active voice.

1. The integrity of professional sports is being destroyed by rampant greed and the resulting adverse fan reaction.
   Rampant greed and the resulting adverse fan reaction are destroying the integrity of professional sports.
2. The new employees were easily manipulated by the office manager.
   The office manager easily manipulated the new employees.
3. After the controversial ruling in the third inning, the game was played under protest by the home team.
   . . . the home team played the game under protest.

4. *Expletives* are the words **there** and **it** used not to stand for anything but simply to occupy the position of sentence subject. Compare sentences #1 and #2 with sentences #3 and #4.

1. A book is on the washing machine.
2. An excited fan kissed the guitar player.

3. There is a book on the washing machine.
4. It was an excited fan who kissed the guitar player.

There and **It** are place holders and do not have a meaning of their own. Such expletive constructions can emphasize the fact that a condition exists. In sentence #2, for example, the transitive main verb (**kissed**) focuses our attention on an action; but in sentence #4 the linking main verb (**was**) and the expletive **It** shift our attention from the action to the fact that an action happened. Because they are wordy, expletive constructions are effective in few contexts (see **14e**, **16a**).

Exercise 3

Eliminate the following expletive constructions and change the sentences to more direct statements.

1. There were thousands of fans greeting the victorious team.
   Thousands of fans greeted the victorious team.
2. It is a wise person who can grasp reality without becoming cynical.
   A wise person can grasp reality without becoming cynical.
3. There were many people present who disagreed with the conclusions of the board.
   Many people present disagreed with the conclusions of the board.

Exercise 4

Create sentences according to the following basic patterns, adding modifiers to create interesting and informative sentences.
Answers will vary.

1. Pronoun—Linking Verb—Noun (Subject Complement)
2. Noun—Intransitive Verb

3. Noun—Transitive Verb—Pronoun (Indirect Object)—Noun (Direct Object)
4. Pronoun—Linking Verb—Adjective (Subject Complement)
5. Noun—Transitive Verb—Pronoun (Direct Object)—Adjective (Object Complement)
6. Noun—Transitive Verb—Noun (Direct Object)
7. Pronoun—Transitive Verb—Pronoun (Direct Object)—Noun (Object Complement)

9 · Modifying with Individual Words and Phrases

9a Words that modify

As we have noted, basic sentences can be expanded by adding appropriate words. In Chapter **8**, we expanded the first sentence below to read as the second sentence.

The boys were pranksters.

The frightened boys were utterly inept pranksters.

The words added to the first sentence are all *modifiers*. They give additional information about the subject and predicate. We could expand this sentence with modifiers indefinitely.

The foolish, confused, frightened boys were utterly inept and harmless pranksters.

Exercise 1

Circle the one-word modifiers in the following sentences, and draw a line from them to the words they modify.

1. Foolishly, the convict attempted a poorly planned and executed escape just one month before his parole hearing.
2. The defendant, dazed and disillusioned by the decision of the court, wept bitterly as she was slowly led from the hushed courtroom.
3. When faced with the incriminating tapes and photographs, the powerful politician made a fiery speech against his accusers, labeling them "witch hunters."

9
b

9b Placement of modifiers

The usual place for adjectives in an English sentence is just before the noun they modify. Adverbs may or may not be next to the words they modify.

adj. adj. adv.
The **inept** and **harmless** pranksters were **soon** discovered by their friends.

Often modifiers can be moved from their usual place so that they receive special emphasis. Note that wherever they are in a sentence, adjectives should be close to the nouns they modify; adverbs are usually more free to be moved throughout the sentence.

adv. adj. adj.
Soon the pranksters, **inept** and **harmless**, were discovered by their friends.

9
c

9c Phrases that modify

Three types of phrases may modify nouns: prepositional phrases, participial phrases, and infinitive phrases. Prepositional phrases and infinitive phrases may also serve as adverbs. Other modifiers may pertain to an entire sentence.

1. *A prepositional phrase* is a preposition, its object, and any modifiers the object might have.

Many people **in the United States** celebrate New Year's Day by watching football **on television**. [prepositional adjective phrases modifying **people** and **football**]

The revelers danced **until twelve midnight**. [prepositional adverb phrase modifying **danced**]

2. *A participial phrase* is a present or past participle plus words acting as the participle's subject, complement, or modifier.

Passively celebrating New Year's Day, Glen slept in front of the TV. [present participial adjective phrase modifying **Glen**]

Martha, **discouraged by her husband's stupor**, gazed out the window at the bleak, cold day. [past participial adjective phrase modifying **Martha**]

3. An *infinitive phrase* is an infinitive plus any modifiers and objects.

All the child wanted was a pet **to treat as a friend**. [adjective infinitive phrase modifying **pet**]

To avoid detection, the smugglers disguised themselves as nuns. [adverb infinitive phrase modifying **disguised**]

4. *Sentence modifiers* are words and phrases that modify the entire sentence rather than a word or phrase within the sentence.

Obviously, he has lost all sense of reality. [adverb as sentence modifier]

To tell the truth, I'm worried about this election. [infinitive phrase as sentence modifier]

5. An *absolute phrase* is a sentence modifier consisting of a noun or pronoun and a participle.

The big day having arrived, we left in a cloud of exhaust.

Her school work finished, the girl saw no reason not to go to the arcade.

When the participle in an absolute phrase is **being** or **been**, the participle may be omitted.

His mother nowhere in sight, the child toddled weeping through the department store.

Exercise 2

Underline the modifying phrases in the following sentences, and indicate whether they function as adjectives, adverbs, or sentence modifiers.

1. On the far side [adv.] of the property [adj.] stretched a tranquil lake.
2. The game having been lost before it started [sent. mod.], our team played like broken robots [adv.].
3. The climber, clinging to his lifeline [adv.], made one last attempt to reach the summit [adv.] of the peak [adj.].
4. Smiling sheepishly [adv.], the youngster announced his intention to join the Navy [adj.], like his father before him [adv.].

9d Effects of modifying words and phrases

Note how much information the sentence below gives:

The foolish, confused, frightened boys were utterly inept and harmless pranksters.

Each adjective with the noun modified carries the same information as a statement, so the phrase **the frightened boys** gives the same information as the clause **The boys were frightened**. In fact, this one sentence has the same information as might be conveyed by seven sentences.

The boys were confused.

The boys were frightened.

The boys were pranksters.

The pranksters were inept.

The pranksters were harmless.

The extent of the ineptness was utter.

The extent of the harmlessness was utter.

Obviously modification is an efficient way to impart meaning, but like all stylistic options it can be abused by over or under use or by imprecise use.

The really beautiful, lovely pond lay under the bright, hot sun.

The student who wrote the sentence above justified doing so by claiming she had made the scene more vivid. She later revised the sentence, though, deleting the vague and redundant modifiers **really, beautiful,** and **lovely** and deleting the overly familiar **bright** and **hot**. She substituted specific images of time and place and used a verb that bore considerably more imagery than **lay**.

Surrounded by low grass banks, the pond shimmered under the August sun.

Modification is like the ingredients in a dish of food: too little, and potential for meaning (or taste) is wasted; too much, and the meaning (taste) is obscured. In fact, a sentence can gain in impact if the writer will delete an adjective or adverb which had at first seemed vivid but on reconsideration seems excessive. For example, compare the sentences below.

The foolish, confused, frightened boys were utterly inept and harmless pranksters.

The frightened boys were inept and harmless pranksters.

Comparing the sentences in a context, we might decide in light of preceding sentences that the ideas of confusion and foolishness and the intensifier **utterly** do not provide sufficient new information to warrant their inclusion; therefore, we might judge that even though the second sentence is shorter, it is stronger and helps the reader focus more clearly on the remaining modifiers.

Exercise 3

Expand the following sentences by adding modifying words and phrases. **Answers will vary.**

1. The young woman enjoyed the movie.
2. The game was important.
3. After the shower, the sky was beautiful.
4. The locomotive puffed.
5. Poverty affects people.

Exercise 4

Combine each of the following pairs of sentences by making one into a modifying phrase. **Answers will vary.**

1. The road was a popular place to park.
   The road was by the lake.
   The road by the lake was a popular place to park.

2. The drive was a long one.
   The drive was to the nearest hospital.
   The drive to the nearest hospital was a long one.
3. The master criminal's scheme was daring and ingenious. His scheme was to blackmail the United States' government.
   The master criminal's scheme to blackmail the United States' government was daring and ingenious.
4. When the bell rang, the boxer collapsed into his corner. The boxer was bleeding from cuts above each eye.
   When the bell rang, the boxer, bleeding from cuts above each eye, collapsed into his corner.
5. The tiny infant began to cry.
   The tiny infant was exhausted from being passed around.
   Exhausted from being passed around, the tiny infant began to cry.

Exercise 5

Combine the sentences in the following passage by changing some of them into one-word modifiers or modifying phrases.

Answers will vary.

Something appeared.
Its appearance was sudden.
Its appearance was mysterious.
It was a spacecraft.
The spacecraft was alien.
The spacecraft had a glint to it.
The glint was metallic.
The spacecraft hovered.
It hovered above the street.
The street was filled with people.
The people were shouting.
The people were pointing.
The spacecraft disappeared.
Its disappearance was sudden.
Its disappearance was mysterious.

Suddenly, mysteriously, something appeared. It was an alien spacecraft with a metallic glint. After hovering above the street filled with pointing and shouting people, it suddenly, mysteriously, disappeared.

10 · Modifying with Clauses

10a Independent and dependent clauses

A *clause* is a group of related words that has a subject and a verb. A clause is *independent* when it can serve as a sentence.

That book offers information on bookkeeping.

Bees swarm.

Note that the example sentences in Chapter **8** are all independent clauses. Basic sentences such as these can be expanded by adding modifying words and phrases (see Chapter **9**), other independent clauses (see Chapter **13**), and modifying clauses. Clauses that modify, called *dependent clauses*, cannot serve as sentences; they must always be included in another clause, where they serve as either adjectives or adverbs. There are two types of dependent clauses: *subordinate* clauses and *relative* clauses.

10b Modifying with subordinate clauses

To form a subordinate clause, you simply add a subordinating conjunction or a relative pronoun to the beginning of an independent clause.

Certain subordinators can make clauses serve as adverbs expressing relationships like those given below.

Time: **when, whenever, after, before, since, while, until, as, as long as, once**

***Until* you have passed the water safety course**, the recreation department will not hire you.

Place: **where, wherever**

Our neighbors hid their house key ***where* no one could find it.**

Condition: **if, provided, since, unless, whether**

***Unless* the rain stops soon**, we will be forced to abandon our homes.

Contrast: **although, even though, as if, though**

***Though* I was initially disappointed at being categorized an extremist**, I gradually gained a measure of satisfaction from the label.

Martin Luther King

Reason: **in order that, so, so that, that**

More and more colleges must increase tuition ***so that* they can continue to operate**.

Cause: **because, since**

I want to climb the mountain ***because* it is there.**

Clauses introduced by subordinating conjunctions can also serve as adjectives.

The moment ***before* dawn breaks** is my favorite time of day.

Most frequently, though, subordinate clauses used as adjectives are formed with the relative pronouns **who, which,** and **that**.

On my eighteenth birthday I learned a lesson ***that* I will never forget**.

An *elliptical clause* is a subordinate clause with certain words deleted.

Those are the shoes **I want**. [The subordinator **that** is deleted.]

If nominated, I will not run. **If elected**, I will not serve. [The subject and the auxiliary verb **I am** are deleted from both clauses.]

William T. Sherman

A common type of elliptical clause occurs in comparisons after the conjunction **than**.

She plays bridge much better **than her husband**. [The verb and the object **plays bridge** have been deleted.]

10c Modifying with relative clauses

When you use a relative pronoun as the subject of a clause, you form a relative clause. Relative clauses usually serve as adjectives.

A fool is a man ***who* never tried an experiment in his life.**

Erasmus Darwin

We got food poisoning in a restaurant ***that* had been rated four stars.**

Exercise 1

In the following sentences, underline the modifying clauses and indicate whether they function as adverbs or adjectives.

1. [adv.] Although experts disagree over how long the earth's resources will last, geologists have noted an accelerating decline in the reserves of several vital minerals.

2. Rudolf Nureyev, [adj.] who is one of the most acclaimed ballet dancers in the world, defected from the Soviet Union

adv.
when he was twenty-three years old.

adj.
3. The film industry's rating code, which has been in effect since 1968, has often been criticized.

adv.
4. Unless new sources of financial aid can be found, many

adj.
students who are now enrolled in college may be forced to drop out of school.

10d Effects of clauses that modify

Like all modifiers, adjective and adverb clauses enrich sentences by embedding information. But because they have subjects and verbs, they modify with greater emphasis than do phrases and single words. For example, in the King James version of Genesis, Adam says to God, "The woman **whom thou gavest to be with me**, she gave me of the tree, and I did eat." Suppose instead of the adjective clause, **whom thou gavest to be with me**, the text gave a participial phrase, "given to be with me." The "woman" would still be modified, but Adam's attempt to escape guilt would be much less emphatic because he would not be stressing that God created the woman in the first place.

Words that introduce modifying clauses also establish a special coherence among ideas in a sentence. For example, the sentence by Martin Luther King quoted earlier expresses a contrast between two attitudes.

> Though I was initially disappointed at being categorized as an extremist, I gradually gained a measure of satisfaction from the label.

If King wanted to stress equally his initial disappointment and his later satisfaction, he might have made both clauses independent.

I was initially disappointed at being categorized an extremist, but I gradually gained a measure of satisfaction from the label.

Instead he subordinated his first clause to his second, so the sentence builds a momentum that forcefully emphasizes his change in attitude.

Exercise 2

Combine each of the following pairs of sentences by making one sentence a modifying clause. **Answers will vary.**

1. Martina Navratilova has reached a rare pinnacle in sports. She makes headlines when she loses.
   Martina Navratilova has reached a rare pinnacle in sports because she makes headlines when she loses.
2. Edgar Allan Poe was fascinated with the workings of the human mind. Poe wrote many stories about the conflict between sanity and madness.
   Edgar Allan Poe, who wrote many stories about the conflict between sanity and madness, was fascinated with the workings of the human mind.
3. Charles Darwin's *The Origin of Species* was published in 1859. *The Origin of Species* continues to have a profound influence on scientific and religious thought.
   Charles Darwin's *The Origin of Species*, which was published in 1859, continues to have a profound influence on scientific and religious thought.
4. Some teachers are skeptical about using computers to teach non-technical subjects. Computers offer one means of providing individualized instruction.
   Although computers offer one means of providing individualized instruction, some teachers are skeptical about using them to teach non-technical subjects.

Exercise 3

Expand the following simple sentences by adding one or more modifying clauses. **Answers will vary.**

1. Television commercials often present women in stereotyped roles.
2. A tall, shrouded figure emerged from the shadows.
3. *Raiders of the Lost Ark* is one of the most popular films of all time.
4. Buying a stereo system can be a complicated task.
5. Some states require students to pass a competency test in order to graduate from high school.

Exercise 4

Combine the sentences in the following passage by changing some of them into subordinate and relative clauses.
Answers will vary.

The alarm rang at 6:00 a.m.
I stumbled out of bed.
I tripped over a stack of books.
The books were lying where I had left them just four hours earlier.
I walked slowly toward the kitchen.
I bumped into a lamp.
The lamp crashed to the floor.
The noise woke up my cat.
He was angry at being awakened so early.
He dug his claws into my leg.
Suddenly I realized the horrible truth.
It was Monday.

When the alarm rang at 6:00 a.m., I stumbled out of bed and tripped over a stack of books lying where I had left them just four hours earlier. As I walked slowly toward the kitchen, I bumped into a lamp, which crashed to the floor. The noise woke my cat, who was angry at being awakened early, so he dug his claws into my leg. Suddenly I realized the horrible truth that it was Monday.

11 · Using Nominals and Appositives

11a Nominals

11 a

Nominals are words or word groups occurring in positions typically occupied by nouns. Infinitives and infinitive phrases, gerund phrases, prepositional phrases, and subordinate clauses may all be used nominally as subjects, complements, and objects.

To know her is **to love her**. [infinitive phrases as subject and as subject complement]

Running a student store is giving Allison ulcers. [gerund phrase as subject]

Near the exit is the best place to sit during this play. [prepositional phrase as subject]

Volunteers in the fire department understood **that they would have no time to enjoy the holiday**. [subordinate clause as object of verb **understood**]

What we have been makes us **what we are.** [subordinate clauses as subject and objective complement] T.S. Eliot

Adjectives can also be nominals.

Bigger is not necessarily **better**. [adjective as subject and subject complement]

Exercise 1

In the following sentences, underline each nominal and indicate whether the nominal is a subject, object, or complement.

1. "Following that act will be tough," moaned the nervous amateur contestant. [subj. written above "Following that act"]

11
b

subj. subj.
2. That the star was glamorous was undebatable; that she couldn't act was unimportant.

object
3. Milt thought that across the state line was too far to ride for a drink, so he gave up alcohol.

subj.
4. To view the proceedings of a typical court on a typical day is to witness first hand the inefficiency and inequity of our system of justice.
complement

complement
5. The boy's favorite activity was watching the harvesters in the fields.

11b Effects of nominals

Nominals provide a means for achieving clear and strong sentences when the thoughts expressed are complex. Consider the sentence below.

1. The parole board rejected his appeal, but **this** did not seem to bother the convict.

This in sentence #1 refers to the whole idea in the clause immediately preceding it. Pronouns such as **it, such, that, this,** and **which** can refer to general ideas expressed in clauses and so are said to have *broad reference*. Broad reference is often abused, however (see Chapter **41**), and we may narrow such constructions by reducing the clause to a nominal and eliminating the broad pronoun. For example, the first clause in sentence #1 can become a subordinate clause nominal replacing **this** as subject.

2. **That the parole board rejected his appeal** did not seem to bother the convict.

We can reword #1 in other ways to achieve similar results. In sentence #3, the first clause's verb has been transformed into a noun.

3. The parole board's **rejection** of his appeal did not seem to bother the convict.

Of course, the context of the sentence should be your guide in determining the wording. Sentence #1 would be most appropriate if you wanted to stress the parole board's judgment and the convict's response as separate, equal acts. Sentences #2 and #3 stress the convict's response, but sentence #2 keeps the parole board as an active agent whereas #3 reduces the parole board to a modifier of a noun.

Note that when the nominal is a gerund, an infinitive, or a clause, it can not only clarify the focus but also strengthen the sense of action.

4a. The students complained bitterly about the exam, but this did not influence their final grades.
b. The students' bitter **complaining** about the exam did not influence their final grades.
5a. An endorsement for this candidate is an investment in disaster.
b. **To endorse** this candidate is to invest in disaster.

In the first pair of sentences, the broad reference (**this**) in #4a has been clarified by a gerund (**complaining**) in #4b. In the second pair, an infinitive subject (**to endorse**) in #5b conveys a greater sense of action than the noun subject (**endorsement**) in #5a.

Exercise 2

Combine each of the following pairs of sentences by changing one sentence into a nominal. Answers will vary.

1. The talk show host had a nightmare that was the worst he could imagine.
   The nightmare was to be locked in a room with William F. Buckley, Jr., Joan Rivers, and Truman Capote.
   The worst nightmare the talk show host could imagine was to be locked in a room with William F. Buckley, Jr., Joan Rivers, and Truman Capote.
2. The students realized something.
   They realized their teacher was not in the mood for jokes.
   The students realized that their teacher was not in the mood for jokes.
3. Something caused Sue to turn pale and tremble.
   Sue turned pale and trembled when she saw a shadow loom quickly behind her.
   Seeing a shadow loom quickly behind her caused Sue to turn pale and tremble.
4. There was a way to go to the isolated city that was best.
   The way was through the mountain pass.
   The best way to go to the isolated city was through the mountain pass.

11c Appositives

An element similar to the nominal is the appositive. *Appositives* are elements that rename or further identify the words they follow. Usually an appositive is a noun or a noun with modifiers that helps define a preceding noun.

Robert Herrick, **the poet**, had an appreciative eye for pretty women, but he never married.

In the dark pit, we saw a teeming population of gnathobdellida, **leeches with teeth and jaws**.

Appositives can always replace the words they refer to in the sentence.

In the dark pit, we saw a teeming population of **leeches with teeth and jaws**.

Appositives may also define other parts of speech. In the sentence below, the appositive defines the infinitive **to rappel**.

After scaling the cliff, he proceeded to rappel, **to slide down using a double rope**.

11d Effects of appositives

Appositives are similar in function to relative clauses (**10c**).

1. My cousin, **who is a man of dark moods**, has been unable to hold any job for long.

If we have a relative clause with a form of **be** as the main verb, as in sentence #1, and if we are unsatisfied with the length and emphasis of the clause, we can reduce the clause to an appositive; we simply delete the relative pronoun and the verb and use the clause's complement as an appositive.

2. My cousin, **a man of dark moods**, has been unable to hold any job for long.

The subject complement of the relative clause in sentence #1 has been used as an appositive in sentence #2. The effects of this revision are to make the sentence more concise, to give less emphasis to the fact that the cousin has dark moods, and thus to focus on the fact that he cannot hold a job for long.

Exercise 3

Circle the appositives in the following sentences and draw a line to the words they rename or help define.

1. The pioneers in this field, Macon and Wickley, claim that the implications of their discoveries are astounding.

2. In Spain we witnessed a bullfight, the ritualistic murder of a noble animal.

3. The manager of the store, a man with strong convictions, refused to go along with the idea of opening for business on Sunday afternoons.

11
d

Expand the following sentences by adding appositives. Answers will vary.

1. The first baseman hit a homerun to win the game.
2. The star of the movie flatly refused to perform without a completely closed set.
3. When John saw what was coming, he looked for a means of retreat.

Exercise 4

Combine the sentences in the following passage by changing some of them into nominals or appositives. Answers will vary.

A ship steamed through the night.
The ship was called *The Riptide*.
The ship had a captain.
The captain's name was Peter Aronson.
Aronson had two major tasks.
One task was to guide the ship.
One task was to keep the crew's morale high.
The captain was a veteran of the sea.
He understood something.
The spirit of the crew was the most important thing on a ship.

A ship called *The Riptide* steamed through the night. The two major tasks of the captain, Peter Aronson, were to guide the ship and to keep the crew's morale high. As a veteran of the sea, he understood that the spirit of the crew was the most important thing on a ship.

12 · Modifying Restrictively and Nonrestrictively

12a Restrictive and nonrestrictive modifiers

Restrictive and nonrestrictive modifiers are illustrated below.

1. Karen invited the neighbors who are her friends to the party.
2. Karen invited the neighbors, who are her friends, to the party.

Sentence #1 implies that not all Karen's neighbors are her friends and states that only those among her neighbors who are friends received invitations. Sentence #2 states that all the neighbors are Karen's friends, and they all received invitations. The two sentences describe two quite different circumstances: we can imagine the Karen of sentence #1 to have a personality less outgoing, a social life more restricted, or a neighborhood less friendly than the Karen of sentence #2.

You will note that the only difference between the two sentences is the use of commas to set off the relative clause in sentence #2. Those commas indicate that the relative clause **who are her friends** is a *nonrestrictive* modifier. Nonrestrictive modifiers are always set off by commas (**21e**). The modifier provides extra information, but it is not required to specify or to establish the meaning of a preceding noun, in this case **neighbors**. We can delete any nonrestrictive modifier and still preserve the essential meaning of the sentence.

3. Karen invited the neighbors to the party.

Sentence #3 preserves the basic message of sentence #2 but omits the extra information that the neighbors were Karen's friends.

In Sentence #1, though, the relative clause is a *restrictive* modifier; it restricts the meaning of a preceding noun, specifying the particular **neighbors** invited. We cannot delete the relative clause from sentence #1 and retain the basic meaning, which is that only certain neighbors were invited by Karen.

When using **that** and **which**, writers usually follow this convention: restrictive adjective clauses are introduced by **that** and nonrestrictive adjective clauses are introduced by **which**.

The practical joke **that** we played on Jeff has backfired on us all.

The bait and switch, **which** we once played on Jeff, can be a disastrous practical joke.

Sometimes this convention is not appropriate. The use of a second **that** instead of **which** in the sentence below would be repetitive.

That was the car **which** tried to run us down.

Like adjective clauses, adjective phrases can modify restrictively and nonrestrictively.

The men **in the blue suits** made their way to the front of the auditorium. [restrictive prepositional phrase specifying the **men**]

Marie, **with eyes flashing,** led the charge of the irate parents. [nonrestrictive prepositional phrase giving extra information about **Marie**]

Appositives can also be restrictive or nonrestrictive.

Bella Abzug, **Congresswoman from New York,** sported the most colorful hats on Capitol Hill. [**Congresswoman from New York** is an additional identification of Bella Abzug.]

William Shakespeare's play ***King Lear*** has some of the most chilling scenes in all literature. [***King Lear*** is required to identify the subject **play**.]

Exercise 1

In the following sentences, underline nonrestrictive modifiers once and restrictive modifiers twice.

1. The swimmer escaped the pull of the current that threatened to sweep him out to sea.
2. At a recent convention, I saw one of my old high school friends, who is now the manager of a large department store.
3. Suzie and Rob, two of the most unpredictable people I have ever met, have just announced that they are going to be married in a bowling alley.
4. Rooftop restaurants, which sometimes revolve 360° in an hour, make me dizzy.

12b Effects of restrictive and nonrestrictive modification

Because restrictive modifiers are necessary, we do not have to employ much judgment to include them in a sentence. We just have to be confident that a noun needs a clause or phrase to identify it fully. And because we exercise little choice in using restrictive modifiers, they are not distinguishing features of a writer's style.

Nonrestrictive modification, however, can be a crucial feature of style. Good writers often take the opportunity to include nonrestrictive modifiers that contribute information efficiently and appropriately.

My old friend Sally, **who has made a name for herself in educational films in New York**, had dinner in Los Angeles recently with another old friend, **who has made a much bigger name for himself in television**. Settling down over late-night brandies, she was stunned when he turned to her and said, "You know, I can't imagine being married to you. I'd panic and run." "Why?" Sally asked, **hurt that their friendship, which had never even touched on the subject of marriage, seemed suddenly flawed**. "You're a star," he said.

Linda Bird Franke

In the passage above, the first two nonrestrictive adjective clauses contribute extensive significant information, and their parallel forms help the reader make all this information coherent. Note how much less integrated are these ideas when the nonrestrictive modifiers have been omitted.

My old friend Sally has made a name for herself in educational films in New York. Another old friend has made a much bigger name for himself in television. Recently they had dinner in Los Angeles.

The third nonrestrictive modifier in Francke's passage, **hurt that their friendship . . . seemed suddenly flawed**, is a complex adjectival construction containing within it a fourth nonrestrictive modifier for **friendship: which had never even touched on the subject of marriage**. Even if you judge this modifier to be too complex, you should keep in mind that judicious use of nonrestrictive elements can profoundly enrich your writing.

Exercise 2

1. Combine the two sentences below to suggest that no student in the school is friendly toward Barry. In doing so, turn the second sentence into a modifier for **students**.
   The students shunned Barry.
   Barry had tried to impress the students.
   The students, whom Barry had tried to impress, shunned him.

2. Combine the two sentences so that the reader will understand that there is more than one department manager.
Louise gave the department manager a surprise birthday party.
Louise had insulted the department manager.
Louise gave a surprise birthday party to the department manager whom she had insulted.
3. Combine the two sentences to indicate that all members of the dance company were rehired.
The choreographer rehired the dancers for the new show.
The dancers were over 5′4″.
The choreographer rehired the dancers, who were over 5′4″, for the new show.

12c Parenthetical expressions

A *parenthetical expression* interrupts a sentence to provide transition, minor digression, additional information, or explanation. Like the nonrestrictive modifier, it is not essential and may be deleted without destroying the sentence.

1. This essay, **therefore**, makes no sense at all. [transition]
2. The only thing wrong with your plan, **if I may say so**, is that it can't possibly work. [digression]
3. There are apparent bonanzas (**piles of firewood, for instance**) that provide the termite with only a temporary food supply. [additional information]

12d Effects of parenthetical expressions

Transitional expressions serve the crucial task of relating ideas; they are discussed further in **5e**. Parenthetical expressions can also communicate the presence of the writer and often can give the impression the writer is tending carefully to the reader's understanding. The transitional device in sentence #1 (**12c**) suggests that the writer is consciously trying to make ideas coherent for the reader. The digression in sentence #2 brings the writer personally into the discourse. And the additional information in sentence #3 demonstrates that the writer indeed wants the reader to understand clearly. Used with care, parenthetical expressions can be an efficient device to achieve coherence and flavor; used to excess, they will slow the discourse and divert the reader.

Exercise 3

In each sentence below add a parenthetical expression. Answers will vary.

1. Love destroyed Mark's appetite for televised football games.
2. That convenience store sells nothing but junk food.
3. The sergeant showed no mercy toward the recruits.

Exercise 4

Combine the sentences in the following passage by using one or more restrictive and nonrestrictive modifiers. Answers will vary.

Ads for suntan products appear on TV.
The ads picture well-tanned youths.
The youths are playing volleyball at the beach.
The youths leap.
The youths dive.
The youths thrash at the volleyball.
The youths are in a frenzy of enjoyment.
The youths never sweat.
The youths' skins never gleam with greasy lotion.

Ads for suntan products appearing on TV picture well-tanned youths playing volleyball at the beach. The youths, who leap, dive, and thrash at the volleyball, are in a frenzy of enjoyment. Yet they never sweat and their skins never gleam with greasy lotion.

13 · Coordinating

13a Coordination

To coordinate, a writer connects two or more language elements that are grammatically equivalent. The connecting may be done with **coordinating conjunctions**, with **commas**, and sometimes with **semicolons**. The coordinated elements may be individual words, phrases, or clauses.

Coordinated individual words must be the same part of speech.

1. "I have nothing to offer but **blood, toil, tears, and sweat**." [nouns]

   Winston Churchill

2. The boy gazed into the **black, dank, silent** cave. [adjectives]
3. The snake **slithered, hissed, coiled, and twisted** in desperation. [verbs]

Likewise, coordinated phrases and clauses should be of the same type.

4. Our purposes in this advertising are **not only to be honest but also to be persuasive**. [infinitive phrases]
5. **After the burglar had found the gun collection and while he was still looking for the silverware**, Aileen climbed out of her bedroom window. [subordinate clauses]
6. **The workers struck, so the stockholders received no dividends.** [independent clauses]

When elements of the same type are coordinated, they are said to have *parallel construction*. When they lack coordination, they have *non-parallel construction*, an error discussed in Chapter **45**.

13b Effects of coordination

13 b

Unlike subordination, coordination relates elements by giving them equal weight. The effect can be like that of a listing. For example, Churchill's statement quoted above lists the things that the British people in 1940 could expect from the immediate future. Adjective clusters like **black, dank, silent** can build vivid impressions if the words are chosen carefully (see Chapter **9**). A string of verbs like **slithered, hissed, coiled, and twisted** can also build impressions while portraying complex actions. Coordinators are especially useful in expressing certain relationships between independent clauses: cause (**for**), exception (**but, yet**), and result (**so**, as in #6, **13a**).

Coordination can easily be abused (see Chapter **16**). Yet when used effectively it has a desirable cumulative effect on the reader, and it makes ideas of equal importance relate coherently. The simplest tactic is to join two elements with a coordinating conjunction as in #4, **13a**. When three or more elements are each joined with a conjunction, the effect is to slow down the reading and emphasize each element: **blood and sweat and toil and tears**. When only commas are used to coordinate, the effect is to speed up the reading and to compress the impressions: "**Hopeful, fearful, bewildered** students jostled in front of the new school."

Exercise 1

Underline the coordinators in the following sentences and tell what types of elements they join.

1. The debate was not only boring but also ludicrous.

   adjectives (subject complements) joined

2. A runaway in the big city faces a life of fear and desperation.

   nouns (objects of preposition) joined

3. The car careened wildly out of control and crashed into the embankment.
   verbs joined
4. The new fall fashions were both practical and colorful.
   adjectives (subject complements) joined
5. The thieves stopped suddenly, for they had left their burglar's tools at the scene of the crime.
   independent clauses joined

Exercise 2

Combine the following groups of sentences by using proper coordination. **Answers will vary.**

1. Lee Harvey Oswald was an ex-marine.
   Lee Harvey Oswald was reputed to be a communist sympathizer.
   Lee Harvey Oswald was an ex-marine and reputed communist sympathizer.
2. Ted Turner owns the Atlanta Hawks.
   Ted Turner owns the Atlanta Braves.
   Ted Turner owns Cable News Network.
   Ted Turner owns the Atlanta Hawks, the Atlanta Braves, and Cable News Network.
3. Thomas Jefferson wrote the "Declaration of Independence."
   Thomas Jefferson led the United States as its third President.
   Thomas Jefferson wrote the "Declaration of Independence" and led the United States as its third President.
4. Success in college requires hard work.
   Success in college requires dedication.
   Success in college requires hard work and dedication.

13 b

Exercise 3

Expand the following simple sentences by adding one or more coordinated elements. **Answers will vary.**

1. Your first year of college can be a wonderful experience.
2. Some students can afford summer-long cross-country treks for vacations.
3. The meteor lit up the sky with an unnatural light.
4. *E.T.* was a major box-office attraction in the summer of 1982.
5. Full appreciation of opera requires a deep sensitivity.

Exercise 4

Combine the sentences in the following passage by using proper coordination. **Answers will vary.**

Young people face many decisions.
The decisions are difficult.
The decisions are crucial to a young person's future.
A young person can pursue an education.
A young person can pursue a career.
A young person can pursue a trade.
Time must be taken with early decisions.
Care must be taken with early decisions.
Mistakes at this stage of life often take years to correct.

Young people face many decisions that are difficult yet crucial for their future. A young person can pursue an education, a career, or a trade. Time and care must be taken with early decisions, for mistakes at this stage of life often take years to correct.

III Writing with Precision and Control

14 · Choosing the Best Words

14a Choose words with appropriate denotation and connotation.

14 a

Mark Twain is reported to have said, "The difference between the almost right word and the right word is the difference between the lightning bug and lightning." The point of this statement is that while one word may adequately serve the meaning of a sentence, another word may superlatively serve the meaning.

The political importance of "almost right" words and "right" words is illustrated below in two versions of the most famous clauses from the Declaration of Independence. The first is from Thomas Jefferson's first draft; the second is from the final draft sent by the Continental Congress to King George III.

Early draft

We hold these truths to be sacred and undeniable; that all men are created equal. . . .

Final draft

We hold these truths to be self-evident, that all men are created equal. . . .

Comparing the two versions leads us to consider differences in denotation and connotation. A word's *denotation* is what the word refers to in human experience. Denotation is the meaning that scholars identify when they prepare definitions for dictionaries. A denotation of **undeniable** is **that which cannot be declared untrue**; a denotation of **self-evident** is **obvious without need of proof or explanation**. Clearly, the members of the Continental Congress felt that

self-evident more effectively communicates what they wanted to say. Unlike **undeniable**, its denotation does more than simply contradict anyone who thinks differently. Saying an assertion is **self-evident** denotes that it carries its own proof within itself and thus forces those who would disagree to search for contrary proof; saying an assertion is **undeniable**, however, can provoke opponents simply to deny the assertion without thinking much about it.

Furthermore, **self-evident** has connotations that must have pleased the Congressional committee that revised Jefferson's first draft. A word's *connotations* comprise the associations and emotional overtones that the word suggests to people. **Self-evident** connotes reasonableness and objectivity. **Evident** things have external evidence that an objective person can perceive. **Undeniable** connotes negativity because of its two negative parts, **un** and **deny**. It suggests closed-mindedness, a reluctance to be open to new information and new perspectives. The Congressional committee thought so well of the term **self-evident** that they deleted the powerfully connotative **sacred** and let **self-evident** stand alone as the only adjective for **truths**.

As a writer, one of your most important duties is to search your vocabulary for words appropriate to your message and audience. When you are not sure of a word, consult a dictionary. When you cannot think of a word, consult a thesaurus.

A dictionary lists a word's denotations so that you may judge if one of them suits the meaning you intend in your writing. A thesaurus groups words of similar denotations so that you may judge which of the words is most appropriate for your writing. In choosing a word from a list in a thesaurus, therefore, you should use a dictionary to check the meaning of the words you do not know. For example, in writing about a lazy condition you once enjoyed, you might consult a thesaurus to find a word to describe most accurately this state. The entry in the index under "laziness" would direct you to a list that includes the words "languor" and "lethargy." A dictionary would reveal that while the two words are close synonyms, "languor" can refer to a contented dreaminess while "lethargy" can refer to an unhealthy sluggishness. With this knowledge you would then be prepared to judge which if either word is the one you need.

Exercise 1

Underline the word with the most appropriate denotation in the sentences below, and compose a sentence that effectively uses the word you do not pick. **Sentence answers will vary.**

1. In his speech, the chairman of the board (inferred, implied) that the company's financial woes were due to narrow-mindedness on the part of management.
2. The burglar alarm rang (continuously, continually) until the police arrived on the scene.
3. The doctor instructed us to administer the medication (orally, verbally) every three hours.

Exercise 2

Underline the word with the most appropriate connotation in the sentences below, and compose a sentence that effectively uses the word you do not pick. **Sentence answers will vary.**

1. The logic behind the ambassador's carefully worded proposal was (blatant, obvious).
2. The defendant's (statement, allegation) that his victim was to blame for the fatal incident was hard to believe in the face of the evidence.
3. The proud father (chuckled, giggled) softly to himself when he saw his daughter in her first ballet recital.

14b Choose synonyms with care.

When two words are synonymous, their denotations are similar. Rarely, however, are two words exactly the same in their denotation and connotation. For example, **belief** and **opinion** are synonymous in many respects, but they are not interchangeable in all contexts.

1. Martin changed his political **opinions** after each election.
2. Nell's political **beliefs** could not be shaken by the results of any election.
3. Carlos formed his political (**opinions, beliefs**) after voting in several elections.

Because **opinion** denotes judgments open to question, that word is appropriate for sentence #1. Less appropriate would be the word **beliefs**, which denotes ideas held with certainty and consistency. On the other hand, these slightly different meanings make **beliefs** more appropriate than **opinions** in sentence #2. In sentence #3, either word could be appropriate depending on the writer's intent.

When you are faced with a choice of synonyms, a good collegiate dictionary is your best guide. Below is a list of words that have some similarity in denotation, but that are not completely synonymous.

ability (the power to do)
capacity (the ability to take in)

adversary (a hostile force)
opponent (someone taking the opposite side)

anticipate (to look forward to with some emotion)
expect (to believe an event will happen)

belief (an idea to which a person is committed)
opinion (a view held at a particular time)

element (a basic part)
factor (a cause)

essential (basic to the essence of something)
necessary (needed with some urgency)

famous (favorably well known)
notorious (unfavorably well known)

fewer (a smaller number)
less (a smaller quantity)

general (not specific)
usual (normal and common)

ignorant (not aware)
stupid (unintelligent)

insignificant (not meaningful)
trivial (of very small importance)

Exercise 3

For the underlined word in the sentences below, substitute a synonym that more accurately reflects the sentence's flavor and meaning. Then compose a sentence that effectively uses the underlined word. **Answers will vary.**

1. The quarterback was known (**notorious**) for his tendency to play poorly in the big games.

2. The parting lovers gave one another a final passionate hug (**embrace**).

3. Before entering the classroom, the students loitered (**lingered**) in the hall for one more glance at their notes.

14c Choose language as concrete and specific as your topic allows.

Concrete language refers to things and experiences that engage our five senses (**apple, hug, sweet**). *Abstract language* refers to ideas, emotions, qualities, and fields of activity (**profit, love, pretty, medicine**). *General* refers to broad classifications (**employment, nation**), and *specific* refers to particular cases (**computer programmer, France**). Specific wording tends to be concrete, and general wording tends to be abstract. Our language provides a range of meanings from abstract to concrete and from general to specific illustrated in the two lists below.

animal—cat—Persian—Abby

move—descend—fall—tumble

A cat is a specific type of animal, a Persian is a specific type of cat, and "Abby" is a particular Persian. Likewise, to descend is to move in a particular way, to fall is to descend in a particular way, and to tumble is to fall in a particular way.

How abstract, concrete, general, or specific your writing should be depends on your topic and your audience. A comparison of two theories on the nature of truth written for readers experienced in philosophical discourse is likely to have a high percentage of abstract and general words. A comparison of two opposing football teams written for readers interested in sports is likely to have a high percentage of concrete and specific words.

Whatever the circumstances, however, a general rule for the philosopher and the sports writer as well as for the college student is to be as concrete and specific as the subject matter permits. Compare the first sentence below with its revised version.

Original

Once after my mother had waxed the kitchen floor, our dog kept falling down on it.

Revised

For days after my mother had waxed the kitchen floor, our poodle could only slide and trip across the linoleum to his food bowl.

Note that the revision offers the reader the more specific **poodle** for **dog** and describes with the more concrete verbs **slide** and **trip** instead of **falling down** how the dog fared on the newly waxed floor. It also specifies more details of time and place with the words **for days, linoleum**, and **food bowl**. The basic message is similar in the sentences, but the revision is richer, more memorable, and so more rewarding for the reader.

Exercise 4

Rewrite the following sentences, using more concrete, specific language to convey greater detail and fuller meaning. **Answers will vary.**

1. The field marshal's conception for the northern front called for more men and more equipment.
   The field marshal wanted more soldiers, weapons, and transport.
2. While the employee's attention was diverted, someone removed money from the premises.
   While the clerk was distracted by the soup cans clattering from the shelves, the thief grabbed a handful of bills from the cash register.
3. A loud noise sounded when the player's bat made contact with the ball.
   The shortstop's bat smacked the ball with a loud crack.
4. After the dance was over the people went home.
   After the Arts Ball was over, the costumed guests trooped out of the ballroom like a cast leaving the set of a fantasy film.

14d Use figurative language to intensify the reader's response and to clarify meaning.

The most common figurative devices, *simile* and *metaphor*, express comparisons between two phenomena by linking two images not usually associated or by linking an abstraction with a concrete image.

The *simile* specifies a comparison with such words as **like, as,** or **than**. Note below how the writer uses two similes to convey the stealth of a soldier passing time during a night ambush.

> Slower than a caterpillar chews on a maple leaf his fingers tore a small paper packet of Kool-Aid, and quieter than a dandelion loses its fluff his hand shook the light purple powder into his Army canteen.
>
> John Sack

By comparing the actions of opening and mixing Kool-Aid to a caterpillar chewing and a dandelion shedding, Sack gives us a keen impression of this act. Note how much less vivid an impression is given by the sentence below.

> Very slowly he tore a small paper packet of Kool-Aid and very quietly he shook the light purple powder into his Army canteen.

A *metaphor* expresses a comparison directly as if the things compared were in fact part of a single phenomenon.

> What does education often do? It makes a straight-cut ditch of a free, meandering brook.
>
> Henry David Thoreau

In this statement, Thoreau has treated education *as if* it were an engineering project to convert a stream to a ditch. Also, the statement implicitly compares **stream** and **ditch** to students who are first free and natural but who are later turned into something rigid and artificial. Of course, we do not take metaphor as fact; we know that students are not really ditches, but we accept the metaphor because it is so suggestive. Note how relatively unstimulating is a literal statement of Thoreau's metaphor.

Education can destroy creativity and spontaneity and can turn students into narrow-minded conformists.

Another common type of figurative comparison is *personification,* in which something non-animal or non-human is given the characteristics of a person.

The future lurks around the corner, even now making plans to mug me for my youth.

The student who wrote this sentence was trying to make vivid her apprehension and uncertainty about the future, so she personified it as a sinister character plotting a theft.

Hyperbole is exaggeration for effect.

Obviously the mosquitoes had organized an effort to suck every drop of blood from me.

As with metaphor, we know that hyperbole is not literally true. We appreciate the sentence above, therefore, for its figurative truth that the mosquitoes seemed *as if* they had organized to bleed the writer dry.

Successful figurative language gives us a heightened sense of what things are like. Unsuccessful figurative language confuses us. Weak metaphors and similes make vague, inappropriate, or trite comparisons.

Vague

He drove to the hospital like a crazy man.

Inappropriate

He drove to the hospital like a bull in a china shop.

The first sentence is vague because **crazy man** is not specific enough to suggest a clear image. The second sentence is inappropriate because there are too few similarities between a person driving toward a destination and an aimless **bull in a**

china shop; this sentence is also trite because of the over-used expression about the bull (see *Cliché*, **14j**).

A *mixed metaphor* combines two incompatible metaphors.

That course in physics was **a dark forest** I couldn't penetrate until Jill began tutoring me; then it became **all sunny weather**.

This passage begins with the figurative idea of a physics course being an impenetrable forest but ends with the unrelated idea of the course being sunny weather. To unmix the metaphor and extend the figurative notion of a course being a type of landscape, **all sunny weather** might be changed to **a broad meadow**.

Exercise 5

Answers will vary.

1. Write a sentence in which you use a simile to describe the atmosphere in a large room where a rollicking party is taking place.
2. Write a sentence in which you use a simile to capture the feeling one might get from finding a hundred-dollar bill in a public place.
3. Use a metaphor to convey the image of a person who has found long-needed hope.
4. Use a metaphor to express your opinion of a popular song or type of music.
5. Use personification in a sentence in which you characterize the '70s (or any other era).
6. Write a sentence using hyperbole to describe a lopsided defeat or victory in an athletic contest or game of some sort.

14e Use a verbal style in preference to a nominal style.

As we suggested in **7j**, expository writers sometimes rely heavily on nouns to convey their messages. For example, note below how many more nouns are used in passage #1 than in passage #2.

1. My preference is for life in a large city because there I would have the freedom to do things that cannot be done in a small town. In a small town a person's life has to be like his neighbors'. There is a need for his conformity to their beliefs regarding proper behavior. If his actions or thinking is different from their general expectations, he will be an object of suspicion. His expression of ideas that are in disagreement with those of others will often have the result of his rejection by them and his isolation from the life around him. Abiding by the standards of a small town means limiting his experience in ways of looking at the world.*

2. I prefer to live in a large city because there I would be free to do things that cannot be done in a small town. In a small town a person has to live the way his neighbors do. He needs to conform to what they believe is the proper way to behave. If he acts or thinks in a way that differs from what they expect, he will be considered suspicious. If he expresses ideas that others disagree with, he will often be rejected by them and isolated from the life around him. If he abides by the standards of a small town, he will experience only a limited way of looking at the world.*

Both passages offer the same message; they differ only in style. Because passage #1 depends so heavily on nouns, we say it has a *nominal style*: "My **preference** is for **life**. . . ." Because passage #2 depends on verbs, we say it has a *verbal style*: "I **prefer** to **live**. . . ." Research has demonstrated that noun-dependent writing is more difficult for readers to understand than verb-dependent writing. Unfortunately, writers are sometimes encouraged to compose in a nominal style. Studies of the written language used in government, the professions, and business reveal that some audiences have grown to expect this style. These audiences tend to assume mistakenly that the writer of a passage like #1 above is a wiser person than the

*Rosemary L. Hake and Joseph M. Williams, "Style and Its Consequences: Do as I Do, Not as I Say," *College English* 43 (September 1981):447–448.

writer of a passage like #2. In fact, verbal style encourages quicker reading and more extensive recall than does nominal style.

To adopt one of these styles, a writer chooses between verbs and nouns derived from verbs. For example, note the related verbs and nouns in the fifth sentences of passages #1 and #2.

Verbs (5th sentence passage #2)	*Nouns (5th sentence passage #1)*
express	expression
disagree	disagreement
reject	rejection
isolate	isolation

A nominal style is also characterized by expletive constructions (**8c**), linking verbs (**7b**), and prepositions (**7g**).

expletive constructions: "**There is** a need. . . ."
linking verbs: "My preference **is**. . . ."
prepositional phrases: ". . . **for** his conformity **to** their beliefs **regarding** proper behavior. . . ."

To eliminate excessive nominal elements from your writing, you might first examine your sentences for expletives, linking verbs, and prepositions. You should then judge if you can become more forceful and clear by revising those constructions requiring nouns to verbal constructions.

You should also realize, however, that an abstract nominal style may be required by the subject matter. When you have no satisfactory alternative to writing in this way, you can still be forceful and clear by supporting your abstract, noun-dependent statements with examples given in a concrete, verbal style. Note how the two styles complement each other in the following two passages from Colette Dowling's book *The Cinderella Complex*.

There is, I have learned, a connection between our feminine urge toward domesticity and those lulling reveries about childhood which seem to lie just beneath the surface of consciousness. It has to do with dependence: the need to lean on someone—the need, going back to infancy, to be nurtured and cared for and kept from harm's way.

At night I prepared big meals and spread them proudly on the groaning board of a real dining room. During the days, I laundered, raked, and mulched. At night, playing helpmate, I would type Lowell's manuscripts for him. Oddly, though I'd been writing professionally for ten years, it felt as if typing for someone was what I ought to be doing. It felt . . . *right* (by which, I now know, I meant comfortable and secure).

To state her thesis, Dowling must establish a certain relationship between concepts, so in the first passage she names her concepts with abstract nouns and relates them with linking verbs and prepositions. Subsequently, she goes on to amplify her meaning for the reader with the concrete, verb-dependent example in the second passage.

Exercise 6

Rewrite the following paragraph, which is written in a predominantly nominal style, by converting to a verbal style. **Answers will vary.**

The regulation and policing of college athletics have become tasks of great difficulty. Officials of the NCAA alone cannot give all the schools the scrutinization necessary for an assurance that no one school gains an advantage through illegal or unethical means. Obviously, there is a need for regulation on the part of the schools themselves. But as long as there is a prevalent attitude of "win at any cost" among many schools, it is unlikely that this self-regulation will exist to any significant extent.

It is difficult to regulate and police college athletics. NCAA officials alone cannot scrutinize all the schools to ensure that no one cheats. Obviously the schools must regulate themselves. But as long as many schools believe they must "win at any cost," self-regulation is unlikely to work.

14f Avoid colloquialisms in formal writing.

To label a term *colloquial* or *informal* is to make a judgment based on experience with language appropriate for different levels of formal and informal discourse. Discourse is colloquial when it is more suitable in conversation than in formal written prose. When dictionaries mark a word *colloq.* or *informal,* they indicate only a judgment that the word is more common in oral than in written language, not an opinion that the word is inferior.

For example, the *American Heritage Dictionary, Second College Edition,* has this entry: "**figure out**. *Informal.* To solve, decipher, or comprehend." Consider the two sentences below.

1. Before Barry had **figured out** the problem, he was **kind of grouchy**, but later he **felt great**.
2. Before Barry had **solved** the problem, he was **rather ill-tempered**, but later he **was in high spirits**.

Each of these statements is suitable for a different context. Sentence #1 would be appropriate in a conversation between two friends discussing a mutual acquaintance; in this context, sentence #2 might sound too formal. On the other hand, sentence #2 would be appropriate in an essay characterizing Barry for an audience of unknown readers; in that context, the readers might find sentence #1 distractingly intimate. Generally, the less familiar you are with your audience or the more formal the occasion, the less colloquial you should be.

14g Avoid slang except in the most informal writing.

Like colloquialisms, *slang* terms are most appropriate in informal discourse. Slang words usually arise within communities whose members desire terms that are vivid and peculiar to their community. By using slang, a person can demonstrate solidarity with group members. Examples of groups that generate slang are ethnic or regional communities, the entertainment world (especially the world of popular music), and young people.

Usually slang terms arise and fade from use quickly. Hippies of the late 60's would **grok** an interesting sight or idea, using the term from the *B.C.* cartoon to mean they would contemplate something; but **grok** is now out of use. Being **hep** meant the same in the 1940's as being **hip** in the 60's and 70's. **Twenty-three skidoo** meant a fast departure to young people in the roaring 20's; it was used in a context similar to that of today's **let's split**. **Spacey, far out**, and **groovy** are other terms from the youth culture.

Some slang words, such as **jazz**, have become appropriate in the most formal written discourse. As a rule, though, slang does not serve readers well, least of all readers outside the community which evolved the terms. Imagine trying to understand this sentence if you did not know that in some groups **freak** means a user of drugs.

You can trust my friends; they're all freaks.

You should keep slang out of your formal writing unless you determine a certain term is appropriate for your audience.

14h Use jargon only for an appropriate audience and always avoid pretentious language.

Like slang, *jargon* is language suitable to an individual community, but unlike slang, it can be appropriate in formal written discourse for the community's members. Most jargon originates in vocational groups. Doctors, lawyers, educators, social scientists, government agencies all use unique technical terms. For example, consider this sentence from a report of research on the type of prose college students can best understand.

This study investigated the effects of problem-solution rhetorical predicates, intersentential cohesive conjunctions, and reference (lexical cohesion) on reading rate and comprehension.*

Technical terms like "intersentential cohesive conjunction" are devised by specialists so that they can refer to phenomena as precisely as possible. This term refers to conjunctions, such as **nevertheless**, that occur between sentences and make them cohere in one of four ways specified by the research. While such prose may be impenetrable to people not members of the community for which it was written, it can make for efficient, accurate communication among the members.

Jargon obstructs comprehension, however, when it is used needlessly or pretentiously. *Pretentious language* results when a writer is trying to impress readers by pretending a mastery of concept. The first passage below is an example of overuse of jargon; the second passage is an example of pretension. Note the *nominal style* (**14e**) of both.

We define motivation . . . as a condition of an organism in which bodily energy is selectively directed in behavioral acts in relation to the environment so as to attain a goal-object that is significant and meaningful to the individual.**

Your subjectively derived belief is not *prima facie* validated as an objectively established construct of reality.

The ideas in these passages can be put more simply.

Creatures are motivated when they try to get something they want.

Your opinion is not necessarily a fact.

A handy principle to guide you in avoiding pretension and unnecessary jargon is that from among synonyms appro-

*Duane H. Roen and Gene L. Piché, "The Effects of Selected Text-Forming Structures on College Freshmen's Comprehension of Expository Prose," *Research in the Teaching of English* 18 (Feb. 1984): 8-25.

**J. Galen Taylor and William M. Alexander, *Curriculum Planning for Modern Schools* (New York: Holt, Rinehart and Winston, 1966), 207.

priate to the context, you should usually pick the word with the fewest syllables: **part** instead of **component, change** instead of **modify, tell** instead of **relate, ask** instead of **inquire, before** instead of **prior to, use** instead of **utilize** or **employ**.

14i Avoid using euphemisms to obscure meaning.

A *euphemism* is a word or phrase that indirectly expresses something which is unpleasant in a particular context. We speak euphemistically when we say someone **passed away** rather than **died**. Rather than say a statement is a **lie** we can say it is **untrue**, or we can be extremely euphemistic and say it is **inoperative**. Euphemisms frequently treat sex, violence, death, the body and its functions, and socially and politically sensitive conditions. Below are listed some recently popular expressions with their translations:

civil disorder	riot
control garment	girdle
dentures	false teeth
encore telecast	rerun
mispeak	lie
negative deficit	profit
nervous wetness	sweat
occasional irregularity	constipation
previously owned	used
released	fired
shortfall	error in planning
substandard housing	slum

Expository writing should be direct but not offensive. While you do not want to hurt particular readers' feelings, neither do you want to mask the truth.

14j Avoid clichés.

A *cliché* is an expression that once may have created vivid impressions but has by now become worn out and boring:

break of day	raining cats and dogs
easier said than done	spread like wild fire
fraught with danger	throw your weight around
picture of health	worse for wear
thrill of my life	not playing with a full deck

Such expressions may enliven conversation, but they can subvert a reader's attention.

Furthermore, like slang terms and euphemisms, clichés can limit the amount of information our sentences provide. Compare the two sentences below.

Original

Waiting during late registration in lines **slow as Christmas** made me **sadder but wiser**.

Revised

Waiting during late registration in lines creeping one body length an hour persuaded me never to miss advanced registration again.

The student who wrote these sentences recognized how clichés can pop into our minds and give us an easy way to emphasize a concept such as "slowness" with a phrase like **slow as Christmas**. By omitting the cliché and by treating the subject specifically in the phrase **creeping one body length an hour**, the student draws readers into empathy with his frustration. Likewise by eliminating **made me sadder but wiser**, the student could be much more informative with a more specific predicate and object: **persuaded me never to miss advanced registration again**. As writers, we should follow this example and give the time and psychological energy to offer our readers as vivid an understanding as possible.

Exercise 7

1. Rewrite the sentences below, eliminating colloquialisms or replacing them with words or terms more suitable to formal written prose. **Answers will vary.**

   a. Actually, Wally was **somewhat** ~~sort of~~ happy when he was **dropped** ~~canned~~ from the football team, but he didn't **reveal his feelings** ~~let on to anyone~~ **to anyone** ~~about his feelings.~~

   b. When Faye heard ~~tell~~ of her sister's impending arrival, she **hurried to** ~~lit out for~~ the train station.

2. Rewrite the sentences below, replacing inappropriate slang with terms more suitable for a general audience.

   a. The police officers were **standing** ~~hanging out~~ on the corner, **discussing** ~~shooting the breeze about~~ the recent crime wave, when **an addict stole** ~~a freak ripped off~~ a woman's purse and **ran** ~~split~~ down an alley.

   b. The whole neighborhood was enjoying the big **party** ~~bash~~ until the **police arrived** ~~heat made the scene~~ and told everyone to ~~put~~ **quiet down** ~~a lid on it~~.

3. Rewrite the sentences below, eliminating jargon and pretentious language.

a. John's ~~superior intimated~~ **boss suggested** that the ~~intended course of action~~ **plan** was ~~not viable in a profit-wise sense.~~ **unprofitable**

b. The post-work life-goals of many people are not in accordance with their future capital intake.
Many people will lack the money to fulfill their retirement plans.

4. Revise the following sentences to eliminate clichés.

a. Not being mentioned during the awards ceremony was a ~~real slap in the face~~ **humiliating insult** for the project's founder.

b. The fog was ~~as thick as pea soup when~~ **so thick that** we stumbled across our missing companion, who was ~~sleeping like a log~~ **sound asleep**.

5. Use appropriate euphemisms to soften the effects of unpleasant ideas in the following sentences.

a. Morris was ~~fired~~ **dismissed** from his job because he was so ~~stupid~~ **unqualified**.

b. I understand that your father ~~shot~~ **wounded** your brother-in-law ~~dead~~ **fatally**.

15 · Writing Concisely

To write concisely means to use only words that contribute significantly to your meaning. Much advice on good writing amounts to a recommendation to be concise.

15a Avoid noun-dependent style.

Consider the wordy sentence below.

There is a requirement in the rules for the establishment of procedures which would be of equal help to visiting and home teams.

In this sentence, we see the characteristics of a noun-dependent style: expletive **there**, linking verbs **is** and **would be**, five prepositional phrases, and four nouns derived from verbs (**requirement, establishment, procedure,** and **help**). Revising these constructions gives us a more concise sentence.

The rules require us to establish procedures equally helpful to visiting and home teams.

Note especially how the objects of the prepositional phrases have been revised. **Rules** has become the subject; **requirement** has become the verb **require; establishment** has become the infinitive **to establish; procedures** has become the object of the infinitive; and **help** has become the adjective **helpful**.

A habit of depending on nouns can thwart concision more subtly and persistently than any other stylistic trait. Sections **7j** and **14e** treat this problem in detail.

15b Avoid needless repetition.

Once you have established a concept for your reader, you usually do not need to repeat it. Note below how the repetitions in the first sentence have been eliminated in the second.

Original

I made the batter first, then **I made** the filling, and last **I made** the topping.

Revised

I made the batter first, then the filling, and last the topping.

The writer has listed three processes, but repeating **I made** slows the sentence and gives unwarranted emphasis to these two words. Needless repetitions often occur in series and are easily revised by eliminating the repeated elements.

Sometimes a word repeated carelessly can retard a sentence.

Original

Marie was worried about her grandfather's **attitude** because a pessimistic **attitude** like his could be dangerous.

Revised

Marie was worried about her grandfather's **attitude**, because **pessimism** like his could be dangerous.

Using two or more synonyms is another form of needless repetition.

Original

The parents ceaselessly **pampered** and **indulged** their child.

Pampered and **indulged** have similar denotations, so together they do not build meaning but instead simply repeat it. In the first revision below, the redundant **indulged** has been deleted. In the second, a verb that gives new information has been substituted for **pampered**.

Revised

The parents ceaselessly **pampered** their child.
The parents ceaselessly **shielded** and **indulged** their child.

Repetition of words or synonyms, called *redundancy*, is usually unnecessary, but occasionally writers use redundancy to achieve emphasis and balance (see **16a**).

15c Avoid empty phrases.

Some words and phrases stretch out a simple meaning beyond what it deserves.

Original

Due to the fact that it is raining, we cannot till our garden.

Revised

Because it is raining, we cannot till our garden.

15 c

Here are some other *empty phrases*: **at this point in time** (now), **for the purpose of** (for), **in order to** (to), **by means of** (by), **in the direction of** (toward). Because such phrases only clutter your sentences, you should avoid them.

Often the subjects and verbs of adjective clauses (**which are, who is, that were,** etc.) can be deleted.

Original

Doctors **who are** squeamish about blood are like mountain climbers **who are** afraid of heights.

Revised

Doctors squeamish about blood are like mountain climbers afraid of heights.

In deciding whether or not to write a modifying clause (**who are squeamish about blood** or a modifying phrase **squeamish about blood**) you should judge how important the modifier's main ideas are. A clause will emphasize these ideas more than a phrase (see **16b**).

Exercise 1

Rewrite the following sentences, making them more concise. Answers will vary.

1. The idea that John has concerning the problem of security

is one that possesses overall merit and worth.

John has a good idea about security.

2. There are many different systems in existence which can be employed for the prevention of burglary.

   There are many different systems for preventing burglary.

3. There was a bad outlook and attitude displayed by the delegation which led to the impossibility of a compromise being reached.

   The delegation's attitude made compromise impossible.

4. It is the fault of the government's policies that the rate of unemployment has risen.

   The government's policies have increased the unemployment rate.

5. The inexperienced and green challenger, who was battered and bleeding, stumbled and staggered back to the corner which was his when the bell rang.

   At the bell, the inexperienced challenger staggered battered and bleeding to his corner.

6. After he checked his own records and after he checked the records of the bank, the depositor concluded that it was the records of the bank which were incorrect, and he decided his own records were correct.

   After checking his records and the bank's, the depositor concluded that his were correct and the bank's were not.

7. The government of the revolutionaries, which was makeshift, quickly weakened and quickly collapsed when its leader was discovered to be corrupt and no good.

   The makeshift revolutionary government quickly collapsed when its leader was found to be corrupt.

8. It is at this moment in time that we are moving in the direction of being under the power of corporate control in all areas and facets of our lives.

   Corporations are gaining control of our lives.

9. There was a tense and strained air and atmosphere on board the ship, and the men seemed to have a mutinous attitude.

   In the tense shipboard atmosphere, the men seemed mutinous.

10. There are specific measures that the council could take in order to assist the members of the league in the establishment of credibility in regard to the public.
    The council could help the league become credible to the public.

Exercise 2

Revise the following paragraph, striving for greater conciseness and clarity. **Answers will vary.**

In my opinion, I personally feel that the solution to the problem of illegal drug use among athletes could be achieved in part through the de-emphasis of the "win at any cost" attitude that is so prevalent and widespread in athletics in this day and time. Particularly in individual sports especially, more stress and emphasis should be placed on striving to fulfill and reach individual potential in a way that is wholesome. If athletes and fans in general would realize that it is the friendly competitive spirit that is more important in sport than the "Winning is not everything; it's the only thing" philosophy in sport, then they would be moving positively in the right direction of eradicating the lamentable and regrettable corruption in sport, of which illegal drug use is the cause.

I feel that the problem of illegal drug use among athletes can be solved by de-emphasizing the "win at any cost" attitude in today's athletics. Individual sports especially should emphasize wholesome development of potential. When fans and athletes realize that the competitive spirit is more important than the idea that "Winning is not everything; it's the only thing," then they will begin to eradicate the lamentable corruption in sport caused by illegal drugs.

16 · Writing with Emphasis

As you plan, write, and revise, you will discern certain ideas and images to be more important than others. These items deserve the greatest emphasis. To achieve emphasis, you will find these tactics useful: repeat the item, put it in an emphatic place or construction in a sentence, or isolate it in comparatively brief sentences or after special punctuation.

16a Repeat for emphasis judiciously.

Section **15b** explains that repetition of words and phrases can destroy conciseness. In special contexts, however, repeated words and parallel, repeated phrases can be emphatic rather than dulling.

> . . . the party in power should never outrage the minority. That means that it must listen to the minority and be moved by the criticisms of the minority.
>
> Walter Lippman

> Youth, which is forgiven everything, forgives itself nothing; age, which forgives itself anything, is forgiven nothing.
>
> George Bernard Shaw

Lippman's passage illustrates how a writer can repeat a word (**minority**) as a means of insisting that the reader note its importance. Shaw's passage illustrates how repetition in parallel word order can emphasize comparisons and contrasts. In your prose, you should use repeated elements at climactic moments toward which you have led your reader. Remember that repeating words is a risky tactic and should be used sparingly, or it will quickly lose its emphatic effect.

16b Use emphatic sentence structure.

Emphasis within the English sentence depends on position as well as grammatical function. The most emphatic place is at the end. A sentence's final words are likely to be relatively easy to remember because they are the last read. The next most emphatic place is at the beginning. Readers are especially alert when they start a segment of text. The least emphatic place is in the middle. After writing the first sentence below, a college student revised it to achieve the greater emphasis in the second sentence.

Original

I dashed up to Fred waving my arms and making faces before he could make a big fool of himself.

Revised

Before Fred could make a big fool of himself, **I dashed up to him waving my arms and making faces**.

The first sentence leaves the reader with the abstract notion of Fred possibly being a fool, and it nests the vivid image of the writer waving and making faces in the unemphatic middle. The revised sentence is more exciting because the most vivid part is at the most emphatic position.

The revision above de-emphasized the subordinate clause **before Fred could make a big fool of himself**. Modifying clauses and phrases can, however, merit emphatic placement in the sentence.

Original

Eyes ringed and bloodshot, tie askew, shirt sagging over his belt, Jack campaigned throughout our city.

Revised

Throughout our city Jack campaigned, **eyes ringed and bloodshot, tie askew, shirt sagging over his belt**.

The original sentence, with its subject and verb at the end, emphasizes Jack's campaigning, but the revised sentence, with the vivid modifiers at the end, emphasizes his appearance.

Note that the phrases describing Jack are arranged according to space, from his eyes, to his tie, to his shirt. Another way to sequence items in a series is according to significance, with the most significant item in the most emphatic position. Note how the listing of items in the first sentence has been rearranged in the second sentence.

Original

The speech made **most people exuberant, some people indifferent,** and **a few people uncomfortable**.

Revised

The speech made **a few people uncomfortable, some people indifferent,** and **most people exuberant**.

Emphasis within the sentence is also influenced by which ideas are expressed as independent clauses and which ideas are subordinated in modifying clauses and phrases. Independent clauses are the most emphatic, subordinate clauses are next most emphatic, and modifying phrases are the least emphatic. The sentences below are ordered so that the blizzard receives decreasing emphasis.

A blizzard was rattling the walls, but we continued to celebrate New Year's Eve.

Although a blizzard was rattling the walls, we continued to celebrate New Year's Eve.

With a blizzard rattling the walls, we continued to celebrate New Year's Eve.

16c Isolate for emphasis.

An especially emphatic technique is to isolate an idea or image in a short sentence or after a colon or dash. The passage below illustrates both techniques.

The traditional way of encouraging children to want to learn the things we want to teach is by giving rewards for success: **prizes, privileges, gold stars. Two grave risks attend this practice.**

Margaret Donaldson

Donaldson's listing of the three **rewards** after the colon gives them special emphasis, and the relative brevity of her second sentence gives special emphasis to her point about the **risks**.

Sometimes a writer can emphasize several impressions by making a series of brief points.

They were very poor. Clothes and boots were a problem. They "made their own amusements." Books were mostly the *Bible* and *The Pilgrim's Progress*. Every Saturday night they bathed in a hip bath in front of the kitchen fire. No servants. Church three times on Sundays.

Doris Lessing

Lessing's passage illustrates the power of the short, emphatic sentence and deliberate fragment. Note, however, that Lessing has varied sentence length and grammatical patterns. The fourth sentence is relatively long and separates the earlier short statements from the two even shorter fragments. A style in which most sentences are of the same length and grammatical pattern will lack emphasis and can make even interesting subjects tedious.

Original

I made the mistake of my life last week. I had asked my fiancée to get a date for an old high school friend. I learned that the date was a very loud and obnoxious person. I thought that we would all have a miserable time, so I decided to take matters into my own hands.

All the main clauses in the passage above are of similar length and have the same subject-verb-object pattern. This repeated structure makes for dull reading. Note in the revision below how varied sentence structures make the passage more emphatic and thus make us more anxious to know how the writer took **matters into [his] own hands**.

Revised

I made the mistake of my life last week. I had asked my fiancée to get a date for an old high school friend, but then I learned that the date was loud and obnoxious. Thinking we would all have a miserable time, I decided to take matters into my own hands.

Exercise 1

Use repetition or parallel structure to create more emphatic sentences below. **Answers will vary.**

1. James attended the opera to become cultured; ~~to~~ **and** the seminar ~~he went~~ to become learned.
2. To overcome this problem we need ~~two things, a definition~~ **to define** and ~~to~~ understand it.
3. The terrorist was cruel, and ~~he also behaved in a~~ cowardly ~~way~~.

Rearrange or rewrite the following sentences in order to put greater emphasis on the underlined element or idea.

1. "Give the bad news to me straight; <u>don't sugarcoat it</u>," the patient said to the doctor.
   "Give me the bad news straight," the patient said to the doctor. "Don't sugarcoat it."
2. <u>As it rumbled down the track</u>, the train had smoke pouring from its engine.
   With smoke pouring from its engine, the train rumbled down the track.
3. The pitcher <u>stormed off the field</u>, frustrated and angry with his error-prone teammates.
   The pitcher, frustrated and angry with his error-prone teammates, stormed off the field.

Exercise 2

Revise the following sentences by incorporating the underlined words into short, emphatic sentences or phrases.

1. We filled our car with everything we thought we could possibly need for the trip, ~~except for gas~~. [. But we forgot gas.]

2. The police finally located ~~his wife~~, the one person who could reason with the unbalanced hijacker. [: his wife.]

3. The graduate thought she would spend her summer visiting relatives and friends, going to the beach, and just relaxing, but her expectations changed two days after the ceremony, [.] ~~because~~ [S]she got a job.

4. The puppy from the animal shelter was painfully thin and weak, [.] ~~and~~ [S]she was obviously a sad case.

Exercise 3

Answers will vary.

Revise the following paragraph, using the emphatic structures discussed in the chapter to make the paragraph more vivid.

A man who had been badly beaten up staggered from an alley into the lights of a passing squad car. Actually, he would have had an even chance in the fight except for one thing, which was the brass knuckles his opponent carried. The results of his adversary's unfair advantage, a broken nose, a chipped tooth, and a split lip, were evident. In the back of the squad car, he promised himself, as a result of this sobering experience, never again to frequent places where that kind of trouble was likely to begin.

A man staggered from an alley into the lights of a passing squad car. He had been badly beaten up. Actually, he would have had an even chance in the fight except for one thing: the brass knuckles his opponent carried. The results of his adversary's unfair advantage were evident—a broken nose, a chipped tooth, and a split lip. In the back of the squad car, he promised himself never again to frequent places where that kind of trouble was likely to begin.

17 · Writing in the Active and Passive Voice

Active and passive structures are explained in **8c**. This chapter examines how voice influences style. Compare the two sentences below.

1. Classic novels produced on television can fascinate illiterate people. [active voice]
2. Illiterate people can be fascinated by classic novels produced on television. [passive voice]

While these two sentences express basically the same information, their different subjects suit them to different contexts. Sentence #1 invites the reader to understand something about televised **novels**, and sentence #2 invites the reader to understand something about illiterate **people**. Sentence #1, therefore, would more likely complement a paragraph about novels adapted for television than would sentence #2; sentence #2 would more likely complement a paragraph about people who cannot read.

Note, though, that the active voice seems more direct and forceful than does the passive. In both sentences the word **novels** names what performs the main action; it tells what **fascinates**. But in #1 **novels** is the subject, the focus of the entire sentence, whereas in #2 it is just the object of an adverbial prepositional phrase (**by classic novels**). By spreading out the reader's attention between a subject that receives action and an agent that acts, passive constructions can make discourse unemphatic, indirect, weak. Passive sentences that omit the agent are especially weak; thus sentence #4 below is more informative and direct than sentence #3 because it names the agent (**recreation committee**) and makes the agent the subject of an active verb (**made**).

3. After the lunch break, little progress was made.
4. After the lunch break, the recreation committee made little progress.

Generally when you face a choice between the active and passive voice, you should choose the active. To use the passive voice wisely, you should determine that your context requires the subject of a sentence to receive action. Consider, for example, that the first sentence in this chapter is in the passive voice and the agent (who it was that **explained**) is missing. We can expand this sentence to read,

Active and passive sentence structures are explained in **8c** by the authors.

In the **active**, it could read as below.

In **8c**, the authors explained active and passive sentence structures.

or

Section **8c** explains active and passive sentence structures.

The reason we two authors wrote that first sentence as we did is that we wanted you the reader to focus on the topic of sentence structures, not authors or sections. Note that in the second sentence, we returned to the active voice, and that except for example sentences, the first sentence is the only passive one in this chapter.

Exercise 1

1. Which of the following sentences would be more appropriate in an essay focusing on the author's personal feelings and experiences?
   a. While I was sunning on the beach, I sipped cool, refreshing drinks served from a shoreside bar.
   b. Bartenders served me cool, refreshing drinks from a shoreside bar while I was sunning on the beach.

2. Which of the following sentences would be most effective in an essay whose purpose is to give pointers on making a tossed salad?
   a. First the produce should be washed and drained, and then cut each ingredient into bite-sized bits.
   ✓b. First wash and drain the produce, and then cut each ingredient into bite-sized bits.
   c. First the produce should be washed and drained, and then each ingredient should be cut into bite-sized bits.
3. Which of the following sentences more forcefully emphasizes the action that is described?
   a. When the two boats collided, a horrifying scream was heard across the waters of the lake.
   ✓b. When the two boats collided, a horrifying scream rang out across the waters of the lake.
4. Which of the following sentences would seem to be more appropriate in an essay about the practice of voodoo?
   ✓a. Voodoo is still practiced by a number of Jamaicans.
   b. A number of Jamaicans still practice voodoo.
5. Which of the following sentences would be more appropriate in a report about women in athletics?
   a. Little League baseball is now successfully played by many girls across the United States.
   ✓b. Many girls across the United States now successfully play Little League baseball.

Exercise 2

The following passage is mainly in the passive voice. Rewrite it in the active voice, and compare differences in focus, emphasis, and effect. Answers will vary.

As the room was entered, I was struck by a joyous sensation. Grandfather was seated in the middle of the room, and the grandchildren were seated around him, laughing and talking. All of Grandfather's birthday presents had already been opened by him, and the wrappings and bows had been scattered about the floor by the kids, creating a colorful and pleasing effect. Great happiness was felt by myself upon having arrived in time to witness this wonderful scene.

Upon entering the room, I felt a joyous sensation. Grandfather sat in the middle of the room surrounded by his grandchildren, who were laughing and talking. He had already opened his birthday presents, and the kids had scattered the wrappings and bows about the floor, creating a colorful and pleasing effect. I was very happy that I had arrived in time to witness this wonderful scene.

V Punctuating and Following Mechanical Conventions

18 · The Period .

18a Use a period to end a declarative sentence (a sentence that makes a statement), an indirect question, or a mild imperative (a directive or command).

For some film makers, special effects are more important than a quality script. [declarative sentence]
The quiz-master asked whether any of the contestants knew who was buried in Grant's tomb. [indirect question]
Please cut the grass and trim the hedges. [mild directive]

18b Use periods after certain abbreviations in accordance with dictionary-recommended usage.

Personal Titles Preceding Names

Mr. Cartright, Ms. Turner, Dr. Jordan

Academic Degrees

B.A., M.A., Ph.D.

Time References

B.C., A.D., a.m., p.m.

Certain Foreign Terms

i.e., etc., e.g.

Note: If an abbreviation comes at the end of a sentence, do not use a second period.

We are leaving for the airport at 5:00 a.m.

18c Do not use a period to separate a part of a sentence from the whole.

Notice how the first period in each of the examples below brings the sentence to a premature close.

Misused

After a long delay**.** The tennis match resumed.

Misused

A fund-raising dinner will be held in the new civic center**.** Which seats almost five thousand people.

In the first sentence a period sets off a prepositional phrase, and in the second a period sets off a relative clause. Each of these sentence parts or *fragments* can be rejoined with the rest of the sentence simply by substituting a comma for the period.

Revised

After a long delay**,** the tennis match resumed.

Revised

A fund-raising dinner will be held in the new civic center, which seats almost five thousand people.

For a more detailed treatment of how to recognize and eliminate fragments, see Chapter **44**.

19 · The Exclamation Point !

19a Use an exclamation point to end an emphatic statement.

Forceful statements

"Get out! I don't ever want to see you again!"

Interjections expressing strong feeling

On no! I'm going to be late.

Emphatic responses to statements or questions

"Can you come back for an interview next week?" the personnel manager asked.
"Yes!" I enthusiastically replied.

Used judiciously, the exclamation point can be an effective stylistic device, as in this sentence by Dr. Martin Luther King, Jr.

Many men cry "Peace! Peace!" but they refuse to do the things that make for peace.

19b Use exclamation points sparingly.

When used habitually for emphasis, exclamation points can easily become artificial, as in the following example.

Overused

According to recent newspaper reports, a chemical company is planning to build a new factory in this area. I am concerned about how such a business might affect the community. It will produce toxic wastes! It will deplete water supplies! And it will drive smaller companies out of business!

Here, the exclamation points call more attention to the writer's emotionalism than to the arguments against the new chemical plant. Periods, on the other hand, are neutral in tone and would allow the reader to judge the evidence on its own merits.

20 · The Question Mark ?

20a Place a question mark after a direct question.

How many people will be at the party tonight**?**
Why do you ask so many questions**?**

20b Use a question mark at the end of a sentence if your purpose is to create a questioning tone.

The library is closing today**?** I thought it would stay open through the weekend.

20c Do not use a question mark after an indirect question.

Misused

I wonder who will win the academy award for best actress this year**?**

Revised

I wonder who will win the academy award for best actress this year.

Punctuation Exercise 1

In the sentences below, insert or change the periods, question marks, and exclamation points wherever necessary. Be able to justify each choice.

1. All complaints, objections, and recommendations should be referred to Dr·Leona Williams, Ph·D·

2. The company's representative, Ms.Pearson, will be in Mr . Watson's office at 9:00 a. m. to conduct a seminar on management problems (e.g.,absenteeism).
3. Tom asked his teachers if he could miss the last day of class before the Christmas holidays.
4. I wonder whether Melissa will ever return my call?.
5. To my surprise, I received an "A" on my history essay!.I have never done that well before!.I've decided to change my major to history!.

21 · The Comma ,

21a Put a comma before a coordinating conjunction (and, but, or, for, nor, so) that links two independent clauses in order to indicate the end of the first clause and prepare for the introduction of the second clause.

Many of the new recruits had looked forward to basic training**, but** some could not adapt to the rigorous physical fitness program.

Note: The comma is optional if the two clauses are short.

I looked for you but I couldn't find you.

21b Use commas to separate the elements of a series consisting of three or more words, phrases, or clauses.

Buses, cars, and trucks skidded on the icy road. [a series of nouns]

The dune-buggy **roared across an open expanse of sand, churned up a hill, and disappeared from view.** [a series of verb phrases]

Some films are successful at the box office but fail with the critics, others are acclaimed by the critics but rejected by the general public, and a rare few appeal to both audiences. [a series of independent clauses]

Note: Although current usage allows for the omission of the comma before a coordinating conjunction preceding the last item in a series, a comma in this position does help to prevent misreading—especially in a long, complex series like the one in the final example above.

21 c

21c Use a comma to separate coordinate adjectives (i.e., adjectives that independently modify the same noun).

Draped across the bed was a **tattered, faded** blanket.

There are two simple ways to test for this kind of coordination. If you can reverse the order of the adjectives or insert the word *and* between them without diminishing the clarity or coherence of the sentence, they are coordinate and should be separated by a comma.

Notice that in the example above, neither of these changes would adversely affect the sentence.

Draped across the bed was a **faded, tattered** blanket. [order of adjectives reversed]

Draped across the bed was a **tattered and faded** blanket. [**and** separating adjectives]

Punctuation Exercise 2

Add commas where necessary in the sentences below. Put a check after any sentences that are correctly punctuated.

1. My brother often returned from school with his clothes torn and his face bruised, but he never would talk about what had happened to him.
2. Whenever the crime rate increases, the people who usually get the blame are lawyers, judges, and the police.
3. I work with a group of happy, cooperative people.
4. The pressure of Christmas shopping often makes people irritable and causes them to purchase gifts they cannot afford. ✓
5. The accident occurred on a dark, lonely road.
6. So-called intelligence tests are not always an accurate measurement of a child's intelligence, and they reveal nothing at all about a person's creative abilities.

21d Use a comma to set off introductory clauses, long modifying phrases, and certain introductory words.

Introductory modifiers

Walking along the beach, I saw hundreds of sunburned tourists.

After a long hike to the lake, we were ready for a swim.

When the climbers reached their destination, they raised a signal flag.

Plans for the new building having been completed, construction began.

Introductory yes or no

Yes, acid rain is a threat to the environment. **No,** the governments of the U.S. and Canada have not yet reached agreement on how to solve this problem.

A name mentioned in direct address

George, please let me know when you will be home.

Note: The comma is optional after brief introductory modifiers.

Soon[,] the economy may improve.

Without thinking[,] I stepped off the curb.

21e Use commas to enclose parenthetical, nonrestrictive, or contrasting elements (i.e., words, phrases, or clauses that could be deleted without changing the essential meaning of the sentence; see Chapter 12).

21 e

Parenthetical words and expressions

This course**, I think,** is going to be more difficult than I anticipated.

In the past, I have always mailed my income tax forms just before they were due. This year**, however,** I am going to finish them early.

Nonrestrictive modifiers

The top of the World Trade Center**, which is over a hundred stories high,** provides a panoramic view of New York City.

The new sports complex**, unlike the old one,** has ample parking.

Nonrestrictive appositives

Ms. Brown**, a local businesswoman,** was recently elected to the university's Board of Trustees.

Possible ill-effects of artificial sweeteners are being studied at Johns Hopkins Hospital**, a well-known research center,** as well as at several other medical centers throughout the nation.

Contrasting elements

Proponents of increased military spending argue that peace**, not war,** is their objective.

Corporal punishment often inspires resentment**, not repentance**.

Punctuation Exercise 3

Add commas where necessary in the sentences below. Put a check after any sentences that are correctly punctuated.

1. Unless the government acts soon to reduce the budget deficit, interest rates will continue to rise.
2. My afternoon classes are all in Taylor Hall, which is the hottest building on campus.
3. Some of my friends suffer from the sweat-suit syndrome, a malady that can be cured only by purchasing a whole wardrobe of sweat-suits and color-coordinated accessories.
4. As soon as I saw the shaving cream on my pillow and the knots in my sheet, I knew that I had been the victim of a practical joke.
5. Some members of Congress have charged that the policies of the Environmental Protection Agency benefit land developers, not the people who use public land for recreation.
6. Last year, the School Board presented an award to my parents, who led several successful fund-raising drives.

21f Use commas to separate names from titles, cities from states or countries, the day of the week from the day of the month, the day of the month from the year, and the salutation of an informal letter from the text.

The letter was addressed to Janet Murdock, **Ph.D.**

Boulder, Colorado, is my home.

On **Wednesday, June 1, 1983,** I began a raft trip down the Snake River.

Dear Aunt Minnie,

Note: When a city and state or date is mentioned within a sentence, a comma comes after the state and after the year. Note also that putting the date before the month eliminates the need for a comma: **1 June 1983.**

Punctuation Exercise 4

Add commas where necessary in the sentences below. Put a check mark after any sentences that are correctly punctuated.

1. The letter was addressed to Leon Gray, M.D.
2. Tomorrow we are leaving for San Antonio, Texas.
3. One of the most controversial U.S. missions of World War II was the fire bombing of Dresden, Germany.
4. July 4, 1976, marked the two hundredth anniversary of the U.S.A.

21g Avoid unnecessary commas.

When used for the purposes discussed in the preceding sections, commas help to clarify relationships between sentence elements and guide the reader to an understanding of what the writer seeks to communicate. But if they are inserted where readers who are familiar with the written code expect no punctuation at all or anticipate a different type of punctuation, commas are distracting and confusing.

If you tend to use commas without knowing why or if you insert them wherever you sense a pause, you may need to review the chapters in Part II in conjunction with the conventions discussed in this chapter. The following suggestions about when not to use commas may also prove useful.

1. *Do not put a comma between a subject and its verb or between a verb and its object or complement.*

Unnecessary commas

The luxury liner *Titanic*, struck an iceberg and sank on its maiden voyage.

I have just read, *The Grapes of Wrath.*

One of the dreams of every serious actor is, to play King Lear.

In all three of these sentences, the comma should be deleted because it unnecessarily interrupts the progress of the sentence and separates its closely related elements.

2. *Do not put a comma before a coordinating conjunction that links compound subjects, verbs, objects, or complements.*

Unnecessary commas

A degree in mechanical engineering, and an unlimited amount of time are the only qualifications anyone needs to assemble the pieces of a typical do-it-yourself kit. [**and** linking compound subjects]

As we walked along the ridge, a hawk soared high above our heads, and alighted on a distant peak. [**and** linking compound verbs]

When I lived near the airport, I was continually disturbed by sonic booms, and shattered glass. [**and** linking compound objects of a preposition]

One summer I was a shoe clerk, and a cook. [**and** linking compound complements]

3. *In general, do not use a comma following a coordinating conjunction.*

Unnecessary comma

This morning, I plan to run five miles, do a few exercises, and, play tennis.

Note: A comma may come after a coordinating conjunction if the comma sets off a parenthetical or nonrestrictive element.

I plan to run five miles and, if I'm not too tired, play tennis.

4. *Do not put commas around restrictive elements: modifiers or appositives that could not be deleted without changing the essential meaning of the sentence (see Chapter* **12***).*

Unnecessary comma

Some colleges will not accept students, who rank in the bottom third of their graduating class.

The comma should be omitted because the relative clause limits the category of unacceptable students to those in the bottom third of the class. If this clause were deleted, the sentence would say that some colleges will not accept students.

5. *Do not put a comma before the first element of a series.*

Unnecessary comma

The new car was equipped with, power steering, cruise control, and a stereo system.

6. *Do not put a comma between non-coordinate adjectives (adjectives that you could not logically link with* **and***) or between an adjective and the noun it modifies.*

Unnecessary comma

At the entrance to the carnival stood a man holding an enormous, helium-filled balloon.

When the game show host grinned, he revealed a mouthful of white, teeth.

7. *Whenever you put a comma between two independent clauses, be sure that a coordinating conjunction follows it. The use of a comma alone or a comma plus a conjunctive adverb (***however, therefore, consequently,*** etc.) in this position will result in a comma splice (see Chapter* **43***).*

Comma splice

I dislike mowing lawns, I detest pulling weeds.

Revised

I dislike mowing lawns, **but** I detest pulling weeds.

Punctuation Exercise 5

In the following sentences, delete any unnecessary commas.
Put a check after any sentences that are correctly punctuated.

1. At present almost anyone, can buy a handgun, a rifle, or even a machine gun.
2. Some of the most outspoken, critics of television believe that it dulls the intellect, and encourages violence.
3. We watched the national news and, then turned off the TV set.
4. The player, who scored the winning goal, was mobbed by her teammates.
5. A battered, foul-smelling lantern hung from the tree limb.✓
6. Excellence in education can be achieved only through the coordinated efforts of, teachers, students, parents, and administrators.

Punctuation Exercise 6

In the sentences below delete unnecessary commas and add needed commas. Be able to explain the reason for each addition and deletion.

1. The brightly, arrayed chieftain, who stood in front of a small stone altar, had a stern, cold face that belied his cheerful apparel.
2. Joining the Army, seemed to be a good idea to the dissatisfied, restless young man until he met his first drill instructor.
3. Scratching, clawing, and biting, the children had to be separated, and taken from the playground.

4. After seeing the grim, reality of war firsthand, the journalist was forced to wonder what on earth could be worth the misery, and despair, that always accompany conflict.
5. Yes, the president of the company, Mr. Danmeyer, authorized this transfer, but he was not aware of the hidden costs in such a project.
6. The challenger had two advantages: youth, and courage.
7. The answer to our problem is, better organization, more attention to detail, and better communication.
8. Leaping the swollen, raging creek, at a single bound, the frantically, baying hound raced off into the forest.
9. The possibility of detection, did not seem to alter the thief's demeanor, or behavior in the least.
10. One of the most interesting people I have ever met is my former philosophy professor, who left the university on May, 15 1977, to search for truth.

22 · The Semicolon ;

22a Put a semicolon between two independent clauses if your purpose is to combine them in a single sentence without using a coordinating conjunction (*and, but, for, or, nor, so*).

If the two clauses are parallel in form and closely related in meaning, a semicolon alone is sufficient to link them:

Rumor breeds mistrust**;** mistrust breeds fear.

If the relationship between the two clauses you wish to join is not obvious, add a conjunctive adverb (**however, therefore, otherwise,** etc.) immediately after the semicolon or within the second clause (see **7h**).

I recently bought a new camera**; however,** I am not satisfied with the pictures I have taken with it.

I recently bought a new camera**;** I am not satisfied**, however,** with the pictures I have taken with it.

or

I recently bought a new camera**;** I am not satisfied with the pictures I have taken with it**, however.**

Note: If you choose a coordinating conjunction rather than a conjunctive adverb as a connective, place a comma rather than a semicolon in front of the linking word (see **21a**).

I recently bought a new camera**, but** I am not satisfied with the pictures I have taken with it.

22b Use semicolons to separate series items that themselves contain commas.

Looking through a television monitor, the department store detective observed **a young man wearing an enormous, overstuffed backpack; a middle-aged woman carrying a large, bulging purse;** and **an elderly gentleman dressed in a long, loose-fitting topcoat**.

If you are uncertain about the appropriateness of a semicolon in a given context, notice its position in the sentence. Except in those rare instances when semicolons are needed for clarity (as in the last example above), this punctuation mark should always come at the juncture of two independent clauses.

22c Do not substitute a semicolon for a colon or comma.

Semicolon misused as colon

The course syllabus listed three basic requirements**; essays, tests, and oral reports**.

Semicolon misused as comma

Because ice had begun to form on the wings; the pilot decided not to take off.

Because semicolons usually promise the end of one independent clause and the beginning of another, their use as colons or commas is confusing. In the first example above, the reader expects another clause after the semicolon and might initially read **essays, tests, and oral reports** as the subject of this anticipated clause. In the second example, the semicolon simply makes no sense because it does not come at the end of an independent clause. **Because ice had begun to form on the wings** is a subordinate clause modifying **decided**.

Even when you can find a grammatical justification for a semicolon, check to be sure that it is your best stylistic option. Used sparingly and purposefully, the semicolon can be an effective means of creating parallelism and balance and of clarifying sentence relationships that might otherwise be confusing to the reader. But if it is employed repeatedly to link two clauses that are only slightly related, it loses much of its freshness and force.

Punctuation Exercise 7

In each of the following sentences add, delete, or change semicolons where necessary. If there are no semicolon errors in the sentence, put a check after it.

1. Critics of the two-party political system often complain; that it arbitrarily limits the number of candidates for any public office.
2. If you are looking for something different; scuba diving is for you.

3. Our society needs vast quantities of energy; however, our petroleum resources are dwindling. ✓
4. Rugby has qualities much admired by American sports fans; speed, violence, and strategy.
5. Making speeches does not have to be frightening; sometimes it can even be pleasurable. ✓

23 · The Colon :

23a Use a colon immediately after an independent clause to introduce a list of appositives, a single appositive, a quotation, or a second independent clause that illustrates or explains something in the first clause.

The student newspaper received the following new equipment**: a word processor, a short wave radio, and a teletype.** [list of appositives specifying the **new equipment**]

On my last fishing trip, I forgot one very important item**: my fishing reel.** [single appositive identifying the **very important item**]

From the editors of *Discover* magazine comes a startling announcement**: "Nessie, the Loch Ness Monster, may be nothing more than a decomposing log."** [quotation]

The members of the Budget Committee soon learned the bad news**: tax revenues were lower than expected.** [independent clause explaining what the **bad news** was]

23b Use a colon to introduce the text of a formal letter, divide hours from minutes, separate chapter from verse in Biblical references, and distinguish the title of a book from its subtitle.

Dear Dr. Johnson**:**
9**:**00 a.m.
Genesis 3**:**1
Billy Budd: *An Inside Narrative*

23c Do not assume that a colon is needed in mid-sentence to signal a series or an example.

Unnecessary colon

For breakfast we had**:** bacon, eggs, toast, and coffee.

The problem here is that the colon separates the complement (**bacon, eggs, toast, and coffee**) from the verb (**had**), thus forcing the reader to pause unnecessarily before the sentence's line of thought is complete.

23d Do not confuse the colon with the semicolon or period.

Colon confused with semicolon

Barry rushed from the house in anger**:** several hours later, he returned and apologized.

In this sentence, the colon is misleading because it tells the reader to expect a further explanation or illustration of Barry's anger, but what actually follows is a second independent clause describing Barry's subsequent actions.

23e Test for appropriate use of colons.

One of the best ways to spot such problems is to look closely at the words to the left of the colon and see if they could be punctuated as a coherent sentence. If not, the colon is unnecessary. Applying this test to the first example above, we find that the words **for breakfast we had** make no sense when detached from the complement. Thus, the colon should be deleted:

For breakfast we had bacon, eggs, toast, and coffee.

If the words to the left of the colon meet the first test, as in the example in **23d** (**Barry rushed from the house in anger** is a complete sentence), notice whether the words following the punctuation mark could also stand alone as a sentence. If there is a second independent clause and it introduces a new idea, change the colon to a period or a semicolon, depending on whether you want to separate or join the two clauses:

Barry rushed from the house in anger**.** Several hours later, he returned and apologized.

or

Barry rushed from the house in anger**;** several hours later, he returned and apologized.

If, on the other hand, you find that the second independent clause defines or illustrates the first, the colon is an appropriate mark of introduction.

Barry rushed from the house in anger**:** he kicked the wall and slammed the door.

Punctuation Exercise 8

In the following sentences, add, delete, or change colons where necessary. If there are no errors in colon usage, put a check after the sentence.

1. Severe depression can result from feelings of~~:~~ loneliness, grief, fear, or inadequacy.
2. I have never really enjoyed chemistry~~:~~ although I do have fun in the laboratory portion of the course.
3. I have developed three areas of my body:my arms, my chest, and my legs.
4. The new Broadway hit was~~:~~ provocative, enlightening, and entertaining.

24 · The Dash —

24a Use a dash as an informal but emphatic mark of introduction.

In a recent biography of Marilyn Monroe, Norman Mailer describes the actress as an angel—a "sweet angel of sex."

I must leave now—without further delay.

24b Use a dash to introduce an independent clause that summarizes the words preceding it.

Shopping malls, condominiums, and convenience stores—these are some of the most prominent features of the modern American town.

24c Use a dash or a pair of dashes to signal an abrupt interruption in thought or an unexpected change in tone.

I am convinced that most—or should I say all—of the claims made by advertisers are exaggerated.

Before every family vacation, my father announced that we could take as many clothes as we wanted—provided that they would all fit in one small suitcase.

24d Use dashes to set off parenthetical elements that warrant special emphasis.

Some members of the Board of Trade—including all the newly elected delegates—are opposed to import quotas.

24e For clarity, use dashes to set off nonrestrictive elements that contain commas.

My aunt—a woman of great charm, intelligence, and patience—has always been one of my favorite relatives.

24f Use the dash for certain stylistic purposes.

When considering a dash, keep in mind that in any given context, it is usually only one of several stylistic options. Both the dash and the colon, for example, are marks of introduction, but each has a different tone and effect. The colon conveys a sense of formality and control, explicitly forecasting what is to follow; the dash, on the other hand, is a freer, less formal mark that usually establishes a more subtle relationship between the introductory statement and the words following it.

Anyone interested in buying a home computer should first learn the meaning of three terms: bits, bytes, and chips.

As the young mathematician contemplated the problem, she closed her eyes and reclined in her chair—gestures that a casual observer might mistake for signs of boredom.

Distinguish also between dashes and other punctuation marks that have the same function of enclosing information. In particular, remember that commas are the standard means of setting off non-restrictive sentence elements and that habitual use of the dash for this purpose diminishes its value as a mark of special emphasis.

24g When typing a dash, use two hyphens with no space before or after.

The members of the dormitory council--without exception--expressed outrage at the new curfew rule.

24h Despite its versatility, the dash is not quite the all-purpose punctuation mark it seems to be. It is not, for example, the equivalent of a period or semicolon; thus, it should not be used to separate or link independent clauses.

Dash confused with period or semicolon

The District Attorney argued that the defendant should be held responsible for his actions—the Defense Counsel claimed that her client was temporarily insane.

In this sentence, the dash leads us to expect more information about the District Attorney's views or the defendant's actions, but instead the writer shifts to the Defense Counsel's argument. Thus, the dash should be replaced with a period if the writer intends to separate the two clauses or with a semicolon if the author's purpose is to coordinate them.

25 · Parentheses ( )

25a Put parentheses around figures or words that you want to include as supplemental information.

Death of a Salesman **(**1949**)** has been acclaimed as a tragedy of the common man.

In the opening section of the essay "Politics and the English Language" **(**pp. 1–2**)**, George Orwell argues that political corruption and language abuse are inseparably related.

World War I **(**the war that was supposed to end all wars**)** ushered in a century of violence.

Many years ago **(**I forget just how many**)** my parents sold their spacious home in the suburbs and moved into a cramped apartment in the middle of the city.

25b Enclose in parentheses numbers or letters that enumerate the items in a series.

In order to be successful at computer games, a player must have the following skills: **(**1**)** good eye-hand coordination, **(**2**)** quick reflexes, and **(**3**)** the ability to concentrate.

25c If you want to set off a parenthetical expression as a sentence in its own right, put the first parenthesis before the capital letter and the second one right after the period.

More and more species of animal life are becoming extinct. **(**Soon, human beings may be added to the list.**)**

25d Whenever you use parentheses to enclose a part of a sentence, place any additional punctuation marks outside the parentheses.

One of the most famous outlaws of the Old West was Bill Harrington **(**alias Billy the Kid**),** who started out as the leader of a New York street gang.

25e Do not overuse parentheses.

Parentheses are distracting if overworked or used to set off constructions that do not warrant special emphasis. Both problems are evident in the following passage.

Overuse of parentheses

It was 2:00 (on Wednesday afternoon) when I entered my first college biology class. The teacher (Mrs. Harper) was already getting out microscopes as I took my seat. Within a few minutes, everyone (that is, almost everyone) was intently examining slides. I saw nothing but dust particles.

In the first sentence above, the parentheses are unnecessary because there is no apparent reason for calling attention to the day of the week, nor is there any indication why the writer encloses the teacher's name in parentheses rather than using commas—the usual means of setting off nonrestrictive appositives. The last set of parentheses, on the other hand, is functional because the words between them forcefully interrupt the sentence and introduce a personal reflection that helps the reader anticipate the outcome of the incident. Even if all three sets of parentheses were stylistically defensible, the number is excessive, especially in a paragraph this short.

Punctuation Exercise 9

Add dashes or parentheses as needed in the following sentences. Be prepared to explain your reason for choosing each mark. **Answers will vary. Students should use the dash as a mark of greater emphasis than parentheses.**

1. "There is a growing guilt about the masses of discarded junk — rusting automobiles and refrigerators and washing machines and dehumidifiers — that it is uneconomical to recycle."
   Anthony Burgess

2. "Whenever I pitched decently (a rarity) I had to tell her so, and then she would smile and say, 'That's nice, dear.'"
   Pat Jordan

3. The final objection to Senator Frampton's appointment (and by far the most damaging one) is his known ties to underworld figures.

4. Famished by the long ride back to school, I rushed up the stairs, threw open my door, and frantically jerked open the refrigerator door. The bottomless pit — my roommate — had struck again, devouring all my food.

5. Long hours, little pay, and less respect — these are the rewards an educator can expect in the long run.

26 · Quotation Marks " "

26a Put quotation marks around all words that you quote verbatim from an oral or written source so that the reader can distinguish your words from those of the writer or speaker you are citing.

Quotation from an oral source

I was one of the millions of people who watched the inauguration of John F. Kennedy and heard him say, "Ask not what your country can do for you but what you can do for your country."

Quotation from a written source

In the words of noted journalist Caryll Tucker, "Perhaps the most poignant victim of the twentieth century is your sense of continuity."

If you quote a passage that already contains quotation marks, replace them with single quotation marks and enclose the entire passage in standard double quotation marks.

Jacques Cousteau has observed that, "One of the most 'human' qualities of the whale is its intense devotion to other whales."

When citing a passage longer than three lines, set it off as a block quotation by indenting ten spaces from the left margin and double spacing. A block quotation requires no quotation marks unless they appear in the source.

> To a professional violinist such as Victor Aitay, concertmaster of the Chicago Symphony Orchestra, nothing compares to the tone that floats from the belly of a Stradivari violin. "Its sound is rich and smooth, with no harshness or shrillness. Music

erupts from it with just a touch of the bow on its strings, and its soothing sound carries to every inch of the concert hall," says Aitay.

Joseph Alper

26b Use quotation marks to distinguish spoken words from words that are not part of the quoted dialogue and to set off the words of one speaker from those of another.

At night the printed page stood before my eyes in sleep. Mrs. Moss, my landlady, asked me one Sunday morning:
"Son, what is this you keep on reading?"
"Oh, nothing. Just novels."
"What you get out of 'em?"
"I'm just killing time," I said.
"I hope you know your own mind," she said in a tone which implied that she doubted if I had a mind.

Richard Wright

26c Use quotation marks to indicate that a word is being used in a special sense.

Some **"convenience"** stores inconveniently run out of the items I always seem to need.

26d Put quotation marks around the titles of essays, short stories, brief poems, short plays, articles in newspapers and periodicals, parts of books, songs and other short musical compositions, and episodes of television and radio shows.

My course in literature and popular culture will begin with a study of George Orwell's essay **"Politics and the English Language,"** W.H. Auden's satiric poem **"The Unknown Citizen,"** a one-act play called **"Act Without Words,"** and the **"Economy"** chapter of Thoreau's *Walden*. Later in the year, we will discuss popular music classics such as The Beatles' **"Let It Be"** and analyze some of the **"Point Counterpoint"** debates from *60 Minutes*.

26e Observe the following conventions when punctuating sentences that contain quotation marks.

1. *Put commas and periods inside quotation marks.*

"The President's plane is going to be late," the press secretary announced to a crowd of disgruntled reporters.

When I asked my new art instructor if I had to buy a drawing board, she replied, **"Only if you want to pass this course."**

2. *Put semicolons and colons outside quotation marks unless they are part of the quoted text.*

At 11:45 the manager announced, **"As soon as you finish your present assignment, take your lunch break";** by 11:46 the office was empty.

Nathaniel Hawthorne explores several major themes in his story **"Young Goodman Brown":** the nature of good and evil, the relationship between dreams and reality, and the conflict between faith and skepticism.

3. *Place a question mark or an exclamation point inside the final quotation mark if the question or exclamation is conveyed by the quoted words alone. If the quoted material is part of a question or exclamation, the appropriate mark should go outside the final quotation mark.*

In answer to a question about how soon the potholes in the city's streets would be repaired, the mayor responded, **"How long will it take to approve new taxes for road improvements?"**

Why, the reader might ask, does Hamlet picture death as an **"untraveled country"?**

26f When quoting from secondary sources, proofread carefully to ensure that you have not inadvertently omitted one or both quotation marks.

The omission of a single mark is confusing because it forces the reader to guess where the quotation begins or ends. The omission of both pairs of quotation marks results in an even more serious problem called *plagiarism*—the appropriation of someone else's words and/or ideas as one's own (see Chapters **54–55** for a full discussion of how to use and document sources).

26 g

26g Avoid unnecessary quotation marks. In particular, do not use quotation marks with conventional, overworked expressions, with nicknames, or with the titles of your own compositions.

Unnecessary quotation marks

When I was younger, my brother and I fought **"**tooth and nail.**"**

My brother **"**Bubba**"** makes friends easily.

"A Critical Analysis of Three Poems by Robert Frost**"** [from the title page of a student essay]

Punctuation Exercise 10

In the sentences below delete unnecessary quotation marks and add needed quotation marks.

1. "After dinner," my grandmother said, "we will take a long walk."
2. "Eleanor Rigby," a wistful yet powerful song by "The Beatles," appears in one anthology as an example of modern "poetry."
3. If you don't study for the final exam, you'll be "up the creek without a paddle."
4. The epitaph of John Keats, author of two famous examples of "Romantic" poetry, "Ode on a Grecian Urn" and "La Belle Dame Sans Merci," reads "Here lies the body of one whose name was writ in water."
5. One critic has observed that "Edgar Allan Poe's short story 'The Fall of the House of Usher' takes the reader on a journey into the dark recesses of the human mind."

27 · Brackets [ ]

27a Use brackets to enclose information that you have inserted within a quoted source.

The "central characters **[in Ernest Hemingway's *A Farewell to Arms*]** are caught in a biological trap from which there is no escape."

Whenever possible, integrate quotations with your own sentences in such a way that brackets are unnecessary.

In Ernest Hemingway's *A Farewell to Arms*, "the central characters are caught in a biological trap from which there is no escape."

27b Substitute brackets for parentheses when parenthetical material occurs within a parenthetical reference.

In *A Critical Guide to Leaves of Grass*, James E. Miller describes Whitman's "Song of Myself" as "the dramatic representation of a mystical experience" (for a conflicting view, see Carl Strauch's "The Structure of Walt Whitman's 'Song of Myself,' " *English Journal*, 27 [**Sept. 1938**]: 597–607).

28 · The Ellipsis Mark . . .

28a Use an ellipsis mark (three spaced periods) to indicate the omission of part of a quoted passage.

Notice, for example, the way in which the author of the second passage below uses the ellipsis mark to condense the original while preserving its essential meaning.

Passage #1

The health-care system of this country is a staggering enterprise, in any sense of the adjective. Whatever the failures of distribution and lack of coordination, it is the giant scale and scope of the total collective effort that first catches the breath, and its cost. The dollar figures are almost beyond grasping. They vary from year to year, always upward, ranging from something like $10 billion in 1950 to an estimated $140 billion in 1978, with much more to come in the years just ahead, whenever a national health-insurance program is installed. The official guess is that we are now investing around 8 percent of the GNP in health; it could soon rise to 10 or 12 percent.

Lewis Thomas

Passage #2

According to the noted medical researcher and essayist Lewis Thomas, the U.S. "health-care system **. . .** is a staggering enterprise**. . . .** Whatever the failures of distribution and lack of coordination, it is the giant scale and scope of the total collective effort that first catches the breath, and its cost. . . . The official guess is that we are now investing around 8 percent of the GNP in health; it could soon rise to 10 or 12 percent.

Three ellipsis dots are sufficient to mark the first deletion above because it occurs within a sentence. But because the second omission comes at the end of a sentence and the third includes an entire sentence, the writer has correctly used a fourth period for terminal punctuation.

Because an ellipsis mark does not tell the reader what or how much has been omitted from a quotation, be careful not to delete words that are essential to meaning or to artificially link widely separated passages.

Notice how the omission of three key words in the second sentence below distorts the first writer's intent.

Source

"Ambition tempered by wisdom is the key to political greatness."

Misleading omission

"Ambition . . . is the key to political greatness."

The first sentence says that those who aspire to political greatness must be wise as well as ambitious. The second states that ambition is the only requirement.

Punctuation Exercise 11

Read each of the sentences or passages below and follow the directions accompanying it:

1. "In certain important ways, *Moby Dick* [1851] carried on methods and themes with which Melville was experimenting in his earlier stories."

   Charles Fiedelson

   a. Add in brackets the information that *Moby Dick* was published in 1851.

b. Revise sentence #1 again so that you add the date of publication without brackets.
Answers will vary. E.g., "In certain important ways, *Moby Dick,* published in 1851, carried on . . . ."

2. "One of William Haast's first jobs, as an airline flight engineer in the 1940's, gave him a chance to pursue both his fascination with snakes(at 12, he had kept them as pets) and his theories on the value of venom research."

Ben Funk

a. Add the punctuation marks needed to indicate that the name **William** has been added by the writer citing the passage.
b. Punctuate the parenthetical statement **at 12, he had kept them as pets** to indicate that it is part of the original quotation.

3. "Modern English, . . . especially written English, is full of bad habits which spread by imitation and which can be avoided if one is willing to take the necessary trouble."

George Orwell

Use the ellipsis mark to condense the passage and at the same time eliminate words that call attention to a type of Modern English. . . .

4. "Salvador Dali (whom, in general, I do not greatly admire) once made the remark that Picasso's greatness consisted in the fact that he had destroyed one by one all the historical styles of painting."

Joseph Wood Krutch

Use the ellipsis mark to condense the passage and also create a more objective tone.

29 a

29 · The Apostrophe '

29a Use an apostrophe to mark the omission of part of a date or word.

The fall of **'82** was unusually hot.

I **don't** want to keep my dental appointment tomorrow.

It's raining.

29b Add 's to the singular form of nouns and most indefinite pronouns (everyone, someone, anyone, etc.) to form the possessive case.

Overexposure to the **sun's** rays can cause serious skin problems.

The professor lectured on **Keats's** poetry.

The speaker appealed to **everyone's** sense of humor.

29c Use an apostrophe alone to indicate the possessive form of plural nouns that end in *s*.

During the **lifeguards'** convention, the hotel pool was always crowded.

29d Use an 's to form the possessive of plural nouns that do not end in *s*.

Several important **women's** rights issues were debated by the legislature.

Children's television viewing habits have been the subject of several recent studies.

29e To denote the possessive case of a compound word (brother-in-law, someone else, etc.) or to indicate joint possession, place an 's after the last word.

We spent the summer at my **brother-in-law's** beach cottage.

George and Martha's parties are always a great success.

Note: An **'s** after George and after Martha would indicate that each gives successful parties.

29f Use an *'s* to indicate the plural form of a number or letter.

My **3's** sometimes look like **5's**.

Some parents reward their children for making a certain number of **A's** and **B's**.

29g Do not use an apostrophe with possessive case forms of the pronouns *his*, *hers*, *its*, *ours*, *yours*, and *theirs*.

The decision is **theirs**.—*not*—The decision is **their's**.

The cat hurt **its** paw.—*not*—The cat hurt **it's** paw.

The insertion of an apostrophe between the **t** and the **s** of the pronoun **its** is particularly confusing because **it's** is the contracted form of **it is** (see also **7c** and **36b**).

29h Do not insert an apostrophe before the *s* ending of a singular verb or plural noun.

There is a new television network that **shows** famous **films** of the past.

Revised

There is a new television network that **shows** famous **films** of the past.

In the first sentence above, the first apostrophe misleads the reader into perceiving the verb **shows** as a possessive noun, and the second apostrophe misleads the reader into seeing plural **films** as a singular **film** that possesses something.

30 · The Slash /

30a Use a slash (also called a "virgule") between the conjunctions *and* and *or* to indicate option.

The instruction sheet that came with my new tent informed me that I could use steel pegs **and/or** aluminum braces for support. [The buyer has the choice of using both types of support or only one.]

Note: Although the **and/or** construction is justifiable in an essay that gives instructions or describes a technical process, it is rarely necessary in other types of prose.

30b Use a slash to separate unindented lines of poetry or poetic drama.

Shakespeare's "Sonnet 73"concludes with the lines, "This thou perceivest, which makes thy love more strong, / To love that well which thou must leave ere long."

30c Use a slash (or a hyphen) to link two words that function as one.

Some universities profess support for the ideal of the **teacher/scholar** but reward publication more than teaching. [The **teacher/scholar** is someone who is both a teacher and a scholar.]

31 · The Hyphen -

31a Put a hyphen between two words that function as a single adjective when the modifier comes before the word it modifies.

The **once-popular** resort area had become a ghost town.

The **ill-fated** mission resulted in high casualties.

Note: The hyphen is unnecessary if the first word in the compound ends in **ly** or if the noun precedes the modifier:

The **previously injured** players returned to action before the end of the season.

The resort area that was **once popular** had become a ghost town.

31b Put a hyphen (or a slash) between two nouns to combine them into a single noun.

The **player-coach** took herself out of the game.

If the compound is formed by the combination of a noun and one or more different parts of speech, consult a dictionary for recommended usage. In one recently published dictionary, words such as **break-in, editor-in-chief,** and **ice-skating** are hyphenated, but similar types of compounds are printed as two separate words (e.g., **boundary line, ice water,** etc.) or as a single unhyphenated word (e.g., **bricklayer**).

31c Use a hyphen to form a compound of two numbers that are written as words.

Twenty-five people have already preregistered for organic chemistry.

The **nineteen-sixties** will be remembered as a decade of discontent.

31d Use a hyphen after a prefix when the root word is a proper noun or adjective or when the omission of the hyphen would result in an awkward repetition of letters or confusion of meaning.

Anti-American sentiment had been building in Iran long before the overthrow of the Shah. [The hyphen links the prefix with a proper noun, **America**.]

I want to **re-lease** (i.e., renew the lease on) this apartment next year. [Without a hyphen, **release** would convey the opposite meaning: **give up**.]

31e If you do not have enough space to complete a word of two or more syllables at the end of a line, divide the word after a syllable and insert a hyphen to indicate that the word will be completed on the next line.

If you are in doubt about where to divide a word, consult a dictionary. It will indicate syllable divisions with raised periods, as in the example below.

ar·chi·tect
bi·ol·o·gist
frac·ture
pre·ven·tion

31f Avoid overusing the hyphen as a mark of syllabication.

Though you might occasionally need to divide a word at the end of a line, a less distracting procedure is to extend the word beyond the right margin or begin it on the next line. Words of one syllable should not be subdivided, nor should words of two or more syllables be split in such a way that a single letter is isolated at the beginning or end of a line. For example, a single-syllable word such as **town** would never be hyphenated, nor would a multisyllabic word such as **amoral** be divided after the **a-**.

31g Do not confuse the hyphen (-) with the dash (--).

Hyphen misused as dash

From my window, I could see a park-a green, fertile oasis in an urban wasteland.

Punctuation Exercise 12

In the sentences below delete or add apostrophes, hyphens, and slashes wherever necessary. Be able to explain the reason for each decision.

1. In the brilliant day-light, the mans eyes squinched involuntarily, causing him to look older than his fifty five year's.
2. Although many stores sell alcoholic-beverages, few tolerate on premise consumption.
3. Ironically, the police officers salaries were not paid due to the robbery of the citys payroll.

4. We are here solely to determine whos to blame for the three victim's suffering.
5. Everyones mind was made up about the councils report on taxes even before it's release.
6. The on/off switch for this unit is located behind the counter.
7. The long-awaited film finally made it's debut.

32 · Italics

32a Italicize (underline) the names or titles of books, magazines, long plays, etc.

Books

The Sound and the Fury, Invisible Man, Cosmos

Plays

Hamlet, A Streetcar Named Desire

Long Poems

Paradise Lost, The Waste Land

Magazines and Scholarly Journals

Cosmopolitan, Esquire, Time, Modern Fiction Studies

Newspapers

The Washington Post (or the Washington *Post*)

Movies, Radio Shows, Television Programs

Gone with the Wind, Mystery Theater, Hill Street Blues

Paintings and Sculpture

Van Gogh's *Starry Night,* Rodin's *The Thinker*

Major Musical Compositions

Verdi's *Requiem Mass,* Bach's *Brandenburg Concertos*

Ships, Planes, Spacecraft

U.S.S. Forrestal, Spirit of St. Louis, Columbia

32b Italicize (underline) foreign words that have not yet been fully absorbed into English.

The ***carpe diem*** theme is one of the central concerns of many seventeenth-century English poets.

I was surprised to find that the chips were covered with combatants, that it was not a ***duellum***, but a ***bellum***, a war between two races of ants.

Henry David Thoreau

32c Italicize (underline) words, letters, or numbers when you refer to them as such.

The word ***evolution*** continues to stir people's emotions.

When I write fast, my ***t***'s look like ***l***'s.

Some people consider the number ***6*** an omen of evil.

32d Italicize (underline) words that warrant special emphasis.

"I will ***never*** resign," the coach shouted.

Note: Use italics for this purpose only on those rare occasions when the denotation or connotation of a word is not sufficient to convey the desired meaning or tone.

32e In the titles of your own compositions, do not italicize any words except those you would italicize in a sentence.

Title

Jay Gatsby and the American Dream [italics unnecessary]

Title

A Study of the American Dream in F. Scott Fitzgerald's ***The Great Gatsby*** [italics needed only for the title of Fitzgerald's novel]

32f Make a distinction between the kinds of names or titles that are customarily italicized and those that are set off by quotation marks.

Robert Hayden's poem "Figure" and Ralph Ellison's novel ***Invisible Man*** both examine the human suffering caused by racism.

33 · Capitalization

33a Capitalize the first word in a sentence, as well as the first word in the salutation and closing of a letter.

Some people go to a medical doctor when they get sick. **O**thers rely on home remedies or nonprescription drugs. **S**till others turn to community healers for advice and treatment.

Dear Mrs. Evans,	**D**ear friends,
Sincerely yours,	**Y**ours truly,

33 b

33b Capitalize proper names and their derivations.

Names of People

Monique **R**ichardson, **N**ick **A**dams, **E**leanor **R**oosevelt

Personal and Professional Titles

General **P**atton, **S**enator **M**cCarthy, **P**rofessor **J**ones, **D**r. **S**trangelove

Names of Nationalities, Races, and Languages

Scandinavians, **S**ioux, **A**fro-**A**merican, **H**ispanic, **E**nglish

Names of Religions and Religious Sects or Denominations

Catholicism, **J**udaism, **P**rotestantism, **M**uslims, **M**ormons, **B**uddists, **U**nitarians

Names for Deity in Different Religions or Cultures

the **H**oly **G**host, **C**hrist, **A**llah, **B**rahma

Names and Abbreviations of Organizations and Institutions

the **D**emocratic **P**arty, the **R**epublican **P**arty, the **B**etter **B**usiness **B**ureau, **AFL-CIO**, **NATO**, **NOW**, **UNICEF**, **FBI**, the **U**nited **S**tates **S**enate, the **H**ouse of **R**epresentatives, the **S**upreme **C**ourt

Names of Roads, Bridges, Buildings, Monuments, Ships, Planes, Spacecraft, and Other Humanmade Structures

33 b

the **B**lueridge **P**arkway, the **G**olden **G**ate **B**ridge, the **M**useum of **N**atural **H**istory, the **T**omb of the **U**nknown **S**oldier, the battleship ***B**ismark*, the ***S**pirit of **S**t. **L**ouis*, the space shuttle ***C**olumbia*

Place Names and Their Derivatives

Denver, **D**ade **C**ounty, **N**ew **J**ersey, the **S**outh, **Y**ellowstone **N**ational **P**ark, **N**ew **Y**orkers, **E**uropeans, **C**hinese

Names of Oceans, Rivers, Mountains, and Other Geological Features

Atlantic **O**cean, **S**nake **R**iver, **M**t. **W**hitney, **C**rater **L**ake, **N**iagara **F**alls

Names of Planets, Galaxies, Constellations, and Related Astronomical Terms

Mars, the **M**ilky **W**ay, **U**rsa **M**ajor, **C**rab **N**ebula

Names for Days of the Week, Months, Holidays, Historical Eras, and Geological Periods

Our **C**hristmas holiday begins about the middle of **D**ecember, usually on a **F**riday, and lasts through **N**ew **Y**ear's **D**ay.

Marine invertebrates first appeared during the **P**aleozoic era.

The eighteenth century was known as the **A**ge of **R**eason.

33c Capitalize the first word and all other words except prepositions, conjunctions, and determiners in the titles of publications, films and other media productions, speeches, paintings, sculpture, and musical compositions.

***T**he **C**atcher in the **R**ye* [novel by J.D. Salinger]

***T**he **N**ew **Y**ork **T**imes* [newspaper]

***P**sychology **T**oday* [magazine]

"**N**otes on **P**unctuation" [a chapter in Lewis Thomas's ***T**he **M**edusa and the **S**nail]*

***C**asablanca* [film]

***W**ide **W**orld of **S**ports* [television series]

***M**ona **L**isa* [painting by Leonardo Da Vinci]

***B**ird in **S**pace* [sculpture by Constatin Brancusi]

Beethoven's ***M**oonlight **S**onata* [musical composition]

33d Do not capitalize common nouns except those which name heads of state (e.g., The *P*resident will soon travel to the Soviet Union to confer with the *P*remier).

One state **senator** has already announced her decision to run for a second term.

Is there a **doctor** on this plane?

At the **high school** I attended, **history** was the most demanding course.

I traveled **south**.

Standing at the rim of the **canyon**, I could see a **river** thousands of feet below.

In all of these sentences, the boldface words are not capitalized because they refer to a general category or class rather than to a specific person, place, or thing. Note, though, that these same words can be used to form proper names, which are capitalized.

One state official, **Senator Kelley**, has already announced her decision to run for a second term.

Is there a **Doctor Johnson** on this plane?

At **Lakeshore High School**, **Modern American History** was the most demanding course.

I traveled throughout the **South**.

Standing at the rim of the **Grand Canyon**, I could see the **Colorado River** thousands of feet below.

34 · Numbers

34a Use figures rather than words for the numbers in dates, addresses, references to pages or volumes, decimals, percentages, degrees, fractions, and quantities requiring more than two words to spell out.

Dates and Other Specific Time References

December **8, 1960** **450** B.C. **3:00** p.m.

Addresses

P.O. Box **21**
401 State St., Apt. **6**

Page and Volume Numbers

p. **10** Vol. **5**

Decimals, Percentages, Degrees, and Fractions

2.75 **60** percent (or %) **30°** Fahrenheit **1 3/4**

Quantities That Require More Than Two Words To Spell Out

34 c

$255.00 **250,000,000** (or **250** million) people **125** coupons

34b When using numbers other than those referred to in the preceding section, spell them out if they can be written as one or two words.

thirty-four customers **six** musicians **one hundred** dancing bears

Ordinal numbers (**first, second, third**, etc.) are customarily written out as well.

34c If you begin a sentence with a number, always spell it out.

Thirty degrees below zero is the lowest temperature ever recorded at this time of year.

34d When referring to numbers in a series, treat them all in the same way regardless of the form they would take if used alone.

The manager of the produce department ordered **135** heads of lettuce, **85** cartons of tomatoes, and **10** bushels of apples.

Whenever you are writing in an academic field and you have a question about which form to use for a given number, consult a manual of style in your discipline for recommended usage.

35 · Abbreviations

35a Abbreviate personal and professional titles when they precede proper names.

Mr. Langston, **Mrs.** Clara Pierce, **Ms.** Murdock, **Dr.** Schwartz, **Rev.** Thomas Barker, **Dr.** Clyde Johnson

Note: The titles **Mr., Mrs., Ms.,** and **Dr.** may be used either with first name and last name or with last name alone. Titles such as **reverend**, **doctor**, **general**, and the like are abbreviated only when they are followed by the person's first and last name: **General** Grant, **Gen.** Ulysses S. Grant; **Reverend** Black, **Rev.** George Black.

35b Abbreviate words such as *street*, *avenue*, *drive*, and the names of states in addresses.

105 West End **Ave.**
Anaheim, **CA**

Note: Current U.S. postal system abbreviations for each state are as follows:

Alabama	AL	Montana	MT
Alaska	AK	Nebraska	NE
Arizona	AZ	Nevada	NV
Arkansas	AR	New Hampshire	NH
American Samoa	AS	New Jersey	NJ
California	CA	New Mexico	NM
Colorado	CO	New York	NY
Connecticut	CT	North Carolina	NC
Delaware	DE	North Dakota	ND
District of Columbia	DC	Northern Mariana Islands	CM
Florida	FL	Ohio	OH
Georgia	GA	Oklahoma	OK
Guam	GU	Oregon	OR
Hawaii	HI	Pennsylvania	PA
Idaho	ID	Puerto Rico	PR
Illinois	IL	Rhode Island	RI
Indiana	IN	South Carolina	SC
Iowa	IA	South Dakota	SD
Kansas	KS	Tennessee	TN
Kentucky	KY	Texas	TX
Louisiana	LA	Utah	UT
Maine	ME	Vermont	VT
Maryland	MD	Virginia	VA
Massachusetts	MA	Virgin Islands	VI
Minnesota	MN	Washington	WA
Mississippi	MS	West Virginia	WV
Missouri	MO	Wisconsin	WI
		Wyoming	WY

35c You may abbreviate names of academic degrees, time references, certain foreign terms,

and names of well-known organizations or agencies.

Academic Degrees

B.A., M.A., Ph.D., M.D.

Time References

B.C., A.D., a.m., p.m.

Frequently Used Latin Terms

e.g.—for example
etc.—and so on
i.e.—that is
et al.—and others

35 c

Names of Well-Known Organizations or Agencies

U.N., U.S., OPEC, NATO

Abbreviations other than the kinds listed here are seldom necessary in most forms of expository writing. However, because abbreviation practices vary considerably from one profession and academic discipline to another, you should supplement these guidelines with a study of the conventions recommended by the standard manual of style for your field (*The Publications Manual of the American Psychological Association* for the social sciences, the *MLA Handbook* for the humanities, etc.).

Punctuation Exercise 13

In the following sentences, correct any errors in the use of italics, capitalization, abbreviations, and numbers.

D 7 1941 J
1. On december ~~seventh~~, ~~nineteen forty-one~~, the japanese
P H
attacked pearl harbor, destroying a large part of the
A
american fleet.

2. Mark Twain's novel The Adventures of Huckleberry Finn
w
influenced numerous twentieth-century Writers, notably
Ernest Hemingway.

eighteenth
3. Yesterday, I had my ~~18th~~. birthday, but the only present I
h
got was a pop quiz in my History class.

S T
4. A number of people devoted to the TV show star trek
fanatically follow "the voyages of the starship
E
enterprise."

5. The word liberal can create very different images and
associations in the minds of different people.

Forty
6. ~~40~~ people began the race, but only a few completed it.

V Avoiding Common Sentence Errors

36 · Errors in the Case Forms of Pronouns and Nouns

In **7c** and **7d** we discussed the ways in which case inflections (changes in word form) help communicate the role of nouns and pronouns in a sentence. In this chapter, we will explore some common problems of case usage and how to avoid them.

36a Make a distinction between subjective and objective case forms of pronouns.

The only kinds of words that have special forms for the subjective and objective case are personal pronouns and the relative or interrogative pronouns **who** and **whoever**.

36 a

Case Forms	*Personal Pronouns*							
Subjective	I	you	he	she	it	we	you	they
Objective	me	you	him	her	it	us	you	them

Case Forms	*Relative/Interrogative Pronoun*	
Subjective	who	whoever
Objective	whom	whomever

A subjective case inflection tells the reader that the pronoun functions as a subject or complement; an objective case form indicates that the word is the object of a preposition, a direct or indirect object, or the object of a participle or infinitive.

subject — object of infinitive
We did not mean to offend **them**.

direct object
The magician fooled **me** with his hat trick.

In short, uncomplicated sentences like these, most writers instinctively use the correct case form. It is unlikely, for example, that anyone would write "**Us** did not mean to offend **they**" or "The magician fooled **I**." In certain kinds of sentences, however, the function of the pronoun may be less obvious and the choice of case more difficult.

1. *Case of personal pronouns after linking verbs*. Sentences in which a personal pronoun follows a linking verb are rare in English because such constructions often sound artificial. But if you should find it necessary to structure a sentence in this way, remember to use the subjective case to indicate that the pronoun is a subject complement.

This is **she**.

The winners were **they**.

Note that written usage differs in this respect from such conversational expressions as "It's me" and "This is him."

2. *Case of personal pronouns in compounds*. Another construction that may confuse the reader is one in which a personal pronoun is joined with another pronoun or noun to form a compound subject, complement, or object.

subject
My brother and I took a long vacation.

complement
The winners were **you and they**.

object
The argument between **the cashier and me** was brief but intense.

When you use a personal pronoun in this way, do not be distracted by the other words in the compound; instead try visualizing the personal pronoun alone in the sentence without the compound elements. For example, if you wanted to check the appropriateness of the pronoun **I** in "My brother and I took a long vacation," you would rephrase the sentence to read "**I** took a long vacation." If you had written **My brother and me**, your rephrased sentence, "**Me** took a long vacation," would make the error obvious. When you cannot appropriately isolate the problem pronoun, as in the final sentence above, you can test for correctness by substituting the plural pronouns **we** or **us** in the same case as the pronoun in the compound. Applying this test to the sentence "The argument between the cashier and me was brief but intense," you would substitute the objective case form **us** for **the cashier and me**.

The argument between **us** was brief but intense.

If you had originally written **between the cashier and I**, rephrasing the sentence with the subjective plural—"The argument between **we** was brief but intense"—would indicate a need for revision.

Note: If the compound is an appositive, both elements should be in the same case as the word(s) to which they refer.

The supervisors, **Ms. Simpson and I**, will conduct a workshop next week.

I is in the subjective case because it is part of a compound appositive that refers to **supervisors**, the *subject* of the sentence. Like all appositives, this one can be substituted for the words to which it refers.

Ms. Simpson and I will conduct a workshop next week.

Similarly, when a pronoun appositive refers to an object, the pronoun is in the objective case:

The teachers condemned their supervisors, Ms. Simpson and **me**, with faint praise.

3. *Case of personal pronouns after* ***than*** *or* ***as***. When you use a personal pronoun after **than** or **as** in an elliptical sentence, think about how the sentence would read with the omitted word(s) included. If the pronoun is the subject of the omitted words, use the subjective case; if it is the object, choose the objective case.

The waiter was more upset with my friends than **I** [was]. [pronoun as subject]

The waiter was more upset with my friends than [he was with] **me**. [pronoun as object]

Note that in these statements, the case of each pronoun leads the reader to a different conclusion. The first sentence explains that both the waiter and the speaker were dissatisfied with the latter's friends. The second sentence states that the waiter was upset with both the speaker and his/her friends.

4. *Case of relative/interrogative pronouns* ***who/whom, whoever/whomever***. **Who** and **whom**, plus their derivatives **whoever** and **whomever**, are the only relative or interrogative pronouns that have different inflections for the subjective and objective cases. Difficulties with these inflections usually arise in three types of sentences.

Although the usual pattern of English sentences is subject-verb-object, this pattern is sometimes reversed in questions. Thus, an interrogative pronoun at the beginning of a question can be in either the subjective or the objective case, depending on its function.

Who are you?

Whom were you calling?

In the first sentence, **who** is in the subjective case because it is the subject of the sentence. In the second sentence, the writer correctly uses the **m** inflection of the objective case to indicate that pronoun is the object of the verb **were calling**.

The function of an interrogative or relative pronoun may also be obscured by a parenthetical expression that separates the pronoun from the rest of its clause. To determine the case of a pronoun in this context, disregard the parenthetical expression and concentrate on the grammatical relationship of the other words.

Who **do you think** will win the election?

Some people will vote for whoever **they believe** will reduce taxes.

Omitting the words **do you think** and **they believe**, we can see that **who** is the subject of **will** and **whoever** is the subject of **will reduce**. Thus both inflections are correct.

Even more troublesome for most writers are sentences in which the function of a relative pronoun within its own clause is different from the function of the clause within the sentence:

Several people saw **who stole the car**.

I want to know the identity of **whoever found the stolen property**.

In the first sentence, the clause in bold type is a direct object, but **who** is in the subjective case because it is the subject of the clause. In the second sentence, the clause in bold type is the object of the preposition **of**, but here, too, the writer has correctly used the subjective case form of the relative pronoun (**whoever**) because it is the subject of the clause.

Another test for **who/whom** inflections can be applied in these three simple steps:

Step 1 Examine only the words following the **who** or **whom** in the sentence. For the sentence "Several people saw who stole the car," the pertinent words would be **stole the car**.

Step 2 Note where a word is needed to make the remaining words a complete sentence: ________ **stole the car**.

Step 3 Fill this slot with **he** or **him**, **they** or **them**. If **he** fits the slot, **who** is appropriate; if **hi*m*** fits the slot, **who*m*** is appropriate. Since **he** fits the slot above, **who** is the correct word for the sentence.

36b Become familiar with possessive case inflections.

Like the subjective and objective cases, the possessive case has only a few inflections:

Nouns	*Indefinite Pronouns (someone, anyone, everyone, etc.)*	*Relative/ Interrogative Pronouns*	*Personal Pronouns*
's or s'	's	whose	my/mine your/yours his, her/hers, its our/ours their/theirs

Many errors in possessive case usage are caused by the writer's failure to recognize which inflections have an apostrophe and which do not. Two of the most frequent errors are evident in the sentences below.

Omitted apostrophe

The bankers account was overdrawn.

Unnecessary apostrophe

The coyote sounded it's mournful cry.

In the first sentence, the writer has omitted the apostrophe before the **s** in **bankers**, thus giving the impression that the word is a plural subject rather than a possessive. The insertion of an apostrophe in **it's** in the second sentence is equally misleading because the apostrophe signals a contraction (**it is**) rather than the possessive case inflection **its**, which never has an apostrophe.

In most contexts, the need for a possessive case inflection is fairly obvious (Few people would write **John** car, for example, or **me** books). The case of a noun or pronoun is more difficult to determine, however, when it comes immediately before a verbal ending in **-ing** (**running, dancing, driving**, etc.). In general, use the possessive case if the verbal is a gerund (i.e., if it functions as a noun) and the objective case if the **-ing** word is a participle (i.e., if it functions as an adjective).

Tom**'s driving** worries me.

Yesterday, I saw **him weaving** in and out of traffic on the freeway.

In the first sentence above, **Tom's** is in the possessive case because **driving** is a gerund used as the subject of **worries**. In the second sentence, the personal pronoun **him** is in the objective case because it is a direct object modified by the participle phrase **weaving in and out of traffic on the freeway**.

36 b

In some constructions you may use either the objective case or the possessive case depending on how you want the reader to interpret the sentence.

I heard **John's** snoring.
I heard **John** snoring.

In the first sentence, **snoring** is a gerund naming what **I heard**. In the next sentence, **snoring** is a participle modifying **John**—John, who is snoring. See Chapter **29** for further discussion of the apostrophe.

Exercise 1

Underline the correct form of the pronoun within the parentheses, and be able to explain whether it is the subjective, objective, or possessive case.

1. (Who, Whom) do you think portrays superspy James Bond more convincingly, Roger Moore or Sean Connery? subjective

2. Just because you scored higher on that standardized test than (I, me) doesn't mean you are smarter than (I, me). subjective subjective

3. I knew that Clifton was working in the cafeteria, but I didn't know that it was (he, him) who was responsible for the luncheon menu. subjective

4. To (who, whom) should I give this paperwork? objective

5. The coach lost his temper when Jerry and (I, me) were late for practice. subjective

6. Working in the community volunteer program gave Sherry and (he, him) a sense of self worth. objective

7. Unfortunately, the rare, old baseball card lost much of (its, it's) value when it was creased. possessive

8. The race for secretary ended in a run-off between the incumbent and (me, I). objective

Exercise 2

Find and correct the case errors in the following passage:

Just between you and I, ~~I~~ me believe that all the turmoil over who~~m~~ gets elected president every four years is pointless. Who^m the voters choose makes little difference. It seems that no matter how hard our leaders try to bring about positive change, their efforts are of no more consequence than the efforts of ordinary citizens such as you and ~~I~~ me. Although some presidents might disagree, our country is truly led and controlled by systems and institutions, not by people. The day might come for ~~we~~ us Americans when our president, like the royalty of England, is more of a symbol than a power.

37 · Pronoun-Antecedent Disagreement

A pronoun and its *antecedent* (the word or words that the pronoun refers to) should always agree in number. A singular pronoun requires a singular antecedent, and a plural pronoun requires a plural antecedent.

The antique **collector** placed **her** bid.

The antique **collectors** placed **their** bids.

A pronoun and its antecedent *disagree* grammatically if one is singular and the other is plural.

Disagreement

singular — plural

An **idealist** will never abandon **their** principles.

Before our eyes reach the direct object in the sentence above, we have construed a singular **idealist** who **will never abandon** something; however, when we read the plural pronoun **their**, our concept of the singular idealist is contradicted, and our reading is temporarily confused.

The causes of such errors in writing vary, but they are most likely to occur when the antecedent is a *collective noun*, an *indefinite pronoun*, or a *compound*.

37a With collective nouns such as *committee*, *team*, *jury*, and the like, use either a singular or a plural pronoun depending on whether you want the reader to think of the members of the group as a unit or as individuals.

The **committee** submitted **its** report to the governor.

The **committee** disagreed about whether **they** should submit **their** report to the governor.

The singular pronoun in the first sentence tells the reader that the committee acted as a single body; the plural pronouns in the second sentence, on the other hand, refer to the members of the committee.

Whenever you use a collective noun, check to be sure that you have not treated it as both singular and plural in the same sentence. For example, a sentence such as "The committee **has** decided to submit **their** report to the governor" would be confusing because the verb **has** signifies that **committee** is singular, but **their**—a plural pronoun—sends the reader a contradictory signal.

37b When using an indefinite pronoun as an antecedent, note whether it is singular or plural and make any pronoun that refers to it agree in number.

Like collective nouns, some indefinite pronouns (any, all, some) may be singular or plural.

Some of the baggage was damaged when **it** fell out of the trunk. [**Some of the baggage** is conceived as a single amount.]

The graduating seniors gathered in the auditorium. **Some** wore **their** robes, and **some** wore **their** school clothes. [**Some** refers to several individuals.]

Several other indefinite pronouns (**both, several, few**) are always plural:

Few remained in **their** homes during the earthquake.

Most indefinite pronouns, however, are always singular. These include such words as **each, every, either, neither, everyone, someone,** and **anyone**. Confusion can arise when words intervene between an indefinite pronoun and its antecedent.

Disagreement

Each of the members of the women's caucus had **their** own motives.

Agreement

Each of the members of the women's caucus had **her** own motives.

Agreement errors are most likely to occur when a singular indefinite pronoun is the antecedent of a personal pronoun. In a sentence such as "**Somebody** left **their** car in the middle of the street" or **"Everyone** has **their** own theory about how to prepare for tests," for example, the plural pronoun **their** is inconsistent with the singular antecedent (**someone** and **everyone** respectively).

Because singular third person personal pronouns referring to humans (he and she) specify sex, constructions like these pose a dilemma for skilled and inexperienced writers alike.

The **somebody** who left a car in the street could be a man or a woman, and **everyone** is a word that includes people of both sexes. The writers of both sentences have attempted to avoid the gender problem in the same way that speakers often do in informal conversations—by using the plural **their**, which can refer to either or both sexes.

A better alternative is simply to delete the pronoun or substitute a plural noun or pronoun for the singular antecedent.

Somebody left a car in the middle of the street.

Students have different theories about how to prepare for tests.

A third option is to join masculine and feminine pronouns with a hyphen, a slash, or the conjunction **or**.

Everyone has **his or her** own theory about how to prepare for tests.

Note, though, that such compounds can convey a stilted tone—an effect that becomes even more pronounced if the combined pronouns are used more than once:

Everyone has **his or her** own preference about how to study for **his or her** tests.

37c To decide whether a pronoun with a compound antecedent should be singular or plural, notice what type of conjunction links the elements in the compound.

In general, a pronoun should be plural if its antecedent is a compound consisting of two or more words joined by **and**.

My brother and his wife like cold weather, but **they** are having second thoughts about moving to Alaska.

Exception: If the elements joined by **and** refer to the same person or thing, treat the entire compound as a singular antecedent and use the singular form for any pronouns that refer to it:

The **famous actor and director** recently completed **his** new film.

Here, the pronoun **his** is singular because the **actor and director** are the same person.

If the antecedent is a compound in which the elements are linked by **or**, **nor**, **either . . . or**, **neither . . . nor**, or **not only . . . but also**, the pronoun should agree with the part of the antecedent that is closest to it.

Neither the lifejacket nor the **flashlight** was in **its** proper place.
Neither the lifejacket nor the **flashlights** were in **their** proper place.
Neither the lifejackets nor the **flashlight** was in **its** proper place.

Note: If the elements of a compound antecedent are different in number, as in the last example above, you can express the relationship between pronoun and antecedent more effectively by changing the connective and—if necessary—the pronoun and verb.

The lifejackets **and** the flashlight were out of **their** proper places.

Exercise 1

Revise each of the following sentences to eliminate pronoun-antecedent disagreement errors. **Answers will vary.**

1. ~~Each~~ I ~~i~~nstructors ~~has~~ have a philosophy of teaching that they follow.

2. The encounter group meets every Tuesday in ~~their~~ the room on the third floor.

3. ~~Neither~~ Both of the campers ~~was~~ were very unhappy with the weather they encountered during the backwoods trip.

4. The committee makes ~~their~~ its recommendations for new by-laws after ~~their~~ its last meeting of the year.

5. The entire coin collection was stolen from ~~their~~ its hiding place.

6. Everyone who has finished ~~their warm-up~~ warming up can begin ~~their~~ the floor exercise.

7. The great doctor and scientist will take a vacaiton only after the completion of ~~their~~ his or **her** research.

8. Some of the logs spilled from ~~its~~ their bin on the back of the truck.

Exercise 2

Correct the pronoun-antecedent disagreement errors in the following paragraph.

Everyone has ~~their~~ a favorite kind of music, but few can tell specifically what makes it appealing. Like the kids on *American Bandstand*, the average music lover can describe ~~their~~ reactions to the music only in general terms, such as "I like the beat" or "It's easy to dance to." These people fail to realize that each of the songs they admire has ~~their~~ distinctive features. By analyzing the appeal of a song, both the enthusiast and the average listener derive greater enjoyment and appreciation.

38 · Subject-Verb Disagreement

In standard written English, a singular subject takes a singular verb, and a plural subject requires a plural verb. When a writer uses a singular form for one and a plural form for the other, the subject and verb disagree grammatically.

Disagreement

Military **advisors has** been sent to Central America.

Fast, effective medical **service are** one of the major goals of an Area Health Center.

38 a

In the first sentence, the plural subject **advisors** leads us to expect a plural verb, but instead we find the singular verb **has**. In the second sentence, the singular subject **service** prepares us for a singular verb, yet the next word is the plural verb **are**.

To avoid such inconsistencies in your own writing, follow closely the conventions discussed in the sections that follow.

38a Do not confuse the plural *s* ending of a noun with the singular *s* ending of a verb.

An **s** at the end of a noun almost always signals that the word is plural, whereas an **s** at the end of a verb indicates that it is singular. Therefore, if you have written a sentence in which the subject and verb both end in **s**, they probably disagree in number.

Disagreement

In the latest air disaster film, two **planes** flying over a large city **collides.**

Here, the **s** at the end of **collide** is unexpected because the **s** at the end cf **plane** prepares us for a plural verb.

Exceptions

1. A few nouns (**news, economics**, etc.) are plural in form but singular in meaning. When one of these singular nouns functions as a subject, its verb should also be singular.

The **news** from Washington **was** all bad.

Economics attracts many students on this campus.

2. When a title is the subject of a sentence, the verb should always be singular—even if the title includes a plural noun or pronoun.

James Fenimore Cooper's ***The Pioneers* takes** place in the West.

***Jaws* has made** some people afraid to go in the water.

Note that in both of these sentences the subject is the title itself, not the words comprising it.

38b When the subject of a sentence is a collective noun, use a singular verb if the noun refers to a group as a unit and a plural verb if the noun refers to the individuals comprising a group.

Collective noun referring to members as a unit

The negotiating **team disagrees** with the ambassador's policy statement.

Collective noun referring to individual members

The negotiating **team disagree** about how to respond to the ambassador's policy statement.

In the first sentence above, the verb is singular because the negotiating team is unified in its disagreement with the ambassador's policy statement. In the second sentence, the verb is plural because the members of the negotiating team respond differently to the ambassador's statement.

Note: If a plural verb following a collective noun sounds unnatural or awkward to you, modify the sentence slightly by adding **the members of** just before the noun:

The members of the negotiating team **disagree** about how to respond to the ambassador's decision.

38c When using an indefinite pronoun as subject, choose a verb form that tells the reader whether the pronoun is singular or plural in meaning.

38 c

Some of the liquid in the beaker **has spilled** on the floor. [**Some** is a singular quantity and therefore needs a singular verb.]

Some of the skateboard artists **were doing** flips as they glided along the sidewalk. [**Some** refers to more than one skateboard artist and therefore needs a plural verb.]

Be sure to make a distinction between these indefinite pronouns and the two other classes of indefinite pronouns: those which are always plural (**several, few, any**) and those which are always singular (**each, every, everyone, everybody, somebody, anybody, either, neither**).

Many speak, but **few listen**.

Everyone has the same problems.

38d Make the verb in a relative clause agree in number with the antecedent of the relative pronoun.

Because a relative pronoun (**who, which, that**) does not have distinctive singular and plural forms, you must locate the antecedent in order to determine the number of the pronoun. You can then make a decision about the verb's number and communicate that information to the reader.

The **person who has** the most experience will receive first consideration. [singular antecedent—singular verb]

The **people who have** the most experience will receive first consideration. [plural antecedent—plural verb]

38e To determine the number of a verb with a compound antecedent, note the type of conjunction(s) used to unite the elements of the compound.

If you form a compound subject with **and**, make the verb plural; if you join the subjects with **or, nor, either . . . or, neither . . . nor**, or **not only . . . but also**, make the verb agree with the part of the compound closest to it.

1. *Compound subjects joined by* **and**.

The highway patrol **and** the national guard **were** available for emergency duty.

Use a singular verb with such constructions only on the rare occasions when you want to indicate that the elements joined by **and** function as one.

The famous **pirate and smuggler was** capable of evading even the swiftest of his pursuers.

Here the singular verb is appropriate because it tells the reader that the pirate and the smuggler are the same person. On the other hand, the use of the singular verb **was** in the previous example would be confusing because the highway patrol and the national guard are separate agencies.

2. *Compound subjects joined by* **or, nor, either . . . or, neither . . . nor**, or **not only . . . but also**.

Neither **reason** nor **intuitions are** infallible.

Either **thunderstorms** or heavy **fog makes** driving difficult.

Though technically correct, both of the above sentences would be improved stylistically if both parts of the compound were the same number.

Neither **reason** nor **intuition is** infallible.

Either a **thunderstorm** or a heavy **fog makes** driving difficult.

38f When you use either a single word or a compound as the subject of the verb *be*, make the verb agree with the subject, not the complement.

A constant **threat** to my garden **is insects**.

In this sentence, some writers might be tempted to use the verb **are** because the noun closest to it, **insects**, is plural. Readers, however, would be confused by **are** because the subject **threat** is singular.

38g If you invert the usual subject-verb order in a sentence or begin with the expletive *there* or *here*, look to the right of the verb for the subject.

1. *Inverted word order.*

Alongside the highway **were** two abandoned **automobiles**.

In this sentence, the verb **were** is plural because its subject is **automobiles**, not **highway**. The prepositional phrase **alongside the highway** serves as an adverb. A good way to test for subject-verb agreement in an inverted sentence is to consider how the sentence would read if the subject came first.

Two abandoned **automobiles were** alongside the highway.

2. *Expletive constructions.*

There is an extra chair on the porch.

Here are the most colorful, exciting real estate ads.

Notice that in each of these sentences the first word is not the subject but a means by which the writer defers the subject (**chair** and **ads** respectively) until later in the sentence.

To test for subject-verb agreement in clauses beginning with **here** or **there**, follow one of these procedures:

If the sentence begins with **there**, think about how the sentence should read with the word deleted.

An empty chair is on the porch.

If the sentence begins with **here**, try moving the word to the end of the sentence and repositioning the verb.

The real estate ads **are here**.

38h Do not be distracted by words that come between a subject and its verb.

1. **Representatives** of a large hotel chain **are** planning to meet with the Builders' Association.
2. The **turntable** as well as the speakers **is** defective.
3. **Postponing** decisions **is** one of my worst faults.

Writers who determine the number of a verb by the number of the noun closest to it might use **is** instead of **are** in sentence #1 and substitute **are** for **is** in sentences #2 and #3. In sentence #1, however, the verb should be plural because its subject is **representatives**; **chain**, the word immediately before the verb, is the object of the preposition **of**.

In sentence #2, the verb **is** agrees with the singular subject **turntable**, not with **speakers**, the object of the preposition **as well as**. One option here would be to substitute a coordinating conjunction for the preposition and make the verb plural:

The turntables and the speakers are defective.

In sentence #3, the subject is a verb phrase consisting of a gerund (**postponing**) and its object (**decisions**). In such constructions, the verb should agree with the **-ing** word not with its object. Thus **is** is the appropriate verb because **postponing** names a single act.

Exercise 1

Correct the errors in subject-verb agreement in the following sentences without changing verb tense.

1. Neither the chief airport official nor the president of the airline ~~were~~ **was** certain that the strike could be averted.
2. If either of the rescue teams ~~get~~ **gets** through in time it will be a miracle.
3. *Star Wars* ~~were~~ **was** a picture that spawned numerous inferior imitations.

4. Statistics ~~are~~ is a required course for computer science majors.

5. The source of the ruler's problems ~~were~~ was the apathy and mistrust of his subjects.

6. Always lurking in the back of the prisoner's mind ~~was~~ were thoughts of escape.

7. Reducing the inefficiencies in production lines ~~were~~ was the main concern of the newly hired consultants.

8. There ~~is~~ are several ivory chess sets in the wall safe.

9. The dancers and their director give~~s~~ a benefit performance yearly for the community.

10. Some outspoken professors at the university ~~has~~ have been attacked in recent newspaper editorials.

Exercise 2

Correct the errors in subject-verb agreement in the following passage.

Two of the biggest problems a college freshman ~~face~~ faces are homesickness and loneliness. Freshmen on their own for the first time often experiences feelings of anxiety and insecurity until they adjust to their new independence. However, once the newest members of the campus community makes the necessary adjustments, solitude and new-found freedoms becomes enjoyable rather than frightening.

39 · Errors in Verb Usage

Subject-verb disagreement, a problem discussed in the preceding chapter, is only one of several common errors involving verb forms. Others include omission or misuse of the **d/ed** inflections; use of nonstandard forms of **be**; confusion of verbs such as **sit/set**, **lie/lay**, and other words that are similar in sound but different in meaning; and unnecessary shifts in tense or voice.

39a Do not omit the *d* or *ed* ending of a regular verb in the past or perfect tense.

Because a final d sound is often inaudible in speech, writers who are guided by the sound of a word rather than by a knowledge of its grammatical form and function are likely to omit the inflection in the past or perfect tenses of regular verbs.

Confusing omission of inflections

I **finish** my research paper yesterday.

The delegates to the convention have **propose** several changes in the constitution.

Whatever the cause, the omission of the **ed** inflection of **finish** and the **d** ending of **propose** in the sentences above is confusing because both verbs have a present tense form, yet they describe actions that have already occurred.

39b Do not use *d* or *ed* to form tenses of irregular verbs.

Misuse of* d/ed *inflections with irregular verbs

The department store manager **choosed** the most successful salesperson for the new customer relations job.

Though common in some spoken dialects, such nonstandard verb forms are distracting to readers who are able to distinguish between regular and irregular verbs and expect to find **chose** in this context.

39c Follow the conventions of written English when using forms of *be.*

Although in some oral dialects, the verb **be** has as few as two forms (**be** and **been**), in standard written English it has eight different forms (**am, are, is, was, were, be, being, been**). Therefore a speaker addressing a listener conversant in the same dialect might say "I **been** to town" or "We **be** ready," but a writer addressing a diversified audience accustomed to the conventions of the written code should conform to that code.

We **are** ready.

I **have been** to town.

39d Distinguish between *sit* and *set*, *lie* and *lay*, and the forms of other irregular verbs that look and sound alike but have different meanings and different inflections for each tense.

Consider the following examples:

Confusing

My grandfather likes to **set** in his rocking chair every afternoon.

I **laid** on the sofa and fell asleep.

Each of these sentences is confusing because the verb conveys a meaning different from that which the writer intended to express.

In the first sentence, the writer has confused **set**, which means **put**, with **sit**, which means **take a seat**. In the second sentence, the writer makes a similar error, using **laid** (**placed**) instead of the expected **lay** (**reclined**).

If you have difficulty distinguishing between these verbs, study the chart below:

Infinitive	*Past Tense*	*Past Participle*
sit (take a seat)	sat	sat
set (place)	set	set
lie (recline)	lay	lain
lay (put)	laid	laid

39e Avoid unexpected and unnecessary shifts in verb tense.

Unexpected shifts

As I **parked** the car, someone **runs** into it.

The runner **circles** the track each time she **won** a race.

Both of these tense shifts are puzzling because they cannot be predicted or explained by anything in the sentence. Notice how much clearer the time relationships in each sentence become when verb tenses are consistent.

As I **parked** my car, someone **ran** into it.

The runner **circles** the track each time she **wins** a race.

Verb tenses should also be consistent within a paragraph and from one paragraph to the next. Look closely at the two passages below and observe how the writer has handled verb tenses.

As a child, I dreamed of all the wonderful things that would happen to me when I became sixteen. Most of all, I looked forward to owning a car and becoming more independent. But when I turned sixteen, I realize that I can't afford to put gas in a car, much less own one, and that my dream of independence is also an illusion. I still had to do homework, mow the lawn, and abide by my parents' rules. In no sense do I feel like an adult.

As a child, I dreamed of all the wonderful things that would happen to me when I became sixteen. Most of all, I looked forward to owning a car and becoming more independent. But when I turned sixteen, I realized that I couldn't afford to put gas in a car, much less own one, and that my dream of independence was also an illusion. I still had to do homework, mow the lawn, and abide by my parents' rules. In no sense did I feel like an adult.

The first passage moves unpredictably between the past and the present. These frequent shifts in verb tense suggest that the writer is unsure about the perspective from which this account of personal experience should be related. At the outset, the point of view seems to be that of an older person reflecting on an earlier time (notice the past tense verbs **dreamed, became, looked, turned**). In sentence 3, however, the writer seems to assume the role of the young person, recording the conflict between dreams and reality in the present tense (**realize, can't, is**). Two additional tense shifts that occur in sentences 4 and 5 simply add to the confusion, further undermining the writer's authority and the reader's sense of continuity. In the revised version, the writer resolves these problems simply by changing the present tense verbs to past tense.

Note: Some shifts in verb tenses are logical and necessary, as in sentences like the following:

Shakespeare **died** in 1616, but his plays **live** on.

Once, great herds of buffalo **roamed** the West; now only a few **remain**.

Exercise 1

In the following sentences, revise nonstandard verb forms, and make verb tense sequences consistent and logical.

1. I ~~laid~~ **lay** in the sun all day and got burned.
2. I ~~use~~ **used** to be shy before I took a course in self-confidence.
3. We ^**have** been writing for at least an hour.
4. The irate fans had ~~came~~ **come** to the conclusion that their team would never be a winner.
5. The banking industry was ~~shook~~ **shaken** by the revelations of corruption in high places.
6. The guests were told to ~~sit~~ **set** their gifts on the hall table and then to ~~set~~ **sit** down in the den.
7. The archaeological team spared nothing in their efforts to

~~rise~~ **raise** the sunken galleon from the harbor bottom.

8. As I walked into the hotel, I ~~spies~~ **spied** the man I had been looking for.

9. I saw many beautiful aspects of nature as I ~~runned~~ **ran** through the park.

10. When the writer was alive, nobody ~~knows~~ **knew** her; when she ~~dies~~ **died**, suddenly everybody ~~would proclaim~~ **proclaimed** what a genius she ~~is~~ **was**.

Exercise 2

In the following paragraph, revise nonstandard verb forms and eliminate inconsistencies in verb tenses.

Only a month after I bought a new car, it was ~~stole~~ **stolen** while I ~~am~~ **was** attending a party. I ^**had** been at the party just a short while when I decided to leave because I was not feeling well. My date and I went to where we ~~remember~~ **remembered** parking the car, but it was not there. After our initial shock, we decided to check and make sure we weren't on the wrong street. However, after we had ~~went~~ **gone** up and down all the nearby streets, we knew that the car was lost. Luckily, my car was ~~recover~~ **recovered** the next day by the police, out of town and out of gas. Apparently someone had merely wanted to take a one-night joy ride; unfortunately, my car ~~happens~~ **happened** to be the most joyful one available.

40 · Errors in Adjective and Adverb Forms

Most problems with the forms of adjectives and adverbs can be traced to the differences between spoken and written English.

40a In writing, do not omit the *ly* ending of adverbs such as *surely*, *really*, *easily*.

40 a

Though common in spoken English, such omissions are unexpected and distracting to most readers because the form of the modifier is inconsistent with its function.

Adjectives misused as adverbs

I can pass the driving test **easy**.

People in coastal areas are **real** unhappy about government's plans to dispose of hazardous wastes in the ocean.

In these sentences, **easy** and **real** have the form of adjectives, but they are used as adverbs (**easy** modifies the verb **can pass** and **real** modifies the adjective **unhappy**).

Such inconsistencies can be eliminated simply by changing the adjective to an adverb.

I can pass the driving test **easily**.

or

I can **easily** pass the driving test.

People in coastal areas are **really** unhappy about the government's plans to dispose of hazardous wastes in the ocean.

40b In writing, do not omit the *d* or *ed* inflection of the past participle of a regular verb.

Confusing omission of inflection

The goods **produce** by the Fly-by-Night Hardware Company were defective.

The picture on the woodworking kit bore no resemblance to the **finish** product.

Although **produce** and **finish** are spelled the way the writer might pronounce **produce*d*** and **finishe*d***, the form of each word conveys a meaning different from that which the writer intends.

In the first sentence, the reader may initially assume that **produce** is the predicate of **goods** rather than an adjective modifying it. The omission of the **ed** ending of **finish** in the second sentence is also misleading because the word at first appears to be a noun. Only after reading further do we discover that the writer intended this word to be an adjective.

40c Follow written rather than oral conventions when using comparative and superlative forms of adjectives.

In some regional dialects, expressions like **most happiest** and **more prettier** are commonplace, but such redundancies are distracting in an essay and should therefore be revised.

Redundant

I am **most happiest** when I am alone.

The flowers are **more prettier** in the spring than in the summer.

Revised

I am **happiest** when I am alone.

The flowers are **prettier** in the spring than in the summer.

Keep in mind, too, that the written code makes a distinction between the comparative and the superlative that is seldom observed by speakers. Writers conventionally use the comparative when referring to two people or things and the superlative when referring to more than two.

Claire is the **more** experienced of the two laboratory technicians on duty this summer. She is also the **most** intelligent member of a large and diversified department.

Someone speaking informally about Claire, on the other hand, might say she was the **most experienced of the two lab technicians.**

Oral and written usage are not always incompatible, of course. In fact, your familiarity with the spoken language will often help you decide the specific form to use for the comparative or superlative degree of a particular adjective—to recognize, for example, that the superlative of **famous** is not **famousest** but **most famous**. If you should have doubts about the appropriate comparative or superlative form of any adjective, consult a dictionary.

Exercise 1

Eliminate the incorrect uses of adjectives and adverbs in the following sentences.

1. All the model ever had for lunch was ~~toss~~ tossed salad.

2. The disgruntled employee did not feel that the lie detector test he was forced to take was administered ~~fair~~ fairly.

3. Both of the cars were quite practical, but the imported

model was ~~most~~ **more** beautiful.

4. Marsha ~~sure~~ **surely** was pleased by the results of her aptitude test.

5. Even though the jacket was on sale, the ~~reduce~~ **reduced** price was still far beyond the means of most shoppers.

6. The survivor's tale was one of the ~~more~~ **most** bizarre stories ever told.

7. The awesome lightning forked ~~crazy~~ **crazily** across the sky.

Exercise 2

Correct the faulty uses of adjectives and adverbs in the following passage.

Aerobic dancing involves performing a series of ~~increasing~~ **increasingly** difficult exercise routines to the beat of popular songs. For the initial ten minutes of class, participants move ~~slow,~~ **slowly** preparing their muscles for the upcoming workout. Then they warm up by doing jumps and twists to the beat of a ~~relative~~ **relatively** slow song. Finally, they dance specific aerobics routines to the driving beat of hard rock. By the time the session is over, the dancers feel like ~~accomplish~~ **accomplished** performers.

41 · Vague Pronoun Reference

The reference of a pronoun is clear if the pronoun has a specific, immediately recognizable antecedent.

Standing at the door was a stern looking **man who** glared at the **customers** as **they** filed past **him** into the theater.

Some products are marked with a special sale **price**, but **this** can be misleading.

At a slower pace, after the flash, came the **sound** of the explosion, **which** some people have no recollection of hearing, while others described it as an earth-shaking roar, like thunder or a big wind.

Alexander Leighton

The reference of a pronoun is *vague* under the following conditions: if the pronoun refers broadly to the idea of a sentence or paragraph rather than to a specific word or word group; if the pronoun normally has an antecedent but none is expressed or implied; or if the pronoun refers ambiguously to more than one antecedent.

41a Avoid excessively broad reference when using the pronouns *this*, *that*, *which*, and *it*.

Some of the effects of such vague references can be seen in the following sentences:

Broad reference

1. One recent report on American education concludes that schools should stay open all year. **This** appeals to some parents.
2. Donnell was annoyed because his friends were late, but **that** did not bother them.

3. The judge ruled that the accident victim's whiplash injury was a hoax, **which** pleased the defendant.

After reading sentence #1, we still cannot be certain what **this** refers to. The only possible antecedent actually expressed in the sentence is **report**, but the report itself does not seem to be what some parents found appealing. The word might refer to the conclusion of the report or to the concept of a longer school year or to the longer year itself. The lack of a specific antecedent for **that** in sentence #2 raises similar questions. **That** could refer to Donnell's annoyance, to his friends' lateness, or to the fact that he was angry with them for being late. And in sentence #3, the reader may at first mistake **injury** or **hoax** for the antecedent of **which** before realizing that the pronoun refers to an unstated antecedent—the judge's ruling.

Vagueness problems of this kind can be eliminated in several different ways.

1. *Include an exact antecedent.*

A recent report on American education concludes with the **recommendation** that schools should stay open all year. **This** appeals to some parents.

2. *Add a noun immediately after the pronoun if the latter is* **this, that**, or one of the other demonstrative pronouns.

Donnell was annoyed because his friends were late, but **that reaction** did not bother them.

3. *Restructure the sentence to eliminate the need for an antecedent.*

The defendant was pleased at the judge's ruling that the accident victim's whiplash injury was a hoax.

Note: The fact that a demonstrative or relative pronoun does not have a one-word antecedent does not necessarily mean that its reference is vague. But if you use a pronoun in this way, its meaning must be clear from the content, as in the following passage.

Most of us are too tired or too harassed to take a computer, a slide rule, and an M.I.T. graduate to market and figure out what we're buying. The makers of the goods we buy know **this**.

Marya Mannes

41b Do not use a personal pronoun such as *they* or *you* as if it were an indefinite pronoun.

Vague reference

I have always wondered when the old house at the edge of town was built. **They** say that George Washington once slept there.

No amount of searching will yield an antecedent for **they** in this sentence. If the writer's intent is to make only a general reference to the townspeople, an indefinite pronoun such as **some** would better serve the purpose.

I have always been curious about when the old house at the edge of town was built. **Some** say that George Washington once slept there.

If the writer has in mind a more specific group of people, that information should be shared with the reader.

I have always been curious about when the old house at the edge of town was built. **People whose families have lived within the area since the Revolutionary War era** say that George Washington once slept there.

A similar problem arises when the second-person pronoun **you** has only a general reference.

When **you** join the college's marching band, **you** must give up other extracurricular activities.

Here the writer seems to be projecting his or her personal experience into a generalized **you** rather than addressing a second-person audience as the pronoun leads us to expect. With the substitution of a first-person pronoun, an indefinite pronoun, or a plural noun, the meaning of the sentence becomes clearer.

When **I** joined the college's marching band, **I** gave up other extracurricular activities.

Anyone who joins the college's marching band must give up other extracurricular activities.

Students who join the college's marching band must give up other extracurricular activities.

41c Avoid ambiguous reference.

Ambiguous reference

When Kellen accused Scott of cheating, **he** was very angry.

Mrs. Posey told her sister that **she** was irresponsible.

In the first sentence, the reference of **he** is ambiguous because its antecedent could be either **Kellen** or **Scott.** The same problem occurs in the next sentence, where **she** may refer to either **Mrs. Posey** or **her sister.**

If you find that you have used a pronoun in this way, rephrase the sentence to eliminate the ambiguity:

Scott was angry when Kellen accused **him** of cheating.

Mrs. Posey criticized **her** sister for being irresponsible.

41 c

Exercise 1

Rewrite the following sentences to eliminate vague pronoun references. Answers will vary.

1. The driver thought he could beat the train to the railroad crossing, but this ^misjudgment^ was fatal.

2. The village was located on top of a peak; ~~it~~ going there was like climbing Mount Everest after a hard day's journey.

3. The children ate like perfect ladies and gentlemen, and they even talked politely during the meal, a behavior which surprised the camp counselor.

4. When the police arrived, the mob dispersed, and that respo[nse] was a relief to the townspeople.

5. Mr. Farnsworth's estate is worth over a million dollars; ~~they~~ some say he started out without a dime to his name.

6. While I was camping in the Appalachians, the first thing I saw every chilly morning was my breath; ~~they~~ natives say that the temperature often drops below freezing even in the summer.

7. When the bride walked down the aisle past her mother, she winked.
The bride winked when she walked down the aisle past her mother.

Exercise 2

Rewrite the following passage to eliminate vague pronoun references. **Answers will vary.**

If you are thinking about investing in a cable television hookup or

41
c

a video recording system, you should consider the disadvantages as well as the advantages of owning such equipment. For instance, you will be able to spend many pleasurable hours in the presence of interesting screen and stage characters, but this activity will reduce the amount of time available for socializing with actual people. ~~They~~ Some also say that the sports fare available through cable is varied and excellent. Of course, the more time you spend watching and rewatching sporting events, the less time you will have to participate in them; in fact, the most exercise anyone will get will probably consist of punching the buttons on the remote control apparatus. The basic rule to remember ~~in this~~ is that if you have a desire to spend more time sitting idly in front of a TV screen, then invest. Otherwise, don't have it a cable hookup or video system installed.

42 · Dangling and Misplaced Modifiers

An adjective, an adverb, or a phrase or clause used as an adjective or adverb should refer to a specific word in the same sentence and be placed close to it so that the relationship is clear to the reader. A modifier is *dangling* if it has nothing to modify, and it is *misplaced* if intervening words obscure the relationship between it and the word it modifies.

42a Avoid dangling modifiers.

Typically, a dangling modifier comes at the beginning of a sentence and takes the form of a participial phrase, a prepositional phrase, an infinitive phrase, or an elliptical clause (a clause with one or more words omitted).

Dangling modifiers

Having cleaned the apartment, the floor was waxed. [dangling participial phrase]

After adjusting the microscope, a slide was placed under the lens. [dangling prepositional phrase]

To lose weight, rich foods should be avoided. [dangling infinitive phrase]

While discussing theories of insect behavior, a fly lit on Mr. Worthington's desk. [dangling elliptical clause]

42 a

All of these sentences are confusing for essentially the same reason: they begin with a reference to someone whom we expect to be identified at the beginning of the following clause, but in each instance this expectation is frustrated. Obviously, a floor cannot clean an apartment, a slide does not adjust a microscope, foods do not lose weight, and a fly is incapable of discussing insect behavior. Yet that is what the structure of these sentences implies.

To avoid such confusion in your own writing, ask yourself this question whenever you use a modifying phrase or clause: To whom or what does this group of words refer? If you cannot find a word in the same sentence that gives you a logical answer, either revise the phrase or clause so that its reference is clear or use an appropriate noun or pronoun as the subject of the independent clause.

After the microscope was adjusted, a slide was placed under the lens.

or

After adjusting the microscope, **the scientist placed a slide under the lens**.

A dangling modifier at the end of a sentence can be corrected in the same way.

Dangling modifier

A ball hit me in the head **while waiting for a tennis court**.

Revised

A ball hit me in the head while **I was** waiting for a tennis court.

42b Avoid misplaced modifiers.

A misplaced modifier is often confusing because the reader may associate it with the wrong word.

Misplaced modifier

A cloud of foul-smelling gas ruined our lunch **from a nearby paper mill**.

By placing the prepositional phrase at the end of the sentence rather than immediately after **gas**, the noun it modifies, the writer seems to be saying that it was the lunch, not the gas, that came from the paper mill.

The solution to such a problem is simply to move the modifier to its appropriate position in the sentence:

A cloud of foul-smelling gas **from a nearby paper mill** ruined our lunch.

Another kind of misplaced modifier (sometimes called a *squinting modifier*) is one that refers ambiguously to the word on either side of it.

The spectators who had been shouting **angrily** protested the official's ruling.

In this sentence, the adverb **angrily** is next to the word it modifies, but we cannot tell which word that is. The writer may mean either that the spectators had been shouting angrily or that they protested angrily. Such ambiguity can usually be eliminated by a shift in the position of the modifier or by a slight change in the wording.

The shouting spectators **angrily** protested the official's ruling.

The spectators who had been **angrily** shouting protested the official's ruling.

The spectators who had been shouting protested **angrily** the official's ruling.

Exercise 1

Rewrite the following sentences to eliminate dangling or misplaced modifiers. **Answers will vary.**

42 b

1. Having missed the flight, ~~the trip was postponed~~. **we postponed the trip**

2. The charred papers were exhibited at the official proceedings that were salvaged from a lit fireplace.
   The charred papers that were salvaged from a lit fireplace were exhibited at the official proceedings.

3. To become a professional dancer, ~~pain and setbacks must be endured~~. **a person must endure pain and setbacks**

4. When studying, ~~noise must be kept to a minimum~~. **students must keep noise to a minimum**

5. After accelerating recklessly through the final turn, ~~the race was easily won by the Italian team~~. **the Italian team easily won the race**

6. The staff members who were working ~~diligently~~ performed their duties **diligently**.

7. Failing to sell enough tickets to break even, the ~~concert was canceled~~ **promoter canceled the concert**.

Exercise 2

Rewrite the following passage, eliminating misplaced and dangling modifiers wherever they occur. **Answers will vary.**

After attending the wedding, a search for the bride and groom's car was undertaken. We soon found it parked about three blocks from the church in an alley. Armed with cans of shaving cream, the windows were quickly covered with foam. Next, we tied tin cans to the rear bumper filled with marbles. Finally, as the newlyweds approached, everyone who had participated enthusiastically shouted, "Surprise!"

After attending the wedding, we searched for the bride and groom's car. We soon found it parked in an alley about three blocks from the church. Armed with cans of shaving cream, we quickly covered the windows with foam. Next we tied tin cans filled with marbles to the rear bumper. Finally, as the newlyweds approached, everyone who had participated shouted enthusiastically, "Surprise!"

43 · Comma Splice and Fused Sentence

The **comma splice** and the **fused sentence** are sentence errors that result from the mispunctuation of independent clauses.

43a Do not link or "splice" two independent clauses with a comma alone or with a comma plus a conjunctive adverb such as *however*, *therefore*, or another such connective (see 7h for a list of conjunctive adverbs).

Comma splices

The coach paced nervously along the sidelines, the kicker sat calmly on the bench.

The coach paced nervously along the sidelines, **however,** the kicker sat calmly on the bench.

Both types of comma splices frustrate readers' expectations. A comma alone following an introductory independent clause, as in the first sentence above, prepares the reader not for a second independent clause but for a nonrestrictive modifier or a series.

43
a

The coach paced nervously along the sidelines, **where the kicker sat calmly on the bench**. [nonrestrictive subordinate clause modifying **sidelines**]

The coach paced nervously **along the sidelines, behind the bench, and among the cheerleaders**. [series of prepositional phrases]

Remember that two independent clauses may be joined by a comma plus a coordinating conjunction (see **13a** and **21a**).

The coach paced nervously along the sidelines, **but** the kicker sat calmly on the bench.

A comma followed by a conjunctive adverb, such as **however**, is also misleading because such words are set off by commas only when they occur within a clause.

The coach paced along the sidelines; the kicker, **however,** sat calmly on the bench.

Note that if the conjunctive adverb were moved to a position between the two clauses, it should be preceded not by a comma but by a semicolon—a punctuation mark that does have the function of linking independent clauses.

43b Do not fuse or run together two sentences by omitting the punctuation mark or connective that marks the boundary between them.

Fused sentence

To some people home remedies are more effective than prescription drugs to others they are a waste of time.

In this sentence, the writer fails to indicate where the first clause ends and the second one begins. As a result, we are likely to misconstrue the words following **drugs** as a continuation of the first clause rather than as a new statement that completes the contrast between the people who value home remedies and those who scorn home remedies.

The key to eliminating both comma splices and fused sentences is being able to recognize independent clauses and to choose the most appropriate means of linking them.

1. *If you want to give separate emphasis to each clause, put a period between them:*

Wind and water erosion are destroying more and more beachfront property each year. People continue to build houses close to the ocean.

2. *If you want to establish a closer but still balanced relationship between the two clauses, link them in one of these three ways:*

With a comma plus a coordinating conjunction (**and, but, or, for, nor, yet, so**)

Wind and water erosion are destroying more and more beachfront property every year, **yet** people continue to build houses close to the ocean.

With a semicolon alone

Wind and water erosion are destroying more and more beachfront property every year; people continue to build houses close to the ocean.

With a semicolon plus a conjunctive adverb

Wind and water erosion are destroying more and more beachfront property every year; **however,** people continue to build houses close to the ocean.

3. *If, after thinking about the problem, you decide that one clause warrants more emphasis than the other, subordinate the less important one.*

If, for example, you wished to emphasize the folly of the people who persist in building houses on the beach, you might subordinate the first clause.

Although wind and water erosion are destroying more and more beachfront property every year, people continue to build houses close to the ocean.

Specific decisions about which construction to use will depend on the context in which the sentence occurs (see Chapters **10, 12,** and **13** for additional suggestions).

Exercise 1

Eliminate comma splices and fused sentences by adding or changing punctuation, or by subordinating one part of the sentence to the other. Put a check after any sentences that are correctly punctuated. **Answers will vary.**

1. We spent several weeks preparing for the admissions

exam, but it was much more difficult than we had imagined. ✓

2. Oysters are good at any time of year; however, some people like to eat them only in the summer.

3. I could see the trail winding toward the bottom of the canyon; about halfway down, something darted across the path and disappeared in the underbrush.

4. Physical changes can be documented rather easily; psychological growth, on the other hand, is difficult to measure.

5. Something may appear to be amiss; however, our procedures are correct. ✓

6. Fog engulfed the airport; no planes were allowed to land or take off.

7. Interest rates have declined slightly during the past month; unemployment, however, has increased.

8. Because many ~~Many~~ stores begin selling Christmas toys right after Halloween, some people are predicting that in the near

future we will be putting up Christmas trees on Labor Day.

9. Organized efforts to censor have increased dramatically, . T two of the chief targets have been *The Grapes of Wrath* and *The Scarlet Letter*.

10. One of the most popular oral legends is a story called "The Vanishing Hitchhiker," ~~it~~ which concerns a woman who returns from the grave each year on the anniversary of her death, hitches a ride with some motorist, and then disappears.

43 b

Exercise 2

Eliminate comma splices and fused sentences in the passage below. **Answers will vary.**

We wear garments of East Indian origin ; our pajamas are made of cotton, a material that was first domesticated in India. The beds that most of us sleep on are built on a pattern that originated in ancient Persia, ; the eiderdown quilts that keep us warm were invented in Scandinavia. After awakening in the morning, we walk into the bathroom . T there we wash with soap, an invention of the ancient Gaul~~s~~, [. W] we then dry ourselves with Turkish towels. Returning to the bedroom, we remove our clothes from a chair, which was invented in the Near East. We put on close-fitting garments, which derive their form from the skin clothing of Asiatic nomads, [and] we fasten our clothes with buttons, which have been in existence since the close of the Stone Age.

Adapted from Ralph Linton's "One Hundred Per Cent American"

44 · The Sentence Fragment

A *fragment* is an incomplete sentence that has been punctuated as if it were a sentence. It either lacks a subject and/or verb, or its subject and verb are part of a dependent clause.

44a Do not punctuate a modifying word, phrase, or clause as a sentence.

Fragments

Suddenly. The door opened. [fragment: adverb modifying the verb **opened**]

The best musician in the orchestra is the lead violinist. **Who practices six hours a day**. [fragment: relative clause modifying **violinist**]

After a two-week strike. The workers returned to their jobs. [fragment: prepositional phrase modifying the verb **returned**]

I couldn't study for my electrical engineering exam. **Because the lights went out.** [fragment: subordinate clause modifying the verb **couldn't study**]

44b Do not punctuate an appositive as a sentence.

Fragment

My cousin is a professional wrestler. **The winner of several championships**.

44c Do not confuse a verbal (part of a gerund or an infinitive) with a verb.

Fragment

As we looked out the window, we saw a rabbit leaping across a ravine. **And a turtle plodding across the highway**. [fragment: a group of words with a subject, **turtle**, but no verb; **plodding** is a present participle]

The *causes* of fragments vary. Some occur because the writer is following the oral rather than the written code of punctuation, translating a prolonged or emphatic pause into a period. Fragments can result from the mistaken assumption that verbals have the same function as verbs. Still others stem from uncertainties about the role of subordinating conjunctions or the careless omission of a subject or verb.

Whatever the specific cause, fragments are confusing because a capital letter at the beginning of a group of words signals the reader that a complete sentence follows, and a period at the end of the word group indicates that the sentence with all its additions is over. When there is no complete sentence between the capital letter and the period, the reader must stop and decide what purpose these words serve. Are they part of a neighboring sentence? Are they meant to express an independent thought as a sentence? Are they part of a sentence not in the text, but in the writer's head?

After identifying a fragment, decide which of the following methods of revision best serves your purpose:

1. *If a fragment belongs in the preceding or following sentence, make it a part of that sentence by deleting the period or changing it to a comma.*

The best musician in the orchestra is the lead violinist**, who practices six hours a day.**

2. *If you want a sentence to be a sentence in its own right, then change, delete, or add words to make it an independent clause.*

The best musician in the orchestra is the lead violinist. **He practices six hours a day**.

Note: Skilled writers sometimes use a fragment purposefully for stylistic effect, as in the following excerpt from Gail Sheehy's book *Passages*:

Without warning, in the middle of my thirties, I had a breakdown of nerve. It never occurred to me that while winging along in my happiest and most productive stage, all of a sudden simply staying afloat would require a massive exertion of will. **Or of some power greater than will**.

This fragment is meaningful because the passage is about psychological fragmentation and because the lack of grammatical completeness calls attention to the "power greater than will." Functional fragments are rare, however, and inexperienced writers should strive for complete sentences until they are relatively certain of English syntax.

Exercise 1

In the examples below, underline each fragment and be able to explain why it is not a sentence. If there is no fragment, put a check after the sentence. **Answers will vary.**

1. For many European explorers, America was El Dorado, t The legendary city of gold.
2. Before making a difficult decision, I like to consider all my options.
3. I have tried hard to talk to my brother a And to understand him.
4. The storyteller related an amusing tale about a hermit. w Who did not enjoy living alone.
5. Lines began forming at 5:00 in the morning. Most people were disappointed, however, because all the remaining tickets for the Rolling Stones concert were sold within minutes after the box office opened. ✓
6. The professor lectured on several characters from *The Canterbury Tales*, g Giving particular emphasis to the Wife of Bath.

7. The Trojan War began. Because Paris stole Helen from her husband.
   b

8. According to one noted author, under a government that imprisons any of its citizens unjustly. The only place for a just individual is a prison.
   t

9. Prospective home buyers should have a good understanding of their special needs before signing a contract. In order to avoid having to move in a year or two.
   In order to avoid having to move in a year or two, prospective home buyers. . . .

10. A family that has no hardships or problems can be found nowhere. Except on television.
    e

Exercise 2

In the following passage, revise each fragment by changing or deleting punctuation or by making the fragment a sentence. **Answers will vary.**

Advertisers use many different strategies to persuade the public to buy new cars. One company proclaims that its **sleek and elegant** cars are works of classic grace and beauty. ~~Sleek and elegant.~~ Another manufacturer emphasizes comfort. , **e**Extolling the plush carpeting and leather upholstery. According to the ads, these cars ~~making~~ make a pleasure cruise out of the longest and most boring drive. A third firm asserts that its luxury cars are so well engineered they last indefinitely~~.~~ ~~And~~ and operate at peak efficiency without regular maintenance. I have pondered these claims all morning~~.~~ ~~While~~ while waiting to get my own new car out of the shop.

45 · Nonparallel Constructions

A *nonparallel construction* is one in which sentence elements of unequal grammatical rank are joined in a compound or series.

45a Be alert to the possibility of nonparallel constructions in compounds and series in which the connective is a coordinating conjunction (*and, but, for, or, nor, so*).

Nonparallel constructions

1. **The house was old**, but **its foundation being solid**.
2. The sun was **bright** and **with intensity**.
3. My chemistry professor is someone **with a photographic memory** and **who also has a dynamic personality**.
4. The porch was littered with **faded newspapers, old clothes**, and **it had broken glass**.

The writers of these sentences seem to be either unable to recognize that an imbalance exists or unaware of its adverse effect on readers. In sentence #1, the comma and the coordinating conjunction **but** immediately following the first independent clause prepare us for a second independent clause. But the expected pattern breaks down at the point where the writer uses the verbal **being** instead of the anticipated past tense verb **was**. Similarly, the **and** after **bright** in sentence #2 seems to forecast another one-word adjective, but instead we find a prepositional phrase (**with intensity**). The relative clause (**who also has a dynamic personality**) at the end of the third sentence also comes as a surprise because the words on the other side of the coordinator—**with a photographic memory**—alert us to look for a second prepositional phrase or another object of the preposition **with**. The third element of the series at the end of sentence #4 frustrates our expectations in much the same way because the clause **it had broken glass** is inconsistent with the adjective-noun pattern established by the first two items, **faded newspapers** and **old clothes**.

If you compare these sentences with the revised versions below, you can see how parallel structure adds coherence.

independent clause — independent clause
The house was old, but **its foundation was solid**.

adjective — adjective
The sun was **bright** and **intense**.

adjective-noun
My chemistry professor is someone with a **photographic memory**
adjective-noun
and a **dynamic personality**.

adjective-noun — adjective-noun
The porch was littered with **faded newspapers**, **old clothes**, and
adjective-noun
broken glass.

45b Whenever you use correlative conjunctions such as *either . . . or, neither . . . nor,*

***both . . . and, not only . . . but also,* place them so that the words following them are parallel.**

Nonparallel constructions

I will **either** take a bus **or** a cab.

The speaker **both** addressed the members of the press corps **and** millions of television viewers.

In the first sentence, we expect the words following **or** to have the same grammatical form as the words following **either**, but **take a bus** is a verb phrase and **cab** is a noun. There is a similar imbalance in the second sentence, where the writer attempts to connect a verb phrase (**addressed the members of the press corps**) with a noun plus a prepositional phrase (**millions of television viewers**).

In both sentences, a slight shift in the position of the first conjunction would eliminate the problem.

noun noun
I will take **either** a bus **or** a cab.

noun + prepositional phrase
The speaker addressed **both** the members of the press corps **and**
noun + prepositional phrase
millions of television viewers.

Exercise 1

In the following sentences, eliminate nonparallel constructions by adding, changing, deleting, or shifting words.
Answers will vary.

1. After the initiation ceremony, the pledges were shown a movie about the club's role in the community, told about ^ its social activities, and presented with a club pin.

2. The agent's mission was to seek out and ~~the destruction of~~ **destroy** secret documents.

3. The philosopher ~~not only~~ commanded respect **not only** from his followers but also from his opponents.

4. The star of the drama performed her part with grace and ~~showed~~ style.

5. The castle was ancient but still ~~having great majesty~~ **majestic**.

6. Having reviewed all the available evidence, the jury decided the defendant neither had motive nor opportunity to commit the crime of which he was accused.

7. The accountant performed her job quietly and ~~with efficiency~~ **efficiently**.

8. Worried and ~~having doubts~~ **doubtful**, the job applicant paced the waiting room floor.

Exercise 2

Revise the following paragraph to eliminate nonparallel constructions. **Answers will vary.**

The day was warm and the waves ~~being~~ **were** perfect, so the water was crowded with surfers. There were short surfers and tall surfers, male surfers and female surfers, ~~and~~ old surfers ~~who were old~~ and young surfers ~~who were young~~. They all had one common goal, however: seeking that "perfect ride" of surfer lore. Nothing kept these enthusiasts from careening wildly down every wave they could catch, bodies plunging and ~~the~~ surfboards ~~would sail~~ sailing. Foolhardy swimmers ~~both~~ had to be on the watchout for both people and fiber glass. When the last ray of sunlight disappeared, the surfers disappeared also, exhausted but ~~having a feeling of exhilaration~~ exhilarated.

VI Eliminating Spelling Problems

46 · Spelling

46a Understand the nature of English spelling.

English suffers the reputation of having a difficult, even capricious spelling system. Writers sometimes despair over the different ways particular sounds are spelled. The **f** sound, for example, can be spelled **f**, **ph**, or **gh**. Why, we might wonder, can we not simply write **fone** instead of **phone** and **ruf** instead of **rough**?

The reason for our rather complex spelling system is that written English reflects more than a sound-symbol relationship. A word's spelling also carries information about smaller units of meaning within it, about families of words to which it is related, about its history in the language, and about its grammatical role in the sentence.

Phone, for example, relates to the family of words derived from the Greek word for "sound," which the Greeks spelled with their letter called "phi." **Rough** comes from the Anglo-Saxon word which ended in a gutteral **gh** sound unlike today's **f** sound. We write **forebode** instead of **forbode** because **fore**, an Old English prefix, communicates the idea of **before**hand. Writing **health** instead of **helth** keeps the root word **heal** intact for the reader.

If English words were spelled strictly according to sound, we would lose such extra information. Indeed, a purely phonetic spelling system would make English more difficult to read. In such a system, for example, we might spell **huts** as we do now, but **hubs** might be spelled **hubz**. Our current system assures readers that they need only perceive **s** or **es** at the end of the vast majority of English nouns to understand the nouns are plural. Plural **s** is thus a grammatical signal to the eye as well as a signal of sound for the ear. Likewise **ed** in regular verbs signals past time regardless of the sound; so we write **heaped**, **arched**, and **peeked** rather than **heapt**, **archt**, and **peekt**. (Irregular verbs depart from this pattern, but often do so in systematic ways: **sleep-slept**, **keep-kept**, etc.)

46b Use special techniques for learning spelling.

Research has shown that good spellers tend to apply knowledge acquired by seeing and understanding words in meaningful contexts. In fact, alert experience with written English discourse seems to be the most powerful teacher of spelling. By being alert to words as you read and write, you naturally develop a feel for the systematic nature of English spelling. When you do encounter trouble with spelling, therefore, you will want to exploit learning strategies that most efficiently increase your understanding of how a word's letter pattern is systematic and meaningful. The techniques below can be helpful in learning to spell words difficult for you.

1. *Study the word in a context that suggests its meaning.* If you have time, write the word in several sentences.

My **intelligence** will help me learn.

Cats have less **intelligence** than dogs.

Intelligence is influenced by environment.

46 b

2. *Relate the word to other words having the same spelling pattern.* Try to remember the word as a member of a group.

-ence words

intellig**ence**
differ**ence**
perman**ence**
refer**ence**

The criteria you develop for classifying a word group can be any that help you see a consistency.

Words with short* i *after double consonant

inte**lli**gence
i**rri**table
mi**ssi**le
i**mmi**grant

3. *Identify meaningful word parts.* Use a dictionary that gives etymologies (word histories). Study the way the word itself imparts meaning.

The verb **persevere** is composed of **per**, a prefix meaning "thoroughly," and **severe**, which as an adjective means "strict, stern, serious." The verb means to remain seriously committed to a goal. Note that **persevere** fits in an **-ere** spelling group: **revere, atmosphere, interfere, adhere**.

The noun **repetition** is composed of the prefix **re** meaning "again," the suffix **-ion** meaning "the act of," and a root from the Latin word **petitius** meaning "gone toward." The word parts add up to the meaning "the act of going to something again," which relates to the modern meaning of the word, "the act of doing something again." Note also that **repetition** is related in spelling and meaning to **petition**.

4. *Pronounce the word accurately.* In conversation we sometimes drop syllables from words, pronouncing "accidently," "probly," and "temperture." If you misspell such words as you pronounce them conversationally, you should study them by learning the pronunciation given in a dictionary. The words below are among those frequently misspelled because of faulty pronunciation.

accidentally	library
athlete	lightning
chocolate	probably
disastrous	strictly
government	temperature
laboratory	umbrella

5. *Use memory aids.* You can learn some pesky words by making especially memorable associations. These memory aids will be most effective if you think up the associations yourself. Some examples are given below.

The princi**PAL** is my **PAL**.

On station**E**ry we find l**E**tt**E**rs.

Old **AGE** is a tr**AGE**dy.

Weak gram**MAR MAR**s my speech.

He was persis**TEN**t **TEN** times in **TEN** days.

Bury all your **E**'s in c**E**m**E**t**E**ry.

46c Learn those spelling rules pertinent to the problems you may have.

1. *Prefixes.* Adding a prefix to a word does not change the spelling of the word.

mis + spell = misspell

pre + fabricate = prefabricate

un + necessary = unnecessary

Prefixes sometimes require hyphens: **K-car**, **anti-hero**, **de-emphasize**. See Chapter **31** for hyphen conventions.

2. ***ie** and **ei**.* The rule is **i** before **e** (fr**ie**nd, rel**ie**ve) except after **c** (rec**ei**ve, c**ei**ling) and when the sound is **a** (sl**ei**gh, w**ei**gh.) Consider the exceptions to this rule to form a group.

either	h**ei**ght	s**ei**ze
for**ei**gn	l**ei**sure	w**ei**rd
forf**ei**t	sh**ei**k	

3. *Suffixes and final consonants.* Some types of words ending in a consonant double the final consonant when a suffix (a word ending) is added, and some types do not. No

words ending in **c** (frolic) or **x** (fix) double the final consonant. When the word is one syllable long and a single vowel precedes any final consonant (except **c** and **x**), *double* the final consonant.

j**a**b—ja**bb**ed
p**u**t—pu**tt**ing
h**o**t—ho**tt**er

When the word is one syllable long and either a pair of vowels or a vowel and a consonant precede the final consonant, *do not double* the final consonant.

p**ea**l—pea**l**ed
h**ur**t—hur**t**ing
l**oo**k—loo**k**ing
l**if**t—lif**t**ing
l**ea**k—lea**k**ing
h**ow**l—how**l**ing
Exception: r**eal**—rea**ll**y

When the word is two or more syllables long, *double* the final consonant *if* one vowel precedes the final consonant *and if* after the suffix is added the last syllable of the root word is stressed.

handi**cap**—handica**pp**ed
be**gin**—begi**nn**er
dis**pel**—dispe**ll**ing

When the word is two or more syllables long, *do not double* the final consonant *if* more than one vowel or a vowel and another consonant precede the final consonant (app**ea**r—appea**r**ing; res**or**t—resor**t**ing). Do not double the final consonant *if* after the suffix is added the last syllable of the root word is *not* stressed (p**ar**don—pardo**n**ed).

rej**oi**n—rejoi**n**ed
entr**ea**t—entrea**t**ing
m**ar**ket—marke**t**ing

4. *Suffixes and final* **e**. Some words ending in a *silent* (unsounded) **e** drop the **e** before a suffix, and some words keep the **e**. If the suffix begins with a vowel, drop the **e**.

ris**e**—ri**si**ng
measur**e**—measu**ri**ng (but, of course, measur**ed**)

Sometimes silent **e** is retained before a vowel to help in word recognition and pronunciation.

mil**e**—mil**ea**ge (instead of milage)

Words ending **ce** and **ge** usually keep silent **e** to retain the soft **c** and **g** pronunciation.

courage—coura**geou**s
peace—pea**cea**ble
knowledge—knowled**gea**ble
change—chan**gea**ble (but changing)
dance—dan**cea**ble (but dancing)

If the suffix begins with a consonant, keep the **e**.

disgrace—disgrac**ef**ul
endorse—endors**em**ent
moderate—moderat**ely**

But sometimes when preceded by a vowel, silent **e** is dropped before a suffix beginning with a consonant.

arg**ue**—arg**um**ent
tr**ue**—tr**ul**y

5. *Final* **y**. Most words ending in **y** preceded by a consonant change the **y** to **i** before all suffixes except the possessive **'s**, suffixes beginning in **i**, and the suffixes **-like** and **-ship**.

46 c

dut**y**—dut**i**es—dut**i**ful
likel**y**—likel**i**hood
def**y**—def**i**ant—def**y**ing (**y** kept before **ing**)
somebod**y**—somebod**y's** (**y** kept before **'s**)
librar**y**like (**y** kept before **like**)

Most words ending in **y** preceded by a vowel do *not* change the **y** before any suffix.

conv**oy**—conv**oy**ing

depl**oy**—depl**oy**ing
gr**ay**—gr**ay**ing—gr**ay**ness

Some exceptions are d**ay**—d**ai**ly, l**ay**—l**ai**d, p**ay**—p**ai**d.

6. *Plurals.* Most nouns are made plural by adding **s** to the singular form.

election**s**	studio**s**
pipe**s**	visit**s**
ring**s**	

Nouns ending in **s**, **z**, **x**, **ch**, or **sh** are made plural by adding **es**.

bu**ses**	bun**ches**
buz**zes**	bu**shes**
bo**xes**	

Most nouns ending in **o** preceded by a consonant add **es** in the plural.

buffa**loes**
he**roes**
toma**toes**

But some nouns ending in **o** preceded by a consonant add only **s**.

e**gos**
pia**nos**
t**wos**

Some nouns ending in **f** or **fe** are made plural by changing the **f** or **fe** to **ves**.

cal**f**—cal**ves**
kni**fe**—kni**ves**

Nouns ending in **y** preceded by a consonant are made plural by changing the **y** to **i** and adding **es**.

ar**my**—arm**ies**

ba**by**—bab**ies**
s**ky**—sk**ies**

But nouns ending in **y** preceded by a vowel simply add **s**.

b**oy**—boy**s**
k**ey**—key**s**

When a compound term is made up of two nouns, the plural is formed on the last noun.

book club**s**
city-state**s**
fairground**s**

When a compound term is made up of a noun and another part of speech, the noun is made plural whatever its position in the term.

mother**s**-in-law
runner**s**-up

Some nouns retain their Latin, Greek, French, and Italian forms in the singular and plural.

datum—data (Latin)
medium—media (Latin)
analysis—analyses (Greek)
beau—beaux (French)
bambino—bambini (Italian)

46d Learn to distinguish homonyms.

Homonyms are words that sound alike but are spelled differently and have different denotations (e.g., **here** and **hear**). Like tense and number markers (**ed** and **s**), homonyms are examples of how the visual appearance of a word can be as important as the sounds it represents. To learn to spell homonyms, you must be sure of the meaning of each similar word and then use an effective study strategy. Below is a list of commonly confused homonyms and near homonyms.

accept (to receive)
except (to leave out)

all ready (prepared)
already (previously)

ascent (a rising)
assent (to agree)

brake (to cause to slow down)
break (to shatter)

capital (the city that is the seat of government)
capitol (a legislative building)

censor (to delete or forbid)
censure (to rebuke)

complement (to improve or reinforce)
compliment (to praise)

descent (a going down)
dissent (to disagree)

desért (to abandon)
désert (an arid area)
dessert (the last course of a meal)

discreet (secretive)
discrete (separate)

elicit (to draw forth)
illicit (illegal)

emigrate (to move away from a country)
immigrate (to move to a country)

ensure (to make certain)
insure (to guarantee)

formally (in a formal way)
formerly (previously)

persecute (to harass)
prosecute (to bring legal action)

principal (of prime importance or head of a school)
principle (a basic law)

stationary (still)
stationery (writing paper)

to (toward)
too (also)
two (sum of one plus one)

VII Writing for Special Purposes

47 · Writing about Literature

Writing that deals with literary subjects is almost always analytical or argumentative. Its purpose is not merely to summarize the surface details of a work but to explore some aspect of its meaning or artistry that would not be apparent to the casual reader.

47a Employ critical reading skills.

To write effectively about literature, you must first be able to read it analytically. One model for literary analysis is described below. Though it deals specifically with fiction, most of the questions it raises and the suggestions it offers are applicable as well to drama and poetry.

1. *What is the relationship between the title and the work itself?* The title can be a valuable aid to interpretation because it usually identifies the central character, situation, or subject—the general issue with which the story is concerned (e.g., love, fate, pride, etc.). It may also foreshadow the outcome of the story or introduce a key image or symbol that is repeated throughout the work.

2. *Who tells the story?* Although your immediate instinct may be to say "the author," the question and the answer are more complex than they at first appear. In some novels and short stories, especially those told from the third-person point of view, the author and the narrator are indeed difficult to distinguish from one another. But in others, particularly first-person narratives, the voice the reader hears is that of a fictional character who may look, think, and act very differently from the author. A writer may even choose to tell a story

from the vantage point of someone whose statements and judgments are so obviously unreliable that the reader cannot accept at face value anything the narrator says.

3. *What events comprise the plot or action of the story, and what is the significance of this narrative structure?* In a traditional plot, the action begins at a certain point, builds through a series of conflicts or complications to a climax, then diminishes in intensity, and finally comes to a resolution. It would be a mistake, however, to expect this type of narrative structure in every story or to find fault with an author for varying from the traditional pattern. For there are many artistically satisfying ways to tell a story. The writer may shift back and forth in time rather than proceeding chronologically, explore the consciousness rather than the actions of a character, or even abandon the conventions of plot altogether by presenting incidents in disconnected fashion. Although plot is seldom the center of interest in a serious work of fiction, it nonetheless deserves thoughtful analysis because it is both a means of characterization and a vehicle for developing theme.

4. *What are the distinctive traits of the characters and what problems do they face?* Judgments about characters should take into account not only what the narrator says about them but also what they say about one another, what they reveal about themselves through words and actions, and what conflicts they are involved in. When analyzing conflict, keep in mind that characters may be pitted against environmental, social, or psychological forces as well as against other human beings.

5. *What is the setting and why is it significant?* To answer the first part of this question, look for specific indications of time and place: dates, references to season or time of day, allusions to historical events or other contextual details, the names of cities, countries or geographical regions, and so on. The results of this analysis, together with a close examination of other details, will help you decide whether the setting is

merely a backdrop for the action or whether it plays a more significant symbolic or thematic role.

6. *What are the tone and theme of the story?* Tone (the author's attitude toward the subject) and theme (the underlying meaning of the total work) are integrally related concepts. A reader who misinterprets tone will very likely misread the author's intent and thus miss the point of the story. When analyzing tone, first think of the word or words that best express what you consider to be the *narrator's* attitude toward the subject (e.g., skeptical, condescending, sympathetic, questioning, etc.) Then, drawing from the knowledge you have acquired from your study of other fictional elements, especially point of view, decide whether the author is sympathetic or unsympathetic toward the narrator's views. This same process of analysis will also help you to determine theme, which you should express in a sentence rather than as a word or phrase.

Because judgments about tone and theme are necessarily subjective, your conclusions may differ from those of other readers. The important thing to remember is that a valid interpretation is one supported by the story and consistent with all its details.

In preparing to write about drama and poetry, you should adapt these questions to suit the genre. In a play, for example, no one tells the story as a fictional narrator does. Instead, the dramatist withdraws from the action, allowing the characters to speak and act for themselves. Also, because a play is intended for stage performance before an audience, anyone who has to rely exclusively on the printed text must imaginatively see and hear what would be tangibly evident to the theater audience. This process of imaginative recreation requires attention both to the characters' language and to any stage directions provided by the playwright. Stage directions usually indicate what the stage set should look like; how and when special effects such as lighting, music, props, and other theatrical devices should be used; when and where characters should enter or leave the stage; where they should stand in relation to one another; and even how the actors should speak their lines.

Poetry also makes special demands on the reader because of its concentrated language and its distinctive artistic conventions. Thus, in addition to studying the implications of a poem's title, analyzing its setting or situation, and exploring other issues raised in the model for fictional analysis, you should pose questions about its language and structure. For example, is the poem written in a continuous series of lines or divided into stanzas? Does the author use rhyme (the repetition of the final stressed syllable in two or more words) and meter (the patterned repetition of stressed and unstressed syllables in a line of poetry) or break with these conventions? Are the lines uniform or irregular in length? Is the language of the poem abstract or concrete? Literal or figurative? Are there any recurrent images or symbols? To what extent and for what purpose does the poet use alliteration (consonant repetition), assonance (vowel repetition), or other sound effects? Such questions will help you identify specific features of the poem; you may then trace the effects of these features, especially how they contribute to the poem's tone and theme.

47b Decide on a topic and a critical approach.

By the time you complete your analytical reading, you should have sufficient knowledge of the work to decide on a topic and a perspective from which to approach it. Here are just a few of the many options available to you:

1. *Decide what the tone or theme of the work is, and write an essay in which you present and analyze the evidence that supports your interpretation.*

Sample topics

Irony in *Desire Under the Elms*

The theme of lost innocence in Gerard Manley Hopkin's "Spring and Fall: To a Young Child"

2. *Explain the purpose and meaning of one of the literary elements you examined in your critical reading of the work.*

Sample topics

The symbolism of the letter *A* in Hawthorne's *The Scarlet Letter*

The role of figurative language in Langston Hughes's "Dream Deferred"

3. *Write an essay that explains the relationship between a part of a work and the whole.*

Sample topics

The drunken porter scene in *Macbeth*

The flawed ending of *Huckleberry Finn*

If your assignment requires you to examine more than one work or to investigate secondary sources (e.g., critical articles and books, biographies, literary histories, etc.), the number of options increases.

4. *Place the work in its biographical, social, historical, or social context.*

Sample topics

Emerson's attitudes toward abolitionism

Social Realism in Kate Chopin's *The Awakening*

5. *Approach the work from the perspective of another discipline, such as psychology, philosophy, the physical sciences, or fine arts.*

Sample topics

A Freudian interpretation of *Death of a Salesman*

The role of music in Wallace Stevens's "Peter Quince at the Clavier"

6. *Compare two or more works on the basis of theme, tone, or technique.*

Sample topics

Conflicting views of death in Emily Dickinson's "Because I Could Not Stop for Death" and "I Heard a Fly Buzz"

The concept of honor in Hemingway's *A Farewell to Arms* and Heller's *Catch 22*

47c Formulate and develop a thesis.

Once you have settled on a topic and a critical approach, formulate a thesis statement that will enable you to analyze and interpret some significant but limited aspect of the topic.

Thesis statement

The letter *A* in Hawthorne's *The Scarlet Letter* is a complex symbol that signifies not only adultery but also ableness, angelhood, and Arthur, the name of Hester's lover. [Topic: The symbolism of the letter *A* in Hawthorne's *The Scarlet Letter*]

The ending of *Huckleberry Finn* is flawed because it is disproportionately long, unrealistic, and inconsistent with the events leading up to it. [Topic: The flawed ending of *Huckleberry Finn*]

If your thesis is precise and restricted, as in the examples above, it will both suggest a plan of organization and guide your selection of supporting examples. To support your thesis, you will want to quote from the text and summarize portions of the work. Your composition should not, however, be merely a string of quotes and summaries. Rather, it should communicate your understanding of the work as a whole and your interpretation of the specific details you cite.

47d Sample essay with preliminary notes

The following essay and the notes on which it was based represent one student's response to a critical reading and writing assignment for a college composition class. Utilizing procedures similar to the ones discussed in the preceding sections of this chapter, the writer began by reading several poems in the class text; raising questions about speaker, audience, situation, structure, language, and other aspects of literary form; and making marginal notations. When he had finished, he reread the poems and his notes in an effort to find the work and topic he wanted to write about.

The poem he eventually decided on was Amy Lowell's "The Taxi," which he had annotated in the manner shown on page 287.

As the student restudied the poem and his responses to it, he made several important discoveries: (1) Most of his comments were concerned with imagery. (2) The images he had identified all seemed related to the speaker's thoughts and feelings. (3) The patterns of imagery in the four sentences comprising the poem each revealed a different emotional dimension.

At this point, the writer was able to formulate a thesis (see the final sentence of the introductory paragraph in the sample essay), devise a plan of organization (a sentence by sentence analysis of imagistic language and its emotional overtones), and write the first draft of his paper. Later, he revised and edited the paper and submitted the version below for evaluation.

47 d

Sample paper

IMAGERY IN "THE TAXI"

In "The Taxi," Amy Lowell explores the thoughts and feelings of a person who is attempting to cope with the reality of being separated from a loved one. We can't tell whether the speaker is talking directly to the unnamed "you" of the poem or addressing this individual

Speaker is the person leaving (or about to leave) in a taxi

Title refers to the type of vehicle we usually associate with travel to airports, railroad depots, bus terminals, etc.

The Taxi

Auditory imagery—Speaker's entire world at this moment described in terms of the dead, muffled, inharmonious sound of a slackened drum

When I go away from you
The world beats dead
Like a slackened drum.
I call out for you against the jutted stars
And shout into the ridges of the wind.
Streets coming fast,
One after the other
Wedge you away from me,
And the lamps of the city prick my eyes
So that I can no longer see your face.
Why should I leave you,
To wound myself upon the sharp edges of the night?

Sound again important ("call out," "shout") Also visual and tactile images ("jutted stars," "ridges of the wind") emphasize futility of effort to communicate

Images of sight, touch, movement—creates sense of panic, emptiness, pain

Night pictured as something threatening—with "sharp edges" that can wound

structure — Four sentences. Each seems to treat a different aspect of her emotional state.
tone — Generally one of depression and despair — though the question at the end suggests that the speaker may have some control over the situation — separation may not be inevitable.
theme — Separation from a loved one can create deep emotional disturbance that affects perceptions of everything else.

47 d

imaginatively while traveling in a taxi toward some unspecified destination, but there can be no doubt of the speaker's emotional condition. For throughout the poem, Lowell uses vivid images to make us aware of this person's frustration and pain.

In the first three lines of the poem, the speaker's mood is one of extreme depression—a feeling that Lowell captures in the auditory imagery of lines 2 and 3: "The world beats dead / Like a slackened drum." A slackened drum is one on which the cover has been loosened, and in this condition it can produce only hollow, muffled sounds. The implication is that the speaker too feels empty and out of harmony with the external world.

In the second sentence (lines 4–5), the speaker calls out to the person left behind. The frustration remains, though, because there is no one to hear the words. The futility of this attempt at communication is reinforced by other images. The distant stars seem "jutted" and threatening, and the wind has "ridges" that shouts cannot penetrate.

In the third sentence (lines 6–10), the poem speeds up as the speaker becomes aware of the "Streets coming fast, / One after another." Images of motion ("coming fast," "Wedge you away from me") convey a sense of panic, which is soon replaced with even stronger emotions in lines 9 and 10: "And the lamps of the city prick my eyes / So that I can no longer see your face."

The poem slows down in the final sentence (lines 11–12). Here the speaker pauses to ask, "Why should I leave you . . .?" but the last line brings the poem to a close as pessimistically as it began. For even the night seems a weapon with "sharp edges" capable of inflicting a "wound" on anyone who has experienced the pain of separation.

Exercise

Read the following poem carefully, and answer the questions that accompany it. When you have finished, choose one question that you consider especially interesting and important, formulate a thesis statement that answers it, and develop it into a short analytical essay.

OZYMANDIAS

I met a traveller from an antique land
Who said: Two vast and trunkless legs of stone
Stand in the desert . . . Near them, on the sand,
Half sunk, a shattered visage lies, whose frown,
And wrinkled lip, and sneer of cold command,
Tell that its sculptor well those passions read
Which yet survive, stamped on these lifeless things,

The hand that mocked them, and the heart that fed:
And on the pedestal these words appear:
"My name is Ozymandias, king of kings:
Look on my works, ye Mighty, and despair!"
Nothing beside remains. Round the decay
Of that colossal wreck, boundless and bare
The lone and level sands stretch far away.

Percy Bysshe Shelley

Questions for Analysis

1. Who tells the story of Ozymandias and his statue? Is this account reported directly to the reader or related at second hand by someone else? What does Shelley accomplish by using this point of view?
2. What is the physical setting of lines 2–14, and why is it important?
3. Approximately how much time has elapsed between the traveler's discovery and the days of Ozymandias's kingship? What contrast between past and present does Shelley develop throughout the poem?
4. What was the nature of the relationship between Ozymandias and the sculptor? How did the sculptor make known his attitude toward the king? What is the evidence on which the traveler bases this inference?
5. What does the inscription on the pedestal of the statue reveal about Ozymandias's character and ambitions? Does the rest of the poem support or contradict the message carried by this inscription? Consider especially the condition of the statue at the time the traveler sees it, the particulars of the physical setting, and the effect of the repeated *b*, *l*, and *s* sounds in the last two lines.
6. What do your answers to the preceding questions suggest is the tone of the poem?
7. What comment does the poem make about the human dream of earthly immortality?

48 · Writing Answers for Essay Examinations

48a Objective tests and essay examinations

Objective tests ask students either to indicate a correct answer from among alternatives (as on multiple-choice and matching items) or to provide a correct answer in a phrase or a brief statement (as on fill-in and short-answer items). Because such tests require only simple marks or a few written words, they may treat a wide range of topics during a relatively short examination time, and they may be scored quickly and objectively. This efficiency makes objective exams a popular type of academic evaluation.

Often, however, college courses endeavor to increase students' ability to communicate at length using new knowledge. Such a goal is not served by tests requiring students simply to indicate a preestablished right answer. Only an *essay item* confronts students with an exam problem requiring them to call up pertinent information and to develop a coherent response. Such writing tasks are similar to those in professional service and commerce, fields which depend on people able to communicate quickly and accurately about problems.

You should respond to essay exam items as you would to other essay assignments, except, of course, you must be faster. Despite time constraints, though, you should undertake all stages of the writing process outlined in Chapter **1**. The one stage of the process students most often overlook is revision. Even if you have only a few moments, you should read over your essay answers not only to correct grammar and usage, but to strengthen points you have made and to add points you have omitted. College professors generally prefer to have significant information added between the lines and incorrect information scratched out than to have neatly written but incomplete answers.

48b Types of essay items

Most essay items request one of the four types of tasks discussed below.

1. *Recalling knowledge.* This type of item requires the student to write down information in a form similar to previously expressed material. The material might be in a textbook, in class notes, or in a non-print medium such as film. The correct answers written by students would differ little from each other in wording. To do well on such an item you must simply be able to recall the information requested and organize it either as it was originally given or as its points relate logically to one another.

Sample item

1. What type of people constituted the major social classes in the eighteenth-century American colonies and what values differentiated these classes?

A good answer to this question would be organized as a brief classification essay (see **4c**). The first paragraph might identify each social class and tell the type of people found in it; a second and final paragraph might describe the social values peculiar to each class. Or each paragraph in the essay might treat the people and values of a particular social class. Recall items do not request judgments or inferences; they simply request evidence that the student remembers the information.

2. *Demonstrating understanding.* Another type of item requests thinking in addition to recall; students are asked to demonstrate comprehension of course content by interpreting

it. Interpretation can involve translating content into your own words or inferring a main idea and its relationship to supporting details. Items that test comprehension may also ask you to discuss implications that are not expressed in the content but that follow directly from it.

Sample items

2. Paraphrase Shakespeare's description of aging in "Sonnet 60," and explain what conclusion he draws from these observations.
3. Specify the intent of Section 3 of the Fourteenth Amendment to the U.S. Constitution and the implicit justification for this intent.

You should read such items carefully, paying special attention to the words identifying the approach you should take ("paraphrase," "specify") and to words giving the focus of the answer ("description," "conclusion," "intent," "justification").

A good answer to item #2 would translate Shakespeare's images of old age into original wording and would express the poet's conclusion that although passing time inevitably takes away all beauty, these verses written by the poet will preserve a record of his beloved's beauty for future generations.

A good answer to item #3 would explain that Amendment XIV, Section 3 pertains to former officials of the United States who have taken part in rebellion against the government. The answer would go on to draw the inferences that such individuals will have broken an oath they took upon becoming officials, and so Section 3 assumes they justly forfeit their right to hold office in the United States again.

3. *Analyzing.* Questions requiring comprehension or recall refer to course content as it may be interpreted or as it is given. Questions requiring you to apply your understanding by analyzing a topic refer to the content's structure (the relations between its parts). Recall and comprehension exam

items specify the particular content you are to treat; you do not have to search your memory for relevant generalizations or evidence because the exam items either identify or provide the actual text of the content you are to treat (e.g., a sonnet or a government document). Analysis items, however, can pose problems, requiring that you search your knowledge for information about a topic, select points relevant to the question, and establish a coherent relationship between the points. When an analysis problem does specify the content, it demands that you take a critical view of the way its parts relate to the whole. For example, instead of simply requesting a demonstration of understanding of Shakespeare's Sonnet 60 as in sample item #2, a question could request an analysis as follows: "Discuss how the images portrayed in Sonnet 60 help develop the poem's theme." To respond to this question, you must not only comprehend the images and the theme but also demonstrate how the images work together to help communicate the theme of the effects of aging on the speaker's attitude toward his beloved.

Types of thinking commonly required by analysis are identifying and describing parts or features, comparing and contrasting subjects, tracing causes and effects, and explaining the principles or patterns according to which content is organized. Because analysis demands such extensive thought and careful exposition, be especially alert in planning your answer. The five-stage planning procedure recommended in **4a** can be particularly helpful.

Sample items

4. Contrast divergent and convergent problem solving.
5. Considering the text and history of Amendment XIV, Section 3 of the U.S. Constitution, explain what the amendment's framers apparently hoped to achieve by its adoption.
6. Study the map given below. Note that features of rainfall, terrain, mineral resources, and natural vegetation are portrayed.

> Describe how the various geographical features would influence the economy of a community made up of people with iron-age skills.

A good answer to item #4 will exploit the principles of comparison given in **4c** (4). Most important, you should identify bases for comparing the two types of thinking; for example, you might contrast them according to differences in (a) the contexts of divergent and convergent problems, (b) the ways information is used in solving the two types of problems, and (c) the types of solutions that result.

Note that sample items #4 and #5 would require only recall if their answers were specified elsewhere in course materials. As an analysis item, #5 would require you to call up pertinent facts from history and to show how they explain the motives behind this section of the Constitution. You might note that Amendment XIV was proposed in 1866 and ratified in 1868, having originated in a U.S. Congress embittered by four years of civil war. Certain congressmen not only wanted to exclude former rebels from political office and to punish the old Southern power structure, they also wanted political power in the South for their own Republican Party. Thus they found it useful to disenfranchise the South's former leaders.

Item #6 would, of course, require you to apply your map-reading skills. You would also have to call up information about the type of agriculture and craft suitable to the geography depicted and to the technological level given for people living in the area. You would then incorporate your information in a description of the ways the various geographical features would influence the economy.

4. *Evaluating.* Questions asking students to evaluate content are relatively rare because the answers can be difficult to grade fairly, especially if the questions invite students to offer personal opinion. Sometimes, though, professors want you to demonstrate that you can apply criteria in describing the quality of something. Evaluative questions require you to

explain such standards as how good or true or effective or valuable something is. The general criteria you are to apply will be stated in the question, which will specify whether you are to treat such notions as "goodness" or "effectiveness." To respond to this kind of question, you must first make specific criteria clear to yourself, and then apply them systematically to the content to be evaluated.

Sample item

7. Explain why according to Lawrence Kohlberg one of the two adolescents described below would be acting on a higher level of morality than the other.

The general criterion requested in item #7 is degree of morality. The specific criteria are psychologist Kohlberg's descriptions of six stages of moral development. Your task would be to call up your understanding of these stages, analyze the behaviors in terms of them, and demonstrate the higher morality of one of the behaviors.

49 · Writing Business Letters

Business letters are written and read to help make transactions possible. Clear, direct, careful, grammatical letters typed in a standard format increase the ease of transactions; wordy, vague letters with non-standard language written in a format that does not conform to readers' expectations make transactions more difficult.

49a Use standard block format.

The most obvious feature of a business letter is its format, commonly called a *block format*. An example of a block format letter with its parts labeled is given on page 298.

1. *Heading.* If you are using *letterhead paper* (stationery with the name and address of a company or institution at the top), the only entry for your heading should be the date; otherwise include your mailing address.

2. *Inside address.* This should be identical to the address on the envelope. Be sure to use an appropriate personal title (**Mr., Ms., Dr.**) and, if pertinent, the business title (**Director, Treasurer**). If the business title is long (**Director of Research Department**), you may put it under the person's name.

3. *Salutation.* The person's or firm's name in the salutation should agree with the name in the inside address. For example, if the letter is addressed to **Dr. Carl Brown**, the salutation should read **Dear Dr. Brown** *not* **Dear Professor Brown**. If the letter is addressed to a firm, repeat the firm's name in the salutation: **Dear Sears and Roebuck**. It is less acceptable today to write **Dear Sirs** instead of the firm's name.

49b Write in a direct, friendly style.

Remember that a business letter's main purpose is to make business easier to conduct. People become willing to do business if they feel a letter treats them as people, not as abstractions; if the letter seems to be written by an individual they might like to meet, not by a computer; and if the attitude of the writer is positive and understanding, not accusing or self-justifying.

You should, therefore, empathize with the recipient of your letter. How might the content affect someone in the position of your correspondent? Might the content worry, anger, or bore the person? The golden rule of correspondence is to write to others as you would have others write to you.

Avoid putting your correspondent on the defensive even if you are frustrated. Instead of writing "Despite my last letter, you still seem confused," write "I believe this letter will make my point more clearly." Instead of writing, "Your lack of cooperation has been discouraging," write "I look forward to our cooperation."

Business is also inhibited by letters that ramble or obscure the writer's intent. Your best approach is to get to the point immediately. Compare the wasted words in the first introductory paragraph with the direct appeal of the second introductory paragraph below.

Original

All of us in this department are busy, and surely you are no exception. Nevertheless, I hope you will take the time to consider the crucial needs of the United Fund.

Revised

The annual United Fund Drive, which begins next week, funds 24 charitable organizations in our community. Without the support of people such as you, these organizations would have to cease their work.

While succinctness is desirable for composition in general, for business correspondence it is at a premium. Pay special attention, therefore, to the strategies for concise writing in Chapter **15**.

Try to keep your letter to one page in length. The prohibition against one-sentence paragraphs common in freshman English courses does not apply in business; if you've made your point in one sentence, go on to the next paragraph. In general, remember that succinctness, politeness, and straightforwardness are more than ethical matters in business; they can make the difference between doing and not doing business. These characteristics are illustrated in the letter below.

Sample business letter

10–15 spaces

Heading

324 River Road
Oak Grove, NJ 07014
January 10, 1985

4–8 spaces

Inside Address

Mr. Robert Williams, Director
Oak Grove Recreation Department
1101 15th Street
Oak Grove, NJ 07014

Salutation **2 spaces**

Dear Mr. Williams:

1 space

Thank you for the Blue Springs Park schedule of events and the guidelines for groups using city recreation facilities.

1 space

Please reserve the open-air theater for the annual picnic of the Oak Grove Little Theater on June 2 from 6:00 to 8:00 p.m. Our group will use the theater to present skits and to make awards to actors and patrons of the 1984-85 season. We will not need any recreational department equipment.

1 space

We are grateful for the opportunity to enjoy this facility, and we gladly agree to abide by the guidelines for its use.

Complimentary Close **1 space**

Sincerely,

Signature Block

Cecilia Rhodes

4 spaces

Cecilia Rhodes, Chairperson
Board of Directors
Oak Grove Little Theater

2 spaces

Enclosure List

Encl. Completed reservation form
       Signed contract

50 · Preparing a Résumé

A résumé is a carefully arranged summary of a person's qualifications for employment. Usually it is mailed with a cover letter by an applicant who is responding to a job opening. Employers read over all the applications they receive and then decide which people to invite for interviews. Obviously, the more clearly your résumé communicates your qualifications, the greater your chances for employment.

You should organize your résumé according to categories of information. The eight entries given below and illustrated in the sample are generally suitable, but your entries should be tailored to your circumstances. One page is the length most welcomed by employers in business and industry.

1. *Give basic information to identify yourself.* Include name, school address (if appropriate), permanent address, and the phone numbers (with area codes) of both addresses.

2. *State your career objectives.* You might write one major objective or write short-range and long-range goals. Word them generally so you can use the same résumé for numerous job applications.

3. *Outline your educational background.* List your educational credentials chronologically, putting your most recent experiences first and your earliest experience last. Include only those details relevant to your career objective.

4. *Cite any honors you may have received at school.*

5. *Outline your work experience.* If you have been out of school for a few years, you may want to put work experience right after your objectives, especially if experience is a strong feature of your application. For each job include the title, the

place, the dates, and a brief description of the tasks you performed.

6. *List professional and extracurricular activities.* Specify organized activities that suggest your ability to help achieve group goals.

7. *List other interests and abilities that indicate an active involvement in the world at large.*

8. *Indicate at the end of your résumé that you will furnish the names of your references on request; there is no need to give the names themselves.*

With your résumé, you should send a cover letter that relates your qualifications to the particular job you are applying for. Your letter should be a business letter in style and format (Chapter **49**). It might open with a reference to how you came to learn of the company or the job. It should include a brief summary of your goals and qualifications most clearly relevant to employment with the firm. It should end with a statement of your availability for further contact with the company.

Sample résumé

MARTIN ALVAREZ

Permanent Address	School Address
1405 Crestline Blvd. Oak Park, NJ 07012	992 Ripley Rd. Fenner, NJ 07112

Professional Objective

To become a successful manager of advertising and promotion.

Education

B.B.A. Degree, Fenner State University, Fenner, NJ, May 1984; marketing major. Completed an invitational "Topics in Management" course, concentrating on marketing management. Average in major 3.4/4.0.

High School Diploma, Oak Park H.S., Oak Park, NJ, June 1981.

Academic Honors

Recipient during junior and senior years of Adele MacIntosh Scholarship administered by Fenner State University Scholarship Fund.

Dean's List, Spring 1982 and Fall 1982.

Work Experience

1982-present; First State Bank, Fenner, NJ. Teller (part time during academic year, full time during summer).

1981-82: Passmore's Men's Shop, Oak Park, NJ. Salesperson and stock clerk (full time during summer).

1978-81: Oak Park, NJ Recreation Department. Lifeguard (full time during summer).

University Activities

Residence Hall Counselor, 1982-83, 1983-84. Duties involved supervising dormitory facilities and counseling resident students.

Member FSU Racquetball Club.

Interests and Skills

Racquetball, swimming, photography.

Proficiency in Basic computer language.

References

Available upon request.

Letter to accompany résumé

1105 Crestline Blvd.
Oak Park, NJ 07012
June 8, 1984

Mr. William B. Simpson
Highland Advertising Agency
4828 Market Road
Newark, NJ 07011

Dear Mr. Simpson:

Professor Fred Baker of the Fenner State University School of Business has told me of a recent opening in your firm. I wish to apply for this position.

Because the job involves soliciting and managing advertising accounts, I feel especially qualified. In my marketing studies, I have specialized in the design and management of just such accounts. Furthermore, working at the First State Bank in Fenner and at Passmore's Men's Shop has given me practical experience in finance, record keeping, and sales.

I am available for an interview at any time on a day's notice. My telephone number is 609-555-2971.

Sincerely,

Martin Alvarez

Martin Alvarez

Encl. Résumé

VIII Writing the Research Paper

51 · Guides for Library Research

51a Approaches to research

Research is a systematic process of exploration and discovery —a means of attaining new knowledge and gaining fresh insights to previously held values and beliefs. Thus, it is both an essential human activity and an indispensable scholarly tool.

Some research activities involve laboratory experimentation. Others require field investigations such as interviews, surveys, and observations of natural phenomena. Still others lead researchers into libraries and archives to explore published and unpublished sources of information.

Different types of research can be reported in different ways. Researchers in the physical and biological sciences usually depend on mathematic notation, tables, and charts as well as prose to present their findings. Psychologists, sociologists, and other social scientists also report quantitative results in tables and charts; like scientists they often use prose to describe the processes of gathering data and the results of analysis of the data.

Scholars in the humanities, on the other hand, are usually more concerned with qualities than with quantities. Historians, literary critics, and philosophers use exposition and argument to propose insights usually derived from a research of written material. These researchers use prose less to describe and report than to interpret and judge.

Although specific aims and methods may vary from one research activity to another, most nonexperimental research tasks will depend on these basic steps:

1. Choose a subject that interests you, and narrow it until it becomes a topic that you can investigate thoroughly and

write about convincingly.

2. Use the resources in your college library to identify books, articles, and other materials pertaining to your topic.
3. Compile a preliminary bibliography of the sources referred to above.
4. Locate, read, and take notes on the sources listed in the preliminary bibliography.
5. Develop a thesis statement and outline based on the evidence you have accumulated.
6. Present results and conclusions in systematic, well-documented written form.
7. Prepare a list of works cited from the preliminary bibliography.

A survey of all types of research and research-based writing would far exceed the scope of this text. The chapters that follow will, however, introduce you to the fundamentals of library research—a form of scholarly investigation that is basic to all disciplines—and help you to develop the skills needed for one important kind of academic research writing, the documented essay usually referred to as a *research paper* or *term paper.*

Although some research topics require interviews, surveys, or the study of documents in off-campus archives, the center for most academic research is the college library. There you will find *primary sources* (examples of the actual subjects being investigated, such as literary works, letters, and the texts of speeches and interviews); *secondary sources* (biographies, scholarly books and monographs, periodical articles, and other works about the subject); and the various reference tools needed to identify and obtain these sources.

51b The card catalog

One indispensable research tool is the card catalog (or its equivalent, the computer catalog), which indexes all the books and bound periodicals in the library's collection. The catalog is usually divided into three sections: (1) an author file, which contains cards for all books arranged alphabetically by author; (2) a title file, which consists of cards for all books and bound periodicals arranged alphabetically; and (3) a subject file, which includes cards for all books arranged alphabetically by subject. The cards in this catalog provide several kinds of information that will aid you in your research:

1. A Library of Congress or Dewey Decimal System **call number** that indicates the exact location of the work in the library.

Sample Cards from Card Catalog

Author card

HV
741 Fontana, Vincent J.
F65 Somewhere a child is crying :
1976 maltreatment--causes and prevention /
Vincent J. Fontana. New York : New
American Library, 1976.
xxii, 264 p. ; 18 cm.
Includes index
Bibliography: p. 239-256.

1. Child abuse--United States.
2. Child welfare--United States.
I. Title

NcGrE EREEac

Title card

```
              Somewhere a child is crying
HV
741       Fontana, Vincent J.
F65         Somewhere a child is crying :
1976      maltreatment--causes and prevention /
          Vincent J. Fontana. New York : New
          American Library, 1976.
            xxii, 264 p. ; 18 cm.
            Includes index
            Bibliography: p. 239-256.


            1. Child abuse--United States.
          2. Child welfare--United States.


NcGrE                      EREEtc
```

Subject card

```
                    CHILD ABUSE--UNITED STATES.

HV
741          Fontana, Vincent J.
F65            Somewhere a child is crying :
1976         maltreatment--causes and prevention /
             Vincent J. Fontana. New York : New
             American Library, 1976.
               xxii, 264 p. ; 18 cm.
               Includes index
               Bibliography: p. 239-256.

               1. Child abuse--United States.
             2. Child welfare--United States.


NcGrE                          EREEsc
```

2. Author, title, and publication data for the book.
3. Brief notes about the book's contents.
4. Cross references to other headings under which each book is listed.

Note: If your library uses a computerized indexing system, you can obtain this information by going to a computer terminal and typing in a user code plus an author, title, or subject descriptor.

51c General encyclopedias and biographical dictionaries

Articles in encyclopedias and other general reference works usually treat their subject so briefly and superficially that there is seldom any need to cite them in a formal research paper. However, they do often provide useful background information, as well as bibliographical references that may lead you to more promising sources.

General Encyclopedias

Collier's Encyclopedia. 24 vols. 1982.
The Encyclopedia Americana. International Edition. 32 vols. 1980.
Encyclopædia Britannica. 30 vols. 1983.
The Random House Encyclopedia. Revised ed. 1983.

Biographical Dictionaries

American Men and Women of Science. 1971–.
American Writers. 1974–.
Contemporary Authors. 1962–.
Dictionary of American Biography.
Dictionary of National Biography (English). 22 vols. 1882–1953.
International Who's Who. 1935–.
New Grove Dictionary of Music and Musicians. 20 vols. 1980.

Notable American Women 1607–1950. 3 vols. 1971.
Webster's Biographical Dictionary. 1976.
Who's Who in America. 1899–.
Who's Who in Finance and Industry. 1972–.

51d Specialized reference works

Many of the subjects covered in general reference works are treated in greater detail in books such as the ones listed below. For additional titles consult such works as Eugene Sheehy's *Guide to Reference Books*, Gavin Higgens's *Printed Reference Material*, or G. Chandler's *How to Find Out: Printed and On-Line Sources*.

The Sciences

McGraw-Hill Encyclopedia of Science and Technology. 15 vols. 1975. Supplemented by *McGraw-Hill Yearbook of Science and Technology*, 1971–.
Encyclopedia of American Agriculture: A Popular Survey of Agricultural Conditions, Practices, and Ideals in the United States and Canada. 4 vols. 1907–1909.
The Cambridge Encyclopedia of Astronomy. 1977.
The Encyclopedia of the Biological Sciences. 2nd ed. 1970.
Grzimek's Encyclopedia of Ecology. 1976.
The Encyclopedia of Chemistry. 3rd ed. 1973.
Encyclopedia of Physics. 1981.
The Planet We Live On: Illustrated Encyclopedia of the Earth Sciences. 1976.
Universal Encyclopedia of Mathematics. 1964.

The Social Sciences

International Encyclopedia of the Social Sciences. 18 vols. 1968.
Dictionary of Anthropology. 1970.

Encyclopedia of Education. 10 vols. 1971.
Encyclopedia of Physical Education, Fitness, and Sports. 1977.
Encyclopedia of Sociology. 1974.
Facts on File. 1940–.
Mythology of All Races. 13 vols. 1916–1932.
Funk and Wagnalls Standard Dictionary of Folklore, Mythology, and Legend. 2 vols. 1949–1950.
The Golden Bough: A Study in Magic and Religion. 12 vols. 1907–1915.
International Encyclopedia of Statistics. 2 vols. 1978.
Encyclopedia of American Economic History: Studies of the Principal Movements and Ideas. 3 vols. 1980.
Encyclopedia of Advertising. 2nd ed. 1969.
A Dictionary of Business and Finance. 1957.
Encyclopedia of American Foreign Policy. 3 vols. 1978.
Black's Law Dictionary. 5th ed. 1979.
Encyclopedia of Psychology. 3 vols. 1972.
A Dictionary of Basic Geography. 1970.

The Humanities

Cambridge History of American Literature. 1943.
Cambridge History of English Literature. 15 vols. 1907–.
Encyclopedia of Philosophy. 8 vols. 1967–1973.
The Encyclopedia of Religion and Ethics. 13 vols. 1908–1927.
Encyclopedia Judaica. 16 vols. 1972.
Encyclopedia of World Art. 15 vols. 1959–1968.
Essay and General Literature Index. 1900–.
Focal Encyclopedia of Photography. 2 vols. 1965.
The Film Encyclopedia. 1979.
Literary History of the United States. 4th ed. 2 vols. 1974.
New Catholic Encyclopedia. 1979.
Oxford English Dictionary. 13 vols. 1933.

51e Periodical indexes and bibliographies

Although the subject headings of the card catalog and articles in encyclopedias and other such reference works will enable you to compile a partial bibliography of books on your topic, you will have to look elsewhere for bibliographical information about books that are not mentioned in these sources and for articles and reviews published in popular magazines, scholarly journals, and newspapers.

Indexes to Articles and Reviews in Popular Magazines

Book Review Digest. 1905–.
Nineteenth Century Reader's Guide to Periodical Literature. 1890–1899.
Poole's Index to Periodical Literature. 1802–1906.
Reader's Guide to Periodical Literature. 1900–.

Specialized Indexes and Bibliographies

Art Index. 1929–.
Biological and Agricultural Index. 1964. Supersedes *Agricultural Index*, 1916–1964.
Business Periodicals Index. 1958–.
Current Index to Journals in Education. 1964–.
Education Index. 1929–.
Humanities Index. 1974–. Formerly part of *Social Sciences and Humanities Index*, 1965–1974.
International Index. 1907–1965. Superseded by *Social Sciences and Humanities Index*, 1965–1974.
Legal Resource Index.
Music Index. 1949—.
MLA International Bibliography of Books and Articles on Modern Languages and Literature. 1919–.
New Film Index.
New York Times Index. 1851–.

Public Affairs Information Service Bulletin. 1915–.
Social Sciences Index. 1974–. Formerly part of *Social Sciences and Humanities Index*, 1965–1974.
United States Government Publications. 1895–.

51f Microfilm resources and computerized information services

Much of the information in written reference works is now stored also on microfilm or in computers. Microfilm indexes such as *Magazine Index*, which lists articles in over 300 popular magazines, are useful because the researcher can easily scan hundreds of items in a few minutes. Even faster are computerized research systems such as Dialog Information Services, which can search thousands of entries for material pertinent to the researcher's interest. Although computer searches are expensive, they are also a convenient and reliable means of gathering bibliographical data on subjects in all academic areas.

52 · Selecting and Limiting the Subject

Unless you are assigned a specific research topic, your first task will be to choose a subject and limit it to manageable proportions.

52a Choose a subject.

Consider, first of all, the requirements of the assignment. Does it limit you to a general subject area such as literature, history, or politics? Does it specify a particular approach or rhetorical mode (e.g., analysis, comparison/contrast, argumentation, etc.)? Does it require the use of certain kinds of sources (e.g., scholarly books and articles, newspapers and general periodicals, media productions, unpublished materials, interview or survey data)? Or does it allow you to make these decisions for yourself?

Once you have answered these questions, make a list of issues or ideas that not only satisfy the requirements of the research assignment but also reflect your own interests or concerns. These might include subjects related to your academic field (e.g., genetic engineering, teacher tenure laws, etc.); ideas derived from the study of poems, plays, novels, or other forms of writing; social and political issues such as abortion, gun control, capital punishment, job discrimination, defense spending, nuclear energy; areas of special knowledge or expertise such as painting, photography, music; and any other promising subjects.

If this self-exploration fails to yield a suitable subject, skim through some of the general reference works discussed in Chapter **51**, or look over recent issues of a general periodical or professional journal to see what kinds of research and documented writing other people are engaged in. You might also generate ideas by talking informally with friends or faculty members.

52b Narrow the subject.

Once you have selected a subject, you will need to narrow it to the point that you can investigate it thoroughly and write about it effectively in the amount of time available to you.

Suppose, for example, that you were interested in doing research on nuclear energy. Although this subject is far too broad to work with, it can be restricted in several different ways.

52 b

One approach is to begin with the general subject and make a list of words or phrases in which each term is more specific than the one before it. Eventually, you should arrive at a researchable topic, such as the final item in the example below:

Nuclear energy—hazards of nuclear energy production—accidents at nuclear plants—the Three-Mile Island accident—causes of the Three-Mile Island accident.

A second tactic is to compose an unstructured list of ideas related to the main subject and then look for patterns or relationships. The result might look something like this:

1. origins of nuclear power
2. safety record of nuclear plants
3. economic benefits of nuclear power
4. thermal pollution
5. radiation leaks
6. how nuclear power is produced
7. hazardous waste problems
8. reliability of nuclear power plants
9. history of the anti-nuclear movement

Background: 1, 6, 9
Advantages: 2, 3, 8
Disadvantages: 4, 5, 7

A third option is to generate ideas by asking questions about the subject:

How do nuclear power plants affect the environment?
What can be done to prevent accidents at nuclear power plants?
Is nuclear energy worth the risks?
Should there be a moratorium on the construction of new nuclear power plants?

Other techniques for generating ideas are given in Chapter **3**. Whatever method you use to find ideas, the topic you select should be one that sets reasonable limits for research and writing and leads you to sources of information that will help you refine your topic, develop a unifying thesis, and organize your first draft.

53 · Compiling the Preliminary Bibliography

As you find references to books and articles that seem pertinent to your topic, record each citation on a separate index card or piece of paper (most researchers use 3 × 5 inch cards for this purpose because cards are easier to file and rearrange).

Each of the cards in this **preliminary bibliography** should include a call number (see **51b**), which will enable you to find the book or periodical (if your library has it), plus all the bibliographical information you need to document the work in your research paper. In this chapter, we have followed the 1984 Modern Language Association (MLA) style because it is the most influential guide for nonexperimental research documentation.

This style, like most others, requires three different types of information for each bibliographical citation: the name(s) of the author(s), the title of the book or essay, and details of publication.

Author Information

1. Put the author's last name before the first name so that you can conveniently alphabetize entries when preparing the final bibliography. If there is more than one author, reverse only the name of the first one.

2. Write out the author's first name and include the middle initial as well, if that information is given in your source.

3. If a work has an editor or translator, indicate that fact by citing the name and the abbreviation **ed.**, or **trans.**

Title Information

1. Include the subtitle as well as the title of a book, and separate them with a colon, even if a different punctuation mark is used in the source.

2. Underline the title of a book or periodical with an unbroken line.

3. Put quotation marks around the title of an essay or of a chapter in a book, the title of an article in a periodical, and the title of a short literary work (a poem, a one-act play, a short story, etc.).

Publication Information

1. If the work cited is a book, give the place of publication (the city alone is sufficient); an abbreviation of the publisher's name (e.g., Heath, Holt, Random, Yale UP, U of Toronto P); and the date of publication (abbreviate months except for May, June, July). If the book is published in more than one volume or is part of a series, indicate that fact as well.

2. If the work cited is a scholarly journal, record the title, the volume number (or the volume and issue number if each issue numbers its pages starting with 1), the date, and the page numbers. If the periodical is a weekly or monthly magazine, include the title, the full date, and the page numbers. Use the same format for a daily newspaper, but substitute section and column number for page numbers.

3. If the work does not fit either of these two categories (if, for example, it is a government document), consult the specific entries in examples that follow.

The most effiecient method of recording this information is to use the appropriate form for each citation in the preliminary bibliography so that you can later prepare the final bibliography simply by alphabetizing the cards and typing them as a single list.

Listed below are sample bibliographical entries for the kinds of sources you are most likely to use in your research paper. To determine the format for a reference, first identify the type of source you are citing (e.g., a book by a single author, an article in a journal, etc.) and find the matching heading. Then use the sample reference as a model for your own entry.

A book by one author

Schlesinger, Arthur M. *A Thousand Days: John F. Kennedy in the White House.* Boston: Houghton, 1965.

A book by two or more authors

If the book cited has two or three authors, list them in the sequence they appear on the title page, giving the first author's name in reverse order. If there are more than three authors, cite only the name of the person listed first on the title page and use the abbreviation **et al**. ("and all") in place of the other authors' names:

Berry, Mary Frances, and John W. Blassingame. *Long Memory: The Black Experience in America.* New York: Oxford UP, 1981.

Berg, Sanford, Jerome Duncan, and Philip Friedman. *Joint Venture Strategies and Corporate Innovation.* Cambridge, MA: Oelgeschlager, 1982.

Danzinger, James N., et al. *Computers and Politics: High Technology in American Local Governments.* New York: Columbia UP, 1982.

A book with an editor

Donohue, Agnes M., ed. *A Casebook on the Hawthorne Question.* New York: Crowell, 1963.

53

A book with more than one editor

If there is more than one editor, follow the multiple-author format, and add the abbreviation **eds**. after the final name:

Wasserman, Elga, Arie Y. Levin, and Linda H. Bleiweis, eds. *Women in Academia: Evolving Policies Toward Equal Opportunities*. New York: Praeger, 1975.

A book with an author and an editor

Chopin, Kate. *The Complete Works of Kate Chopin*. Ed. Per Seyersted. 2 vols. Baton Rouge: Louisiana State UP, 1969.

A book in translation

Baudelaire, Charles. *The Flowers of Evil, and Other Poems*. Trans. Francis Duke. Charlottesville: U of Virginia P, 1961.

A book in more than one edition

Bartels, Robert. *The History of Marketing Thought*. 2nd ed. Columbus: Grid, 1976.

A multivolume book

Davis, Richard Beale, *Intellectual Life in the Colonial South, 1585–1763*. 3 vols. Knoxville: U of Tennessee P, 1978.

A book in a series

Robe, Stanley, L., ed. *Hispanic Legends from New Mexico: Narratives from the R. D. Jameson Collection*. Folklore and Mythology Studies, 31. Berkeley: U of California P, 1980.

A book with a corporate author

Carnegie Commission on Higher Education. *The Academic System in American Society*. New York: McGraw, 1974.

A pamphlet

Unsigned

Marijuana: The National Impact on Education. Rockville: American Council on Marijuana, 1982.

Signed

Benedick, Richard E. *Population Growth and the Policy of Nations*. U.S. Department of State. Bureau of Public Affairs. Office of Public Communication. Washington: GPO, 1982.

An article in an encyclopedia

Schmitt, Barton D., and C. Henry Kempe. "Child Abuse." *The Encyclopedia Americana*. International ed. 1980.

An article in a scholarly journal

References to scholarly journals (e.g., *American Literature, Journal of Marketing, Journal of the American Chemical Society*) follow one of these patterns:

Quirk, Tom. "Fitzgerald and Cather: *The Great Gatsby*." *American Literature* 54 (1982): 576–591.

Henderson, Bruce. "The Anatomy of Competition." *Journal of Marketing* 47.2 (1983): 7–11.

In the first entry, the volume number alone (54) is sufficient because this journal is continuously paginated (i.e., the page numbering of each issue in a volume begins where the previous issue stopped). In the second entry, the number 47.2 indicates that this journal is separately paginated and that this article is in volume 47, issue number 2.

Article in a weekly or monthly magazine

Unsigned

"How to Stop Crib Deaths." *Newsweek* 6 Aug. 1973: 79.

Signed

Browne, Malcolm W. "Locking Out the Hackers: There Are Ways to Keep Trespassers Out of Computer Systems." *Discover* Nov. 1983: 30–40.

A work in an edited collection or casebook

When citing a work published or reprinted in a book, include bibliographic information for both sources:

Fogle, Richard H. "Ambiguity and Clarity in Hawthorne's 'Young Goodman Brown.'" *New England Quarterly* 18 (Dec. 1943): 448–65. Rpt. in *A Casebook on the Hawthorne Question*. Ed. Agnes M. Donohue. New York: Crowell, 1963.

Beach, Ruth. "A Case History of Affirmative Action." In *Women in Academia: Evolving Policies Toward Equal Opportunities*. Ed. Elga Wasserman, Arie Y. Levin, and Linda H. Bleiweis. New York: Praeger, 1975.

Note that the writer of the first entry includes publication data as well as the author and title of the essay to indicate that "Ambiguity and Clarity in Hawthorne's 'Young Goodman Brown'" is a reprint of an article published originally in *New England Quarterly*. No such information accompanies "A Case History of Affirmative Action" because the essay had not been previously published.

Magazine review

Cowley, Malcolm. Rev. of *The Grapes of Wrath*, by John Steinbeck. *New Republic* 3 May 1939: 382.

Article in a newspaper

Haverman, Joel. "Time Running Out for Congress to Act on Deficit." *Los Angeles Times* 7 Nov. 1983: 1A, col. 2.

Note: If this article had appeared without a by-line, the entry would begin with the title rather than the author.

A film

When citing a film, give the director's name first and put the abbreviation **dir.** after it. Immediately following the title, cite the main actors' names and the name of the studio.

Brooks, James L., dir. *Terms of Endearment*. With Shirley MacLaine, Debra Winger, and Jack Nicholson. Paramount, 1983.

A television or radio program

The Day After. ABC. 20 Nov. 1983.

A personal interview

Thomas, Carlyn. Personal interview. 5 Jan. 1984.

54 · Locating Sources and Taking Notes

When you have finished the preliminary bibliography, the next step is to locate sources and take notes on them. As you gather information, keep in mind that you are under no obligation to use everything you record in your notes. Some of the sources that first seem most promising may later prove to be irrelevant or unreliable, whereas references that initially appear to have little value may furnish exactly the evidence you need to explain a key point or clinch an argument in your research paper.

54a Locate sources listed in the preliminary bibliography.

If you have not already checked the card catalog to find out which of the sources listed in your bibliography are in the library and what their call numbers are, you will need to do so now. Once you know the call number, you can find the work by consulting the maps or other location guides posted in the library or by filling out a book request form, depending on whether your library has open or closed stacks.

Under ideal circumstances, all the sources in your bibliography would be listed in the card catalog and shelved exactly where the call number indicates they should be. In reality, however, conditions may be different. You may discover, for example, that some of the books and journals you have found in bibliographies or other reference works are not in your library's collection or that the particular volume or issue you need is missing. If any of these sources seem essential to your research you may be able to obtain them through interlibrary loan. This is usually a slow process, however, so you should file interlibrary loan requests well in advance of your deadline for completing your note taking. If you have only a limited time in which to conduct research and write your research paper or if most of the sources in your preliminary bibliography are available only from other libraries, you may need to search for additional sources or even consider changing your topic.

54b Take accurate notes.

First, skim over each source to determine whether it is relevant to your topic and—if so—how extensively it should be cited in the research paper. Obviously, a book is more difficult to assess quickly than an article or chapter, but you can learn a good deal just by reading the introduction and by studying the table of contents and the index.

When you have identified the most promising sources, reread them carefully and take notes, following these procedures:

1. Record information on index cards (4 × 6 inch cards are more suitable for note taking than the smaller bibliography cards) or on sheets of paper.

2. Use a separate card or page for each piece of information and write only on one side so that you can conveniently arrange sources when you write your research paper.

3. At the top of each note, sum up the author's main point in a word or phrase. Later, when you are ready to write, these topical headings will let you quickly identify the contents of

each note and help you decide whether the material should be cited and—if so—when it should be introduced.

4. Just below the topic heading, write the author's name (or the name and a short title if you intend to cite more than one work by the same person) and the page number. This information will refer you to the complete entry for the source in your bibliography.

5. For each note, record information in one of the following ways.

(a) Photocopy the page on which the information appears and mark the relevant passage, or write down the exact language and punctuation of the original and enclose the passage in quotation marks, as in the example below:

Permanent effects of physical abuse

Elmer p. 44

"Multiple fractures of the extremities, if not properly treated, may result in some permanent disability, such as a limp or limitation of motion, while subdural hematomas, suffered by a number of the children, may prevent the brain from growing normally and thereby cause permanent mental retardation."

(b) Paraphrase the desired information by completely rewriting it in your own language and sentence structure, using approximately the same number of words as the source:

Permanent effects of child abuse

Elmer p. 44

In one study group of abused children, many of the victims had suffered serious physical injuries, including fractured limbs and head injuries severe enough to cause blood clots. Unless these children receive the medical care they need, some of them may never walk or move normally again, and others will suffer permanent brain damage.

(c) Summarize information by shortening as well as rewriting the original:

Permanent effects of child abuse

Elmer p. 44

Abused children in one study group showed signs of serious, permanently debilitating injuries, some of which may prevent normal body movement or cause irreversible brain damage.

(d) Combine a quotation with a paraphrase or a summary:

Permanent effects of physical abuse

Elmer p. 44

In one study group of abused children, many of the victims had suffered severe, long-term injuries. Some of these children had "multiple fractures of the extremities," which could cause a permanent "limp or limitation of motion." Others had been struck on the head so forcefully that blood clots or "subdural hematomas" had formed, causing "permanent mental retardation."

Notice that the information at the top of each note card is keyed to the bibliography card for this source:

HV
741
E 48c
1977

Elmer, Elizabeth. *Children in Jeopardy: A Study of Abused Minors and Their Parents.* Pittsburgh: U. of Pittsburgh Press, 1977.

Of these note-taking strategies, the first two are the most widely used. Some researchers prefer to quote all or most of their information when they take notes so that they can evaluate all the data and arrive at a definite thesis before deciding specifically how to incorporate each piece of evidence into the research paper. Others choose to paraphrase most of their sources in the note-taking stage so that when they begin writing, they can transfer the notes directly into their papers. The safest course, however, is to vary your note-taking methods.

54c Avoid plagiarism.

Plagiarism is *the unacknowledged use of someone else's words or ideas.* It occurs when a writer omits quotation marks when citing the exact language of a source, fails to revise completely a paraphrased source, or gives no documentation for a quotation or paraphrase. The best way to avoid this problem is to be attentive to the following details:

1. When you copy a quotation directly into your notes, check to be sure that you have put quotation marks around it. If you forget to include them when you copy, you may omit them in the paper as well.

2. When you paraphrase, keep in mind that it is not sufficient to change just a few words or rearrange sentence structure. You must completely rewrite the passage. One of the best ways to accomplish this is to read the material you want to paraphrase, then cover the page so that you cannot see it and write down the information as you remember it. Then, compare your version with the original and make any necessary changes in the note. If, after several attempts, you cannot successfully rewrite the passage, quote it instead.

The difference between legitimate and unacceptable paraphrases can be seen in the following examples:

Source

"What is unmistakably convincing and makes Miller's theatre writing hold is its authenticity in respect to the minutiae of American life. He is a first-rate reporter; he makes the details of his observation palpable."

From Harold Clurman's introduction
to *The Portable Arthur Miller*

Unacceptable paraphrase

What is truly convincing and makes Arthur Miller's theatrical writing effective is its authenticity. He is an excellent reporter and makes his observation palpable.

Legitimate paraphrase

The strength of Arthur Miller's dramatic art lies in its faithfulness to the details of the American scene and in its power to bring to life the reality of ordinary experience.

The differences between these two versions of Clurman's statement are enormous. The first writer has made some token changes, substituting a few synonyms (**truly** for **unmistakably**, **excellent** for **first-rate**), deleting part of the first sentence, and combining the two parts of the second sentence into a single clause. Otherwise, this is a word-for-word copy of the original, and if the note were copied into the paper in this form, the writer would be guilty of plagiarism. The second writer, on the other hand, has changed the vocabulary of the original passage and completely restructured the sentence so that the only similarity between the note and the source is the ideas.

3. Check to see that each note has the correct name and page number so that when you use this information in your paper, you will be able to credit it to the right source.

4. If you have any doubts about the way in which you have handled material from printed sources, confer with your teacher before you submit your paper.

55 · Planning and Writing the Research Paper

When you have finished gathering information and taking notes, you should be ready to begin writing your research paper.

55a Formulate a thesis statement.

The thesis should be a single declarative sentence that sums up what you have learned about the topic through your research and what you want your readers to learn from your research paper. A precise, clearly phrased thesis sentence will guide your selection and arrangement of information and, at the same time, alert the reader to the design and direction of the essay as a whole. Notice how the thesis statements below combine these functions.

Anorexia nervosa, a condition that affects thousands of young women every year, has both psychological and social origins.

In *The Grapes of Wrath*, John Steinbeck affirms the universal values of unity, sacrifice, courage, and faith through his portrayal of the Joad family.

Contrary to the popular belief that food additives are unnatural or harmful, these substances provide vital nutritional supplements, prevent spoilage, enhance appearance, and aid in food processing.

55b Prepare an outline.

Once you have formulated your thesis, carefully reread your notes, discarding any that do not pertain directly to this central idea or proposition. Then, using the thesis statement as a guide, list the main points of your explanation or argument in the order in which you plan to discuss them, assign a Roman numeral heading to each, and group your remaining notes under these broad categories. Your Roman numeral headings will in turn suggest subgroupings of ideas and examples that help develop each main point.

The result should be a detailed outline such as the one below (for additional information about outline form, see **4b**).

```
                The Value of Food Additives

Thesis Statement: Contrary to the popular belief that food
additives are unnatural or harmful, these substances provide
vital nutritional supplements, prevent spoilage, enhance
appearance, and aid in food processing.

Introduction
I.   Misconceptions about food additives
     A. Belief that additives are unnatural
     B. Belief that additives are harmful
II.  Value of food additives as nutritional supplements
     A. Vitamins
        1. Riboflavin (B2)
        2. Alpha tocopherol (E)
        3. Cobalmin (B12)
     B. Amino acids
        1. Tysine
        2. Tryptophan

     B. Colors
        1. Caramel
        2. Carotene
        3. Paprika
V.   Value of additives in food processing
     A. Emulsifiers
        1. Glycerides
        2. Sorbitan
     B. Leavening agents
        1. Sodium bicarbonate
        2. Potassium acid tartrate
Conclusion
```

55 b

55c Compose a rough draft.

When you have finished gathering information, begin working your notes into the first draft of your research paper. As you write, keep in mind this is not the version of the paper that you will submit for evaluation but a working draft that can be expanded, reorganized, or changed in other significant ways as the paper develops. More specifically, this early draft will give you an opportunity to organize related notes into paragraphs, move sentences around within paragraphs to achieve coherence, and arrange paragraphs in the order indicated by the outline so that you can test the logic and coherence of your original organizational scheme.

As you compose your essay, you can copy from your notes material that you have already expressed in your own words or recorded by combining short quotations with original statements or paraphrases. Extended quotations, on the other hand, will require further evaluation, for they can be used in numerous ways.

Suppose, for example, that you were writing an expository essay on the nuclear arms race and that you had quoted in your notes the passage (top of p. 331) from Fletcher Knebel and Charles Bailey's *No Higher Ground*.

One option would be to quote the passage in full (or condense it by using an ellipsis mark) and introduce it with a statement such as the following:

At a time when the threat of nuclear war seems greater than ever before, the nations of the world would do well to remember what happened on the morning of August 6, 1945, when a single atomic bomb devastated the city of Hiroshima:

> First came heat. It lasted only an instant but was so intense that it melted roof tiles, fused the quartz crystals in granite blocks, charred the exposed sides of telephone poles for almost two miles, and incinerated nearby humans . . . ~~so thoroughly that~~

Heat—detrimental effects on Hiroshima

Knebel and Bailey p. 181

"First came heat. It lasted only an instant but was so intense that it melted roof tiles, fused the quartz crystals in granite blocks, charred the exposed sides of telephone poles for almost two miles, and incinerated nearby humans so thoroughly that nothing remained except their shadows, burned into asphalt pavements or stone walls. Bare skin was burned up to two and a half miles away."

> ~~nothing remained except their shadows, burned into asphalt pavements or stone walls~~. Bare skin was burned up to two and a half miles away (Knebel and Bailey 181).

Another approach would be to select portions of the quotation and adapt them to the grammatical structure of your own sentence, as in the following paragraph:

> First, the people of Hiroshima felt an intense heat which "lasted only an instant," yet generated enormously high temperatures that changed roof tiles into running lava, "fused the quartz crystals in granite blocks," burned the exposed sides of telephone poles, and vaporized nearby people, leaving only "their shadows, burned into asphalt pavement and stone walls" (Knebel and Bailey 181).

A third alternative would be to rewrite the passage, as in the following paraphrase:

> Peter Knebel and Charles Bailey explain that the heat generated by the nuclear bomb dropped on Hiroshima lasted only a moment, but its effects were devastating. The heat was so intense that it liquified roof tiles and rock crystals, charred telephone poles two miles from

the blast, vaporized anyone near the center of the blast, and burned the skin of people who were over two miles from ground zero (181).

All three of these passages represent an effective and legitimate use of sources. The words that have been taken verbatim from the notecard in the first and second examples have been enclosed in quotation marks, the borrowed ideas in the second and third examples have been expressed in a language completely different from that of Knebel and Bailey, and the source and location of the quoted or paraphrased material have been clearly identified (see the next chapter for specific suggestions on documentation).

Throughout this preliminary stage of the writing process, keep in mind that you have at least as much to contribute as any of the sources you cite. For example, the thesis statement and most or all of the introduction and conclusion should be in your own language and should reflect your own insights. You will also require original language and thought to write the topic sentences around which you organize your paragraphs, the transitions that lead from one sentence or paragraph to the next, and the words or phrases that introduce and identify quotations and paraphrases. Furthermore, as you write you should not be reluctant either to revise your previous work or to alter your plans for the paper.

55d Document sources fully and accurately.

Although you need not acknowledge a source for generally known information such as the dates of the Civil War or the names of the ships that carried Columbus and his followers to the New World, you must identify the exact source and location of each statement, fact, or idea you borrow from another person or work.

There are many different ways to acknowledge sources, but one of the simplest and most efficient is the MLA documentation system (1984 version), which requires only a brief parenthetical reference in the text of the paper keyed to a complete bibliographical entry in the list of works cited at the end of the essay.

For most parenthetical references, you will need to cite only the author's last name and the number of the page from which the statement or idea was taken, and if you mention the author's name in the text, the page number alone is sufficient. This format also allows you to include within the parentheses additional information, such as title or volume number, if it is needed for clarity. Documentation for some of the most common types of sources is discussed in the sections below, and additional examples of documentation in the context of a student research paper can be found in Chapter **56**.

References to Articles and Single-Volume Books

Articles and single-volume books are the two types of works you will be referring to most often in your research paper. When citing them, either mention the author's name in the text and note the appropriate page number in parentheses immediately after the citation or acknowledge both name and page number in the parenthetical reference, leaving a space between the two. If punctuation is needed, insert the mark outside the final parenthesis.

Author's name cited in the text

Marya Mannes has defined euthanasia as "the chosen alternative to the prolongation of a steadily waning mind and spirit by machines that will withhold death or to an existence that mocks life" (61).

Author's name cited in parentheses

Euthanasia has been defined as "the chosen alternative to the prolongation of a steadily waning mind and spirit by machines that will withhold death or to an existence that mocks life" (Mannes 61).

Corresponding bibliographic entry

Mannes, Marya. *Last Rights.* New York: Morrow, 1973.

If the work you are citing has two or three authors, cite all their last names in parentheses, and follow the conventions for spacing and punctuation noted above. If there are more than three authors, include the last name of the author listed first on the title page, plus the abbreviation **et al**.

Sample parenthetical references

(Berry and Blassingane 125)
(Berg, Duncan, and Friedman 85)
(Danziger et al. 28)

Corresponding bibliographic entries

Berry, Mary Frances, and John W. Blassingame. *Long Memory: The Black Experience in America.* New York: Oxford UP, 1981.

Berg, Sanford, Jerome Duncan, and Philip Friedman. *Joint Venture Strategies and Corporate Innovation.* Cambridge: Oelgeschlager, 1982.

Danzinger, James N., et al. *Computers and Politics: High Technology in American Local Governemnts.* New York: Columbia UP, 1982.

References to Works in an Anthology

When referring to a work in an anthology, either cite in the text the author's name and indicate in parentheses the page number in the anthology where the source is located, or acknowledge both name and page reference parenthetically.

Author's name cited in text

One of the most widely recognized facts about James Joyce, in Lionel Trilling's view, "is his ambivalence toward Ireland, of which the hatred was as relentless as the love was unfailing" (153).

Author's name cited in parentheses

One of the most widely recognized facts about James Joyce "is his ambivalence toward Ireland, of which the hatred was as relentless as the love was unfailing" (Trilling 153).

Corresponding bibliographic entry

Trilling, Lionel. "James Joyce in His Letters." In *Joyce: A Collection of Critical Essays*. Ed. William M. Chace. Englewood Cliffs: Prentice, 1974.

References to More Than One Work by an Author

When you paraphrase or quote from more than one work by an author, give the title as well as the name of the author and the page reference so that the reader will know which work is being cited.

If you mention the author's name in the text, you need not duplicate it in the parenthetical reference. Just cite the title (or a shortened version of it), skip a space, and insert the page number, as in the second example below. If you do not mention the author's name in the text, cite it first in the parenthetical reference, put a comma after it, skip a space, and insert the title. Then skip a space again and insert the page number (see the third example below).

Title cited in text

Stephen Gould asserts in his article "Singapore's Patrimony (and Matrimony)" that "Some historical arguments are so intrinsically illogical or implausible that, following their fall from grace, we do not anticipate any subsequent resurrection in later times and contexts" (22).

Title cited in parentheses

Stephen Gould asserts that "Some historical arguments are so intrinsically illogical or implausible that, following their fall from grace, we do not anticipate any subsequent resurrection in later times and contexts" ("Patrimony" 22).

or

In the words of one contemporary scientist, "Some historical arguments are so intrinsically illogical or implausible that, following their fall from grace, we do not anticipate any subsequent resurrection in later times and contexts" (Gould, "Patrimony" 22).

Corresponding entries in the list of works cited

Gould, Stephen Jay. *Ever Since Darwin: Reflections in Natural History.* New York: Norton, 1977.

---."Singapore's Patrimony (and Matrimony)." *Natural History* May 1984: 22–29.

References to Works of Unknown Authorship

If you borrow information or ideas from an article or book for which you cannot determine the name of the author, cite the title instead, either in the text of the paper or in parentheses, and include the page reference as well.

Title cited in the text

According to an article entitled "Going Back to Booze," surveys have shown that most adult alcoholics began drinking heavily as teenagers (42).

Title cited in parentheses

Surveys have shown that most adult alcoholics began drinking heavily as teenagers ("Going Back to Booze" 42).

Corresponding bibliographic entry

"Going Back to Booze." *Time* 31 Nov. 1979: 41–46.

References to Multivolume Works

55 d

When you borrow from one volume of a multi-volume work, cite the volume of your source in parentheses as an arabic number *without* the abbreviation **Vol.**, and put a colon after it. Then skip a space and insert the page reference.

Sample references

Frazer points out that scapegoat rituals have been common throughout history, not only in primitive societies but also "among the civilized nations of Europe" (9: 47).

Scapegoat rituals have been common throughout history, not only in primitive societies but also "among the civilized nations of Europe" (Frazer 9: 47).

Corresponding bibliographic entry

Frazer, Sir James G. *The Golden Bough: A Study in Magic and Religion.* 3rd ed. 12 vols. New York: MacMillan, 1935.

References to Information Gathered from Interviews

When citing an oral source, either mention the informant's name when you introduce the quotation or paraphrase, or give the name in a parenthetical reference.

Informant's name cited in text

When asked to comment on conditions in the dormitories, one of my informants, Sherry Cobb, complained that the worst thing she could think of was the insect problem. "You just wouldn't believe how bad things are around here," she said. "I walked into the bathroom this morning and came face to face with the biggest roach on record."

Informant's name cited in parentheses

When asked to comment on conditions in the dormitories, one of my informants complained that the worst thing she could think of was the insect problem. "You just wouldn't believe how bad things are around here," she said. "I walked into the bathroom this morning and came face to face with the biggest roach on record" (Cobb).

Corresponding bibliographic entry

Cobb, Sherry. Personal interview. 10 Apr. 1982.

References to Literary Works

When citing works of literature, observe the following guidelines for each genre.

Novels and other prose works subdivided into chapters or sections

Begin the parenthetical reference with author's last name and page number (the author's name may be omitted if it is mentioned in the text of the paper or if the authorship is evident from the context) and insert a semicolon. Then skip a space and give the number of the chapter (with the abbreviation **Ch.**) as well as the number of any other subdivisions.

Sample reference

At the beginning of *The Great Gatsby*, Nick Carraway characterizes himself as someone who has "a sense of the fundamental decencies" (Fitzgerald 1; Ch. 1)—a trait that he displays throughout the novel.

Corresponding bibliographic entry

Fitzgerald, F. Scott. *The Great Gatsby*. New York: Scribner's, 1925.

Poems

When quoting or paraphrasing a poem that is divided into sections, cite the number of the book, part, or canto plus the line number(s). There is no need for abbreviations such as **bk.** (book) or **l.** (line), but the first time you cite the work write out the word **line** or **lines** so that the reader will not mistake the line numbers for page references. If the poem you are citing has no subdivisions, line numbers alone are usually sufficient to identify the source—provided that the author and title are identified in the text of the paper.

Sample reference to a poem with subdivisions

One of Byron's satiric techniques is to juxtapose the comical with the serious, as in this passage from *Don Juan*:

But I am apt to grow too metaphysical:
"The time is out of joint,"—and so am I;
I quite forget this poem's merely quizzical,
And deviate into matters rather dry
(9 lines 321–24).

Note: If you omit the word **lines**, put a period after the number of the section (in this case Canto 9) and, without spacing, insert the line number(s): (9.321–324).

Sample reference to a poem without subdivisions

One of the questions that must be answered in any analysis of Jeffers's "Hurt Hawks" is whether the author's viewpoint is reflected in the narrator's statement "I'd sooner, except the penalties, kill a man than a hawk" (line 18).

Corresponding bibliographic entries

Byron, George Gordon, Lord. *Don Juan*. In *Lord Byron: Don Juan and Other Satirical Poems*. Ed. Louis Bredvold. New York: Odyssey, 1935.

Jeffers, Robinson. "Hurt Hawks." *Selected Poems*. New York: Random, 1928.

Plays

When citing a play, give the act and scene number without abbreviations, plus the line numbers if the work is in verse.

Sample reference

Shakespeare repeatedly describes Denmark in images of unnaturalness as in Horatio's comparison of Denmark with Rome just before Caesar's murder, when "The graves stood tennantless and the sheeted dead / Did squeak and gibber in the Roman streets" (I. i.115–16).

Note: Upper-case Roman numerals are traditionally used for act numbers and lower-case Roman numerals for scene numbers.

Corresponding bibliographical entry

Shakespeare, William. *Hamlet*. In *Shakespeare: Twenty-Three Plays and the Sonnets*. Ed. Thomas Parrot. Rev. ed. New York: Scribner's, 1953.

55e Revise and edit your paper.

A good way to identify potential problems in the rough draft is to answer the following questions:

1. Have you included enough information from your sources to support your thesis?
2. Are all paragraphs relevant to the thesis and consistent with the outline?
3. Have you accurately quoted or paraphrased all ideas and information you have drawn from your sources?
4. Have you acknowledged each source in the text through parenthetical documentation as recommended in section **d** of this chapter?
5. Have you made your own judgments an integral part of the essay?
6. Do your conclusions follow logically from the evidence you have presented?

Don't be surprised if you have to answer *no* to some of these questions. The value of a rough draft is that it enables you to get ideas on paper without stopping to correct all mistakes. You can eliminate errors in subsequent drafts. If you discover any paragraphs that are irrelevant to the thesis, delete or revise them. If you find that your original plan of organization is flawed, rearrange those sentences and paragraphs that seem out of place. If you notice that more information is needed to support a particular point, go back to your notes for other examples or return to the library and do some additional reading. If you have strung together a series of quotations or paraphrases without transitions, add appropriate connectives or interpretive comments.

When you are able to answer affirmatively all the questions posed at the beginning of this section, proofread and edit your paper. At this point, you should be concentrating on the smaller elements of the essay, searching for errors in grammar and punctuation, misspellings, inappropriate word choice, inconsistencies in point of view or verb tenses, and the other common problems discussed in Parts **II** and **III** of this text.

55f Prepare the final list of works cited.

After you have revised and edited the text of your paper, use your preliminary bibliography cards to prepare a list of all the works you have cited in your essay. (This list should be titled either **Bibliography** or **Works Cited**, without quotation marks or underlining.) If you have recorded author, title, and publication information in the bibliographic format recommended in Chapter **53** or followed the conventions prescribed by another style manual approved by your teacher, you will have all the information required for your paper's bibliography page. You need only alphabetize the cards for sources you used in the paper and type them as a single list. When you have finished, check to be sure that every source cited in the text appears in the final bibliography and that the entry for each source is complete and accurate.

55g Compose the final draft.

When you are satisfied that you have fulfilled all the requirements of the research assignment and that your paper is ready for submission, prepare the final draft.

Since manuscript requirements vary, you should consult your teacher to find out what kind of paper is acceptable; how wide the margins should be; whether there should be a separate title page and, if so, what information it should include; whether a formal topic or sentence outline should be included with the paper; and what other guidelines you should observe when typing your final copy.

In addition, you should observe these generally accepted conventions of manuscript form:

1. Double-space the text of the paper including block quotations, which should be indented ten spaces from the left margin and cited without quotation marks unless quotation marks appear in the original (see p. 2 of the sample research paper).

2. Double-space entries in the list of works cited and within entries that cannot be completed on a single line.

3. Put your title at the top of the first page even if you have included a separate title page (remember that there is no need to underline or put quotation marks around your own words).

4. Do not number the title page or the first page of an outline. To number an outline of more than one page, use lower-case Roman numerals (ii, iii, iv), beginning with the second page.

5. Using Arabic numbers, number the pages of the paper and the list of works cited consecutively, starting with the second page. Only the number should be placed in the upper right corner of each page.

When you have completed the final copy, proofread it carefully, checking for reversed letters, omitted words or punctuation marks, and other typographical errors. If you note typographical errors and you don't have time to type corrections, make the correction neatly in ink; draw a single line through letters you want deleted.

56 · Sample Research Paper

The research paper that follows was written by a student in a second semester composition class. Based on the conventions of the 1984 edition of the *MLA Handbook for Writers of Research Papers*, this essay—together with the introductory notes and page-by-page annotations that accompany it—provides a practical guide to parenthetical documentation style, techniques for using sources, methods of organization, revision strategies, and other important aspects of the research writing process.

Background

The research assignment

The assignment on which the sample paper is based required students to choose a researchable subject and limit it to manageable proportions, gather information from at least six different sources, and present results and conclusions in an informative or argumentative paper of 5–8 pages. Additional requirements for the final written draft included a title page, a topic or sentence outline with a thesis statement, the text of the paper in a format consistent with MLA documentation style and manuscript form, and a list of works cited.

Circumstances of composition

Sarah Poindexter, the author of the sample paper, decided almost immediately that she wanted to investigate the problem of child abuse—partly because she had already read several magazine and newspaper articles on the subject but even more so because her own close family ties made her sympathetic to the plight of abused children and curious to learn more about them.

Because Sarah already had some familiarity with her subject, she decided that there was no need to consult encyclopedias or other general reference works, so she began her research by compiling a selected bibliography of books listed in the card catalog under the subject heading "child abuse." For each source, she recorded the call number plus pertinent bibliographical information on a 3 × 5 inch card. Then she went to the reference room, checked under the same subject heading in recent volumes of the *Reader's Guide to Periodical Literature* and several other periodical indexes, made additional bibliography cards for ten articles that seemed especially promising, and looked up the call number of each periodical in another reference room resource—the serials catalog.

Below are several entries from the preliminary bibliography. Note that the writer has taken the time to convert the publication data for each book or article into the format appropriate for that source.

WA
320
P967
1980

Garbarino, James, et al., eds. *Protecting Children from Abuse and Neglect*. San Francisco: Jossey-Bass, 1980.

(Essay collection with more than three editors—modeled on the sample entries on pp. 317–18.)

HV
741
J272
1975

James, Howard. *The Little Victims: How America Treats Its Children*. New York: David McKay, 1975.

(Book by a single author—modeled on the sample entry on p. 317.)

AP
2
N 6772

"The Hard Case." Newsweek
16 July 1972: 66.

(Unsigned article in a weekly magazine—modeled on the sample entry on p. 319.)

After reading the essay collection edited by Garbarino, Sarah made additional bibliography cards for each of the essays on which she took notes. Notice that in the example below the author's name and the title of the essay are cited first:

Gottlieb, Benjamin. "The Role of the Individual and Social Support in Preventing Child Maltreatment." In Protecting Children from Abuse and Neglect. Eds. James Garbarino, et al. San Francisco: Jossey-Bass, 1980.

(Essay in an edited collection—modeled on the sample entry on p. 320.)

Next, Sarah used the call numbers and bibliographical information to find the books and periodicals in her preliminary bibliography and began reading. At first, she skimmed quickly over each work, noting major ideas and reflecting on how she might restrict her subject. Through this process, she eventually discovered her topic—the effects of child abuse on its victims—and formulated the thesis statement that appears at the top of the outline page. She was then able to devise a plan of organization and develop a preliminary outline with the following subdivisions:

Introduction
Profile of the typical child abuser
Characteristics of abused children
Physical abuse and its effects
Emotional abuse and its effects
Neglect and its effects
Conclusion

These decisions in turn helped Sarah determine the kinds of information she needed to record in her notes: definitions of the general concept of child abuse and the specific forms of abuse identified in the preliminary outline, statistical data indicating the scope and seriousness of the problem, and explanations and examples of the effects of abuse. With these considerations in mind, she began a process of intensive reading and note taking that continued for several weeks. As she accumulated information, she grouped related notes under the outline headings she had decided upon earlier; later, after she had finished her research, she rearranged material within each section, discarded notes that seemed repetitious or irrelevant, and prepared a more detailed outline. When she was satisfied that she had adequately covered each of the main points she had set out to discuss and that her organization was sound, she wrote the first draft of her research paper.

As soon as she had finished this preliminary draft, which consisted mainly of the quotations and paraphrases recorded in her notes, she started revising. First, she concentrated on the large elements of composition. She rearranged sentences to achieve emphasis, inserted transitional words and phrases to improve coherence within and between paragraphs, and added her own comments to explain or interpret her sources.

Turning next to smaller details, she varied her word choice to eliminate unnecessary repetition, revised several weak passive voice constructions, consulted a dictionary to confirm the spelling of several words that were not part of her usual vocabulary, and checked for possible errors in grammar and punctuation. When she finished, she compiled a list of works cited from her preliminary bibliography, prepared a title page, made a few minor adjustments in her outline, and typed the final copy of the manuscript. Then she proofread the paper once more to ensure that it was free of typographical errors and submitted it for evaluation.

Sample Research Paper

Title Page Format

A title page usually includes at least four pieces of information, centered and spaced in a balanced arrangement as on the opposite page.

1. The title of the paper
2. The author's name
3. The course and section numbers
4. The date of submission

If you include the teacher's name, place it between the course information and the date.

Alternative Format

If you are not required to do a title page, follow these procedures:

1. Beginning one inch from the top of the page, put your name, the teacher's name, the course number, and the date, double-spacing between the parts of the heading.

2. Double-space after the last line of the heading and type the title of the paper in the center of the page.

3. Double-space after the title and begin the text of the paper.

The Effects of Child Abuse

by

Sarah Jo Poindexter

English 1200

April 14, 1983

Outline Page

The outline accompanying this paper follows the topic format discussed in **4b**. Suggestions for developing a sentence outline can be found in the same chapter.

Outline

Thesis Statement: For the survivors, child abuse is more than the momentary pain and humiliation of a blow or an insult or even a sexual attack; it is a lifelong trauma.

Introduction

I. Types of child abusers

A. People who take pleasure in inflicting pain on others

B. People who have difficulty coping with stress

C. People with various types of personality problems

D. People who were themselves abused children

II. Typical victims of child abuse

A. Infants

B. School-age children

III. Major forms of child abuse and their effects on the victim

A. Physical abuse

1. Definition

2. Effects

B. Emotional abuse

1. Definition

2. Effects

C. Sexual abuse

1. Definition

2. Effects

D. Neglect

1. Definition

2. Effects

Conclusion

Manuscript Form

If you include a separate title page, repeat the title on the first page of the essay, as in the model research paper, and double-space between it and the first line of text.

Use and Documentation of Sources

The first paragraph of Sarah Poindexter's research paper exemplifies several characteristics of effective research writing:

1. Quotations and paraphrases are skillfully intermixed with original statements.

2. Passages quoted verbatim are varied in length and unobtrusively imbedded in the writer's own sentences.

3. Quotations are transcribed exactly as they appear in their sources and enclosed by quotation marks.

4. Each source is clearly identified by a parenthetical reference in the format recommended in **55d**. The quotation from David Walters, for example, is acknowledged by page number alone because his name is mentioned in the text. Fontana's name, on the other hand, is not mentioned in the essay; therefore, it is included within parentheses, along with the page numbers and the title of the book from which the quotation was drawn. Usually, the title would be unnecessary but it is essential here because the author of the research paper cites two different works by the same author. A third variation of the format for parenthetical documentation can be found in the reference to "Abused Child," which is the title of an unsigned magazine article.

Content and Organization

The first paragraph accomplishes several related purposes: it introduces and defines the subject, alerts the reader to the severity of the problem, identifies the forms of abuse that will be analyzed in the body of the paper, and concludes with a statement of the thesis.

The Effects of Child Abuse

¶1 One of the most serious but least reported crimes in the United States is child abuse, a term which "denotes a situation ranging from the deprivation of food, clothing, shelter and paternal love to incidences where children are physically abused and mistreated by an adult, resulting in obvious physical trauma to the child and not infrequently leading to death" (Fontana, The Maltreated Child 10). The number of child abuse incidents in a given year cannot be determined exactly because only about one case in eight is reported ("Abused Child" 41). But according to David Walters, "Child abuse is pandemic in the United States" (3). Most of these cases involve one or more of the following types of maltreatment: physical abuse, sexual abuse, emotional abuse, or neglect. All have serious immediate consequences--especially physical abuse, which frequently results in death--but for the survivors, child abuse is more than the momentary pain and humiliation of a blow or an insult or even a sexual attack; it is a lifelong trauma.

¶2 To understand the effects of child abuse, we must first understand what motivates or provokes it. Some abusers are sadists or psychopaths who inflict pain on others "for the joy of it" (Fontana, Somewhere a Child Is Crying 70). Most, however, are otherwise normal people who have difficulty

Manuscript Form

On this page (as well as on the ones following) the page number has been placed in the upper right corner about $\frac{1}{2}$ inch from the top.

The block quotation is indented ten spaces and double-spaced, with doublespacing also between the passage and the text above and below it. Note that the indentation eliminates the need for quotation marks unless they appear in the original.

Use and Documentation of Sources

Paragraphs 2 and 3 illustrate a wide range of techniques for using sources. In paragraph 2, for example, the writer uses information from five different sources. Some she quotes or summarizes in a few words; others she treats at greater length.

Note, too, the use of the ellipsis mark to indicate the omission of words in two of the quotations in paragraph 2. In citing the passage from Gabarino and Stocking, the writer omits three words—"a parent's own"—to make the first element of the series parallel with the ones following it. In the indented quotation, she eliminates a substantial amount of the original text to enhance the dramatic effect of the informant's self-revelations.

Content and Organization

Paragraphs 2 and 3 treat points I and II in the outline. Note in particular the specificity of the topic sentence that begins each paragraph and the fullness of the supporting evidence.

2

coping with stress (Friedman and D'Agostino 31) or overcoming the effects of "emotional deprivation in . . . childhood, low levels of empathy, low self-esteem, social aloofness, and a variety of other personal characteristics" (Garbarino and Stocking 7). The one characteristic that most child abusers have in common is their family history. According to a 1976 article in U. S. News and World Report, "80% of all abusive parents were themselves abused as children" (84), but even more revealing than the bare statistical data are the sentiments expressed by one child abuser in an interview with Brandt F. Steele:

> Our defense mechanisms make it difficult to read us, but look to see what went into our lives to make us this way. It's true that we are socially alienated, most of us with good reason. Ninety percent of us were abused as children. . . . Since most of us grew up viewing others as part of negative, harmful relationships, why should we form more relationships now? . . . Child abusers are going through hell. (3)

¶3 These parents in turn pass on their legacy of bitterness and hostility to their own children. Often this abuse is directed at infants, especially babies who require expensive medical services at birth; unwanted or unplanned children;

Use and Documentation of Sources

In paragraphs 4 and 5, as in the preceding paragraphs, the writer skillfully integrates source material into the grammatical structure of her sentence. The quotation in the first sentence of paragraph 4, for example, is an excerpt from the longer passage on the note card below:

> Physical abuse — definition
>
> Chase p. 1
>
> "Child abuse is the deliberate and willful injury of a child by a caretaker — hitting, beating with a belt, cord or other implement, slamming against a wall, burning with cigarettes, scalding with hot water, locking in a dungeon, hogtying, torturing."

(The first part of this quote is deleted in the text of the paper.)

Also effective is the use of information from an oral source in paragraph 5, which is devoted entirely to a case of child abuse recounted by the author's sister.

Content and Organization

With paragraph 4, the writer begins the central portion of her paper. In this paragraph, the writer defines physical abuse (section III, A of the outline) and explains its damaging effects on the body; in the following paragraph, she treats its long-term psychological consequences.

and infants who for one reason or another fail to measure up to their parents' expectations (Steele and Pollock 130). Older children also suffer abuse. Of the reported incidents of child abuse each year, approximately half involve school-age children (Steele and Pollock 130). "At this age," Vladimir de Lissovoy observes, "the child must make a transition from the primary group of the family to the world outside" (12), a transition that brings changes in attitudes and behavior which may provoke acts of parental abuse.

¶4 One of the most common forms of child abuse, as well as the most frequently reported, is physical maltreatment such as "hitting, beating with a belt, cord or other implement, slamming against a wall, burning with cigarettes, scalding with hot water, locking in a dungeon, hogtying, torturing" (Chase 1). For children who survive these brutal attacks, the effects range from bruises and other minor injuries to permanent disabilities. Among the most serious complications are the ones cited by Elizabeth Elmer in Children in Jeopardy:

> Multiple fractures of the extremities, if not properly treated, may result in some permanent disability, such as a limp or limitation of motion, while subdural hematomas, suffered by a number of the children, may prevent the brain from growing normally and thereby cause permanent mental retardation. (44)

Use and Documentation of Sources

In paragraphs 6 and 7, the writer develops her ideas mainly through paraphrases drawn directly from her notes. A good example of the paraphrase technique can be found in the second and third sentences of paragraph 7, which are based on the following passage from Robert Bates's "Child Abuse and Neglect: A Medical Priority":

> Abusive language and verbal expressions of hostility are present in a high percentage of severely abusing families. Some parents state bluntly that they hate their children and never wanted them. Others wish their deaths and desire to kill them. Frequently they are yelled at and called derogatory names such as "idiot" and "monster."

Note that the writer has included a parenthetical reference to acknowledge the source of the idea even though she has changed the language and structure of the passage.

Content and Organization

Paragraphs 6 and 7 continue the line of development established in the outline by defining and explaining the effects of emotional abuse (section III, B of the outline).

An interesting technique here is the placement of the topic sentence at the end of paragraph 6 rather than at the beginning. By this means the writer calls attention to the words "emotionally abused" individuals and prepares for the fuller discussion of emotional abuse in the next paragraph.

4

¶5 In the long run, physical abuse may also lead to attitudinal or behavioral problems, as in the case of a twelve year old, seventh grade classmate of my younger sister Valerie. In a recent personal interview, Valerie informed me that in 1983 this young adolescent was beaten with a broom handle, which left his arms red, scraped, and bruised. The year before, his mother had burned him with an iron. Thus far, he has suffered no debilitating injuries, but each instance of abuse provokes him to misbehave at school by throwing temper tantrums or refusing to obey his teacher--actions that bring additional parental punishment and start the cycle all over again.

¶6 When children have caring parents and a warm home environment, they will most likely become parents their children will love also. Exactly the opposite is true of children living in homes where love is seldom or never shared (Rogers 57). Robert Bates aptly characterizes these children as "emotionally abused" individuals who "feel unwanted, angry, and bad" (53).

¶7 Emotional abuse includes not providing attention, normal living opportunities, and necessary supervision (Rogers 48). People who abuse children in this way constantly belittle them by calling them names, saying "I hate you," or telling them they were never wanted. Abuse such as this often causes

Use and Documentation of Sources

In paragraphs 8 and 9, the writer continues to vary the ways in which she uses information from her notes. The wording of the sources paraphrased in the second sentence of paragraph 8, for example, is the same as the phrasing on the respective note cards. The two short quotations imbedded in the last sentence of paragraph 9, on the other hand, are taken from different sections of the long quotation on the note card below:

> Effects of sexual abuse on psychology and personality of victim
>
> Burgess and Groth p. 79
>
> "Even a physically mature child is not mature enough emotionally to cope with sexual demands by an adult. The child can easily be taken advantage of by an adult and although the child may agree to and cooperate with the sexual activity, the child does so without awareness or appreciation of the impact such activity may have on his or her subsequent psychological development. That is, his personality formation, attitudes and values, identity issues and the like."

Content and Organization

Paragraphs 8 and 9 take up the issue of sexual abuse—the third main type of child abuse (section III, C of the outline). Note the clarity of such transitional elements as the following:

Another serious form of child abuse is. . . .
More commonplace are. . . .
The long-range effects of sexual molestation are. . . .
It may also interfere with. . . .

children to see themselves as worthless. Furthermore, most children suffering from emotional abuse see their situation as hopeless because they know they cannot fight back and win (Rogers 48). Emotionally abused children can be helped, but in most cases they must be placed in foster homes while the parents undergo counseling (Bates 53).

¶8 Another serious form of child abuse is sexual exploitation or assault. Because the offender is usually a close relative of the child, many families are reluctant to report such cases ("The Hard Case" 32), but according to one source, sexual abuse may occur even more frequently than physical abuse (James 39). In fact, the two are difficult to distinguish in cases involving sexual assault in which "the offender may directly confront the child with sexual demands in the context of verbal threats, . . . intimidation with a weapon, . . . or direct physical assault" (Burgess and Groth 81). More commonplace are non-violent incidents of abuse, which usually involve "exhibition of sexual organs, genital and nongenital petting or fondling, mouth-genital contacts, and attempted penetration without force" (Bates 51).

¶9 The long-range effects of sexual molestation are difficult to assess because little data is currently available (Bates 51), but many authorities agree that such abuse may adversely affect children's sense of self-confidence and

Use and Documentation of Sources

In paragraphs 10 and 11, the writer relies chiefly on case studies to develop ideas. First she relates the story of a child who died as a result of parental neglect. Then she quotes from a published interview the words of a woman who had survived the various forms of abuse inflicted upon her as a child but carried the emotional scars of those experiences into her adult life.

Content and Organization

Paragraph 10, which deals with child neglect (section III, D of the outline), completes the analysis of the four different types of child abuse and their effects on the victim.

Neglect is also mentioned at the beginning of paragraph 11; however, the writer's purpose here is not to continue the discussion of this particular form of child abuse but to link neglect with the three forms of abuse discussed earlier and at the same time prepare for the conclusion.

self-respect. It may also interfere with what Ann Burgess and Nicholas Groth refer to as the "subsequent phychological development" of the victims, their "personality formation, attitudes and values, identity issues, and the like" (79).

¶10 More difficult to document are the effects of neglect, the fourth main type of child abuse. Unlike physical, emotional, or sexual abuse, child neglect is, in the words of Dale Rogers, a "passive negative treatment characterized by a parent or custodian's lack of care and interest, and includes not feeding, not clothing, not looking after, not nurturing" (41). Therefore, only the most extreme cases are likely to be publicized. An especially graphic example of neglect is the case in which a mother left her young child unattended in a car with all the windows closed. She had intended to be gone for only a short time, but she was delayed, and by the time she returned, the child had died from the extreme heat (Walters 12). Usually, however, neglect has a more subtle influence, affecting not just the child's physical well-being, but also his or her ability to function normally in later life.

¶11 In this sense, neglected children are much like those who have been subjected to other types of abuse. All of them must seek comfort, love, and acceptance in the outside world, but they are poorly equipped to make this transition,

Use and Documentation of Sources

Rather than drawing information from external sources at this crucial point in her essay, Sarah expresses her own view about the information she has presented. Therefore, no quotation marks or parenthetical references are needed.

Content and Organization

The conclusion accomplishes three things: it re-emphasizes the magnitude and complexity of the problem, it sums up what the writer learned from her analysis of the effects of different types of child abuse, and it in effect extends the boundaries of the essay by leaving the reader with the thought that child abuse is a self-perpetuating cycle.

7

as Janice Zemdegs convincingly demonstrates in an essay entitled "Outrage: What It Feels Like to be an Abused Child." Especially informative are the words of the young woman whose experiences are the focus of Zemdeg's study.

> I remember when I finally left home to attend nursing school . . . my main purpose in life was to be released from the war mentally and physically intact. . . . What I never realized was I didn't know how to cope in a normal environment. (104)

¶12 Child abuse, then, is a complex and far-reaching problem. Abused children obviously have a disadvantage in life from the beginning, for the physical and psychological pain they experience in their childhood remains in their memories. It blights their adult lives and dooms many of them to continue the destructive cycle in which the abused child of one generation becomes the abusive parent of the next.

Bibliography

The format for the works cited list on the opposite page follows the conventions discussed in Chapter **53** and **55d**.

1. Pages are numbered consecutively with the text, and the number of each page is placed in the upper right corner.
2. The title **Works Cited** is centered one inch from the top of the page, with a double space between the title and the first entry.
3. Each entry starts at the left margin. If more than one line is necessary, the second line and any additional lines are indented five spaces.
4. Double spacing is used between entries and within entries of two or more lines.
5. Works are alphabetized by author's last name except under the following circumstances:
   a. If more than one work by the same author is cited, the author's name is given only in the first entry. In subsequent entries, three unspaced hyphens take the place of the name (see the references to Fontana's *The Maltreated Child* and *Somewhere a Child Is Crying* on the opposite page). Note, too, that such works are listed in alphabetical sequence by title.
   b. If the author's name is not given, the entry should be alphabetized by title.
   c. The works cited on the opposite page are modeled on the sample entries in Chapter **53**. The only variation from that format occurs in the entries for the five essays by Bates, Burgess and Groth, de Lissovoy, Friedman and D'Agostino, and Zemdegs, all of which were published in *The Maltreatment of the School-Aged Child*, edited by Richard Volpe, Margot Breton, and Judith Mitton. To avoid repeating the publication information from the essay collection six times, the writer includes a complete bibliographical entry for this work (see the entry for Volpe) and keys each of the separate essay entries to it through an abbreviated reference.

8

Works Cited

"Abused Child." Today's Education. Jan. 1974: 40-42.

"Authorities Face Up to the Child-Abuse Problem." U.S. News. 3 May 1976: 83-84.

Bates, Robert. "Child Abuse and Neglect: A Medical Priority." Volpe, Breton, and Mitton 45-57.

Burgess, Ann W., and Nicholas Groth. "Sexual Victimization of Children." Volpe, Breton, and Mitton 79-89.

Chase, Naomi. A Child is Being Beaten. New York: Holt, 1975.

de Lissovoy, Vladimir. "The Behavioral and Ecological Syndrome of the High-Risk Child." Volpe, Breton, and Mitton 11-17.

Elmer, Elizabeth. Children in Jeopardy: A Study of Abused Minors and Their Families. Pittsburgh: U of Pittsburgh P, 1967.

Fontana, Vincent. The Maltreated Child: The Maltreatment Syndrome in Children. 2nd ed. Springfield: Thomas, 1971.

---. Somewhere a Child Is Crying: Maltreatment Causes and Prevention. New York: Macmillan, 1973.

Friedman, Robert M., and Paul D'Agostino. "The Effects of Schools upon Families: Toward a More Supportive Relationship." Volpe, Breton, and Mitton 27-41.

Garbarino, James, and S. Holly Stocking. "The Social Context of Child Maltreatment." In Protecting Children from Abuse and Neglect: Developing and Maintaining Effective Support Systems for Families. Eds. James Garbarino, et al. San Francisco: Jossey, 1980.

Note that when only one work in a collection is cited, full publication data for both the work cited and the collection are included in the same entry (see the citation for Steele and Pollock on the opposite page).

9

"The Hard Case." Newsweek. 16 July 1973: 32.

James, Howard. The Little Victims: How America Treats Its Children. New York: McKay, 1975.

Poindexter, Valerie. Personal interview. 5 Apr. 1984.

Rogers, Dale E. Hear the Children Crying. Old Tappan: Revell, 1978.

Steele, Brandt F. "Working with Abusive Parents: A Psychiatrist's View." Children Today. May-June 1975: 3.

Steele, Brandt F., and Carl B. Pollock. "A Psychiatric Study of Parents Who Abuse Infants and Small Children." In The Battered Child. Eds. Ray E. Helfer and C. Henry Kempe. 2nd ed. Chicago: U of Chicago P, 1974.

Volpe, Richard, Margo Breton, and Judith Mitton, eds. The Maltreatment of the School-Aged Child. Lexington: Heath, 1980.

Walters, David R. Physical and Sexual Abuse of Children: Causes and Treatment. Bloomington: Indiana UP, 1975.

Zemdegs, Janice. "Outraged: What It Feels Like to Be an Abused Child." Volpe, Breton, and Mitton 91-107.

Glossary of Usage

a, an Use **a** as an article before words beginning with consonant sounds, and use **an** before words beginning with vowel sounds.

a field
an opener

Note: **a** unit (**u** sounding as consonant **y**)
an honest person (**h** being silent)
a historian (**h** pronounced)

accept, except The verb **accept** means "to receive"; the verb **except** means "to leave out." The preposition **except** means "other than."

The club **accepted** almost everyone who applied.
It **excepted** only people too young to purchase alcoholic beverages.
No one objected **except** a few young people.

affect, effect The verb **affect** usually means "to influence"; the verb **effect** means "to cause" or "to bring about." The noun **effect** means "a result."

The drought has **affected** the corn crop.
The lobbyists could not **effect** a change in the administration's farm policy.
An **effect** of the drought has been increased prices for food.

aggravate, irritate **Aggravate** means "to make worse," and **irritate** means "to make uncomfortable" or "to annoy." In informal use the two words are sometimes synonymous.

My poison ivy was **aggravated** by sunburn.
Poison ivy causes an **irritating** rash.

agree to, agree with, agree on To **agree to** means "to consent to" something; to **agree with** means "to be in accord with" someone; to **agree on** means "to decide by mutual consent."

The club members **agreed to** a five dollar assessment.
I **agreed with** the majority of the members.
The committee **agreed on** a course of action.

all ready, already **All ready** means "prepared." **Already** means "by this time" or "before now."

Fortunately the musicians were **all ready** to take their places, for the audience was **already** restless.

all right In formal writing use **all right** to mean "wholly correct" or "satisfactory," but not "acceptably."

FORMAL: The meal was **all right,** but the service was poor.
INFORMAL: Jerry may be sloppy but he can cook **all right**.

Alright is a misspelling.

all together, altogether **All together** means "collectively" or "in a group." **Altogether** means "entirely."

The campers emerged **all together** from the woods; they were **altogether** tired and discouraged.

allusion, illusion An **allusion** is "an indirect reference." An **illusion** is a "false impression."

Shelley's poem "Adonais" has many **allusions** to classical Greek culture.
The defeated team realized that their invincibility was an **illusion**.

almost, most **Almost** means "nearly." **Most** means "the greatest part." The two are sometimes confused.

Insects have infested **almost** (not **most**) the entire supply of grian.
Insects have infested **most** of the grain.

among, between **Among** refers to a relationship involving three or more, whereas **between** refers to a relationship of two.

We found great optimism **among** the President's economic advisors.
For dessert you may choose **between** pie and custard.

amount, number **Amount** usually refers to an uncountable quantity. **Number** refers to a countable quantity.

In a small **amount** of dirt you will find a great **number** of microorganisms.

and/or This construction can be appropriate in legal documents, but it is a needless complication in most other contexts.

anyone, any one **Anyone,** like **anybody** and **everyone,** is an indefinite pronoun. **Any one** is the pronoun **one** modified by the adjective **any**.

As **anyone** can tell, **any one** of these books would take a long time to read.

as, because To avoid confusion, do not use **as** to mean "because."

We used a spray painter **because** (not **as**) a brush would have taken too long.

as, like In formal usage **as** may be a conjunction, but **like** may not be a conjunction.

You should do **as** (not **like**) the instructions direct.

assure, ensure, insure **Assure** means "to state confidently" or "to promise." **Ensure** means "to guarantee." **Insure** is sometimes used synonymously with **ensure**, but **insure** also means "to contract for protection" against loss.

The director of parks and recreation **assured** us the old playground would be popular again.
The renovations and new equipment **ensured** that children would enjoy themselves.

In the unlikely event that someone will get hurt, the city has **insured** the parks for $100,000 against liability.

awful, awfully In formal usage **awful** means "awe inspiring" or "terrifying." Less formally it is used to mean "bad." **Awful** and **awfully** as substitutes for "very" are informal and trite.

He was **very** (not **awfully**) upset.

a while, awhile The phrase **a while** is an article plus a noun naming "a short time." **Awhile** is an adverb meaning "for a short time."

They rested **awhile**. (**awhile** modifying **rested**)
They rested for **a while**. (**a while** object of preposition **for**)

bad, badly **Bad** is an adjective; **badly** is an adverb. Avoid confusing their grammatical roles.

The patient felt **bad**. (**bad** a subject complement)
The patient had cut himself **badly**. (**badly** modifying **cut**)

being as, being that Avoid these wordy, awkward substitutes for "because."

Because (not **being that**) Barry is claustrophobic, he would rather climb stairs than ride in an elevator.

beside, besides Both words are prepositions; **beside** means "next to," and **besides** means "except for." **Besides** is also a conjunctive adverb meaning "moreover" or "in addition."

The young prodigy had few good traits **besides** musical ability.
Three old cars were rusting **beside** the shack.
We should leave the party now. Most of our friends have left, and **besides**, the band will stop playing in ten minutes.

burst, bust **Burst** means "to come apart suddenly." Its past participle is **burst** (not **bursted**). **Bust** and **busted** are non-standard.

can, may In formal prose **can** denotes ability, and **may** denotes permission. In informal use, **can** denotes permission also.

The child **can** ride a bicycle, but he **may** not ride over two blocks from his home.

capital, capitol **Capital** means "chief" or "primary," or the city that is the seat of a government. **Capitol** refers to a building that houses a legislature.

In our nation's **capital**, Washington, DC, the legislature meets in the **Capitol** building.

center around This is an illogical phrase; use **center on** instead.

The speech **centered on** the theme of civic responsibility.

climactic, climatic **Climactic** is the adjective for "climax" and refers to "a culminating moment" or "turning point." **Climatic** is the adjective for "climate" and refers to the weather.

The play's **climactic** moment came in the second act.
Some meteorologists specialize in studying the **climatic** conditions that give birth to tornadoes.

compare to, compare with Use **compare to** to emphasize similarities (often of a figurative nature) and use **compare with** to emphasize differences or to discuss similarities and differences.

One critic **compared** the rock group's music **to** a cat fight.
Compared with professional tennis, our club's annual tournament is of little interest to the public.

complement, compliment The verb **complement** means "to add to" or "to bring to perfection"; the noun **complement** means "that which brings to perfection" or "the quantity needed to complete or improve."

The model's manner **complemented** her appearance on the stage.
The architecture was a **complement** to the landscape.

The verb **compliment** means "to praise"; the noun **compliment** means "an act of praise."

The teacher **complimented** his students on their achievement.
We got many **compliments** on our successful performance.

comprise, compose **Comprise** means "to include" or "to consist of." **Compose** means "to form" or "to make up."

The trailer **comprises** two bedrooms, a kitchen, a living room, and two bathrooms.
The trailer is **composed of** (not **comprised of**) five rooms.

continual, continuous **Continual** means "happening again and again." **Continuous** means "occurring constantly without break."

In the British House of Commons, speakers are **continually** interrupted by the members.
The police siren sounded **continuously** for fifteen minutes.

criterion, criteria **Criterion** is singular; **criteria** is plural.

There are many **criteria** for success, but perhaps the simplest **criterion** is money in the bank.

datum, data In formal usages **datum** is singular, **data** is plural. "Result," "fact," or "piece of information" are commonly used instead of the singular **datum**.

The **data** from the public opinion poll **are** interesting but not surprising.
One fact from the survey stands out.

differ **Differ from** means "be unlike." **Differ with** means "disagree with."

Sue **differs from** most students because she continually **differs with** her professors.

different from, different than Generally use **different from** instead of **different than**.

Barry's reasons for liking Allison were **different from** mine.

Increasingly, however, writers are choosing **different than** as less wordy when a clause follows.

The outcome of the play was **different than** I remember.
The outcome of the play was **different from** the one I remembered.

discreet, discrete **Discreet** means "cautious," "tactful," or "unobstrusive." **Discrete** means "separate," "distinct."

At the divorce hearing neither spouse was **discreet** in describing the other's behavior.
The painting was composed of thousands of **discrete** colored dots.

disinterested, uninterested **Disinterested** means "unbiased." **Uninterested** means "not interested" or "feeling no concern."

In Olympic competition, gymnasts hope the judges will be **disinterested**, whatever the nationalities of the competitors.
Erwin remained **uninterested** throughout the irrelevant speech.

due to This phrase is most appropriate when used as an adjective meaning "attributable to" rather than as a preposition meaning "because of." **Due to**, therefore, most often follows a form of the verb "to be."

The team's losing streak is **due to** the coach's pending resignation.
The team is losing **because of** the coach's indifference.

each and every This is a wordy phrase that usually fails to achieve the emphasis a writer wishes. Use **each** or **every**, but not both.

The promoter counted **every** person who entered the stadium.

enthuse This verb is not as appropriate in formal usage as its corresponding noun, adjective, or adverb.

Marty was **enthusiastic** (not **enthused**) about her upcoming vacation.
She spoke **enthusiastically** (not **She enthused**) about her plans.

especially, specially **Especially** means "mainly" or "to an unusual degree." **Specially** means "for a particular reason."

The crew was **especially** pleased with the new sail, which had been **specially** made for their boat.

etc. **Etc.** is an abbreviation for the Latin phrase **et cetera**, meaning "and others" or "and so forth." Avoid using it in formal writing. In informal writing **etc.** can be appropriate at the end of a list to indicate that only unimportant items remain to be listed.

Like their predecessors, this year's incoming freshmen report that they have come to college to get an education, to find a spouse, to prepare for a lucrative vocation, **and so forth**.
Backpackers depend on lightweight provisions: dried meat, freeze-dried vegetables, dried cereal, nuts, **etc.**

every day, everyday **Every day** is an adverb phrase. **Everyday** is an adjective.

Every day the factory whistle blew at noon.
Dessert was not an **everyday** treat for our family.

every one, everyone In the phrase **every one, every** modifies the pronoun **one**; **every one** means "each individual" and usually precedes **of**. **Everyone** (like **everybody**) is an indefinite pronoun.

Every one of the musicians had dyed his hair on unnatural color.
Everyone was shocked at their appearance.

farther, further These words are sometimes used as synonyms, but in formal usage **farther** refers to distance in space, and **further** refers to other types of extent.

The cyclists had **farther** to go than they thought.
His behavior got him **further** into trouble.

fewer, less **Fewer** refers to countable quantities. **Less** refers to degrees or amounts in general.

Frieda has **fewer** bad habits than Mark, but he has **less** conceit than she.

finalize Avoid this pretentious verb.

We will **finish** (not **finalize**) the plan as soon as we have all the information we need.

flaunt, flout To **flaunt** is "to show off." To **flout** is "to defy or scorn."

The peacock **flaunts** his exotic tail.
The drunk driver **flouted** every rule of the road.

formally, former, formerly **Formally** means "in a formal way." **Former** as a noun denotes the first of two persons or things named previously. **Formerly** means "at a previous time."

Although you have seen Ted before, I will **formally** introduce you at the party tonight.
Formerly we were close friends, but now we have little to do with each other.
The carpenter and the plumber both finished at the same time, but only the **former** remained to clean up the litter.

got Avoid using **have got** for "have" in formal prose.

I **have** (not I **have got**) no money at all.

great Use "excellent" or "fine" instead of the informal "great."

It has been a **fine** day.

good, well **Good** is an adjective and should not serve in place of the adverb **well**.

The young violinist played very **well** (not **good**).

hanged, hung As the past tense of **hang, hanged** means "executed" and **hung** means "suspended."

The war criminals were **hanged**.
Original paintings were **hung** in every room of the house.

have, of **Have** can be an auxiliary verb, but **of** should never be used as a verb.

We **should have** (not **should of**) left before now to avoid the crowd.

herself, himself, myself, ourselves, yourself These are reflexive pronouns and should not be substituted for **her, him, me, us,** and **you**. Intensive constructions use both the personal pronoun and the reflexive pronoun: **she, herself**.

You (not **Yourself**) can repair this car.
The only person who can repair this car is **you, yourself**.

hopefully In informal usage **hopefully** can mean "I (or we) hope that." Strict formal usage requires **hopefully** to modify a verb and to mean "in a hopeful manner."

The politician spoke **hopefully** about the future.
We hope (not **Hopefully**) it will not rain tomorrow.

imply, infer **Imply** means "to hint" or "to suggest." **Infer** means "to draw a conclusion."

In her welcoming speech, the club president **implied** that membership would be more expensive than the new members had been led to believe.
The new members **inferred** that belonging to the club would be more expensive than they had thought.

in, into **In** refers to position, condition, or direction. **Into** refers to movement or change. **Into** meaning "interested in" or "involved in" is not suitable for formal prose.

The dog is **in** his house.
He is **in** a bad mood.

Hastily the cook dumped dough **into** a baking pan and shoved the pan **into** the oven.
My parents are **interested in** (not **into**) meditation.

inside, outside Use **inside** and **outside** without the word **of**.

Our whole family was **outside** (not **outside of**) the house during the thunderstorm.

irregardless **Irregardless** is a double negative and is nonstandard. Use **regardless**.

Regardless of the weather, the workers will continue building the pipeline.

is when, is where Avoid using these inaccurate phrases in definitions.

Courage is the ability to control fear in the face of danger. (not Courage **is when** a person controls fear in the face of danger.)

its, it's **Its** is the possessive form of **it,** just as **his** is the possessive form of **he. It's** is a contraction meaning **it is** or **it has**, just as **he's** is a contraction meaning **he is** or **he has**.

The dog broke **its** leash.
It's not the type of dog I want.

kind of, sort of **Kind of** and **sort of** are informal for "rather" and "somewhat."

She appeared to be **rather** (not **kind of**) interested in the play, but later she confessed that she had been thoroughly bored.

leave, let **Leave** means "depart" and **let** means "permit." They are synonymous when used with **alone**.

If this cold weather lasts, even the winter birds will **leave**.
Let (not **leave**) the child sit where he wants.
Leave (or **let**) her alone.

liable, likely In formal usage, **likely** refers to probability, and **liable** refers to legal obligation or to responsibility.

If you forget your raincoat, you're **likely** to get wet.
A law suit might establish that you are **liable** for damages.

lie, lay **Lie** (**lay, lain**) means "to recline." **Lay** (**laid, laid**) means "to place." **Lie** (**lied, lied**) means "to say something untrue." To help your memory, think of the following sentence as meaning that the speaker is not going to recline but is going to put feathers (down) on the sofa: "I am going to **lay down** on the sofa."

Most of my friends **lie** (not **lay**) in the sun for hours at a time.
Only once have I **lain** (not **laid**) in the sun so long.
Lay your beach towel where our friends have **laid** theirs.

literally In formal usage, **literally** means "word for word" or "in actuality." Avoid using it as an intensifier to mean "virtually" or "extremely."

The marathon runners were **almost** (not **literally**) dying from the heat.

lots **Lots** and **lots of** are informal terms for **a great deal of, many,** and **much**.

He had **many** (not **lots of**) opportunities to win.

may be, maybe **May be** is a verb phrase. **Maybe** is an adverb meaning "perhaps."

The coach **may be** depressed after losing the game. **Maybe** we can cheer her up by taking her out to dinner.

neat In formal usage, avoid using **neat** to mean "pleasing" or "good."

Our treasurer had a **good** (not **neat**) idea for saving money.

nice **Nice** is an overworked adjective that is less informative than terms such as "appealing," "pleasant," and "polite."

Our waiter seemed **polite** (not **nice**) but shy.

nowhere near **Nowhere near** is informal for **not nearly**.

Although basketball is **not nearly** (not **nowhere near**) as violent as football, some people consider it should, like football, be classified as a contact sport.

off of Formal usage requires **off** or **from** rather than **off of**.

The police took several weapons **from** (not **off of**) the prisoners.

on account of In formal usage, **because** is more appropriate.

They lost the contract **because** (not **on account of**) the competing firm promised to lower expenses.

ourselves **Ourselves** refers to two or more persons. **Ourself** is used only in the special context of a king, queen, or Pope speaking in the first person singular.

Barry and I found **ourselves** suddenly in pitch dark.
"Let the traitors be brought before **ourself**," commanded Queen Elizabeth.

persecute, prosecute **Persecute** means to "oppress" or "harass." **Prosecute** most commonly means to "carry out legal proceedings against."

Minorities are often **persecuted**.
The attorney general **prosecuted** everyone who had tried to bribe the police officers.

plus The preposition **plus** means "in addition to" or "increased by." Avoid using it as a conjunction meaning "furthermore."

Reimbursement for travel includes cost of an airline ticket **plus** cost of transportation from the airport.
The consultants were late; **furthermore** (not **plus**), they were unprepared.

precede, proceed **Precede** means "to come before." **Proceed** means "to go on" or "advance."

The senior class officers **preceded** their classmates into the auditorium.
The graduating class **proceeded** to their seats in single file.

principal, principle The noun **principal** refers to a school's chief administrator or to an amount of money. The adjective **principal** means "first in importance." The noun **principle** means a "fundamental law" or "rule."

The **principal** disciplined those students who had participated in the food fight.
The **principal** reason for the committee's inaction was the indifference of its members.
The Magna Carta is founded on the **principle** that no individual is above the law.

prior to **Before** is less wordy.

We understood our minister's philosophy **before** (not **prior to**) his first sermon to us.

raise, rise **Raise** is a transitive verb meaning "to cause to be elevated." **Rise** is an intransitive verb meaning "to go up."

Many college students **raise** their grade point average in their junior and senior years.
Members of the press corps **rise** when the President enters a press conference.

real, really **Real** is an adjective meaning "actual" or "authentic." **Really** is an adverb meaning "in reality" or "actually." In formal usage, avoid using **real** as an adverb.

One thief brandished a **real** gun while the other held a toy pistol.
The customers were **really** (not **real**) afraid.

reason is that (because) Writing "the reason is because" is redundant. Write "the reason is that . . ." or "because" by itself.

The **reason** for the German failure to repulse the Allied invasion

was that (not **because**) the Germans could not concentrate their forces.
The Germans failed to repulse the Allied invasion **because** they could not concentrate their forces.

in reference to, in regard to, relative to, with respect to All these terms are wordy constructions for "about," "concerning," or "on."

We have corresponded **about** (not **relative to**) an advertising program.

sensual, sensuous Both are adjectives meaning "pertaining to the senses," but **sensual** often suggests sexuality.

The dancer aroused the audience with suggestive, **sensual** movements.
The orchestra moved the audience with its **sensuous** music.

set, sit **Set** is a transitive verb meaning "to place." **Sit** is an intransitive verb meaning "to take a seat."

Set your tray on the floor.
Yesterday we **set** all our house plants outside.
Sit down and relax.
Yesterday we **sat** by the stream.

shall, will Modern usage requires little distinction between these two verbs. **Shall** is sometimes used to communicate determination. **Shall** is usually used in questions that serve as invitations.

Our foe **shall** not succeed.
Shall we try one more time?

sometime, sometimes The adverb **sometime** means "at an unknown time." The adverb **sometimes** means "occasionally."

The economists hope their prediction will come true **sometime** soon.
Sometimes the economy responds to government initiatives.

such a To avoid vagueness, do not use **such a** as an intensifier unless it is followed by a subordinate clause beginning with **that**.

We had **such a** good time at the amusement park **that** we plan to return next year. (not We had **such a** good time!)

supposed to, used to Always retain the **d**.

He use**d** to attend church regularly.
Mary was suppose**d** to bring the Frisbee.

sure **Sure** is an adjective meaning "certain" or "reliable." It is nonstandard when it is used as an adverb.

To play shortstop you will need **sure** hands.
The laser **certainly** (not **sure**) has become a versatile device.

than, then Do not confuse the conjunction **than** with the adverb **then**.

The brown bear is larger **than** (not **then**) the black bear.
First the male bear slouched into the clearing: **then** came the female followed by her cubs.

that, which, who In strict formal usage, **that** serves in restrictive clauses, and **which** serves in non-restrictive clauses. Use **that** and **which** to refer to things and **who** to refer to humans.

Suicide is a response **that** only the most desperate people make.
Suicide, **which** is a desperate act, occurs most often during bad economic times.
The person **who** saved the mayor's life remained anonymous.

their, there, they're **Their** is a possessive pronoun. **There** is an adverb or expletive. **They're** is a contraction of "they are."

We found a site where the ancient Indians had built **their** campfires.
It will be very expensive to go **there**.
They're unhappy because they don't have enough money.

try and Formal usage requires **try to** rather than **try and**.

Often I **try to** imagine the future.

unique **Unique** means "one and only" or "unlike any other." Avoid the informal meaning of "remarkable" or "strange." Avoid modifying it with "very" or "most" as if there were degrees of uniqueness.

Boy George's appearance is **unique** (not **very unique**).
Our garden is **strikingly** (not **uniquely**) colorful in the spring.

utilize **Utilize** is often a pretentious substitute for **use**.

Use (not **utilize**) your common sense.

very This word is not needed as often as it is used. Omitting it lets an adjective speak for itself.

The dog was friendly and eager to please, but even its owners had to admit it was **ugly** (not **very ugly**).

wait for, wait on To **wait for** is "to remain while expecting" something. To **wait on** is "to serve."

If you arrive before 7:00 a.m., you will have to **wait for** the store to open.
The short-order cook could **wait on** three people at the same time.

who's, whose **Who's** is a contraction meaning **who is** or **who has**; **whose** is the possessive form of **who**.

She's a comedian **who's** funny and serious at the same time.
The voters will never approve of a candidate **whose** policies are so radical.

Glossary of Grammatical Terms

absolute phrase A noun (or pronoun) and a participle that modify an entire clause.

The snow having melted, we found the landscape had lost all its charm.

active voice See **voice.**

adjective A word that modifies a noun or pronoun.

We sold that **rickety old** car.

Most adjectives can indicate degree:

COMPARATIVE DEGREE: old**er,** health**ier,** grand**er**
SUPERLATIVE DEGREE: old**est,** health**iest,** grand**est**

adjective clause See **subordinate clause.**

adjective phrase An infinitive phrase, a participial phrase, or a prepositional phrase that modifies a noun.

The plate **of spaghetti** lay untouched before the nervous child.

adverb A word that modifies a verb, an adjective, or another adverb.

We dressed **quickly**.

adverb clause See **subordinate clause.**

adverb phrase A phrase (usually an infinitive or participial phrase) that modifies a verb, an adjective, or another adverb.

The assistant manager worked **behind the service counter**.

antecedent The word or words to which a pronoun refers.

The **consultant** was so confident, **she** predicted that if **her** recommendations were followed, the company's profits would increase twenty percent. (**Consultant** is the *antecedent* of **she** and **her**.)

appositive A noun or noun phrase that renames or further identifies the noun or pronoun it follows.

Dr. Wilson, **the superintendent of schools**, is an excellent golfer.

article The noun-marking words **a** and **an**, which are *indefinite articles*, and **the**, which is the *definite article*. See **determiner**.

auxiliary verb See **helping verb**.

case The form nouns and pronouns take to help indicate a role in the sentence. Pronouns take a *subjective* form and an *objective* form, but nouns have the same form whether they are subjects or objects.

She (*subjective*) saw **him** (*objective*).

Nouns and pronouns take a *possessive* case form.

Mary's (*possessive noun*) pleasure is **your** (*possessive pronoun*) pain.

clause A group of words comprising a subject and a predicate. See **independent clause** and **subordinate clause**.

collective noun A noun that names a group (**team, club, faculty**).

comparative degree See **adjective**.

complement A word or phrase that completes the predicate. *Subject complements* follow linking verbs and are also known as *predicate nouns* or *predicate adjectives*.

For several years, Norman was a **carpenter** (*predicate noun*).
The mayor was **tired** (*predicate adjective*).

Object complements are nouns or adjectives that follow and identify or modify a direct object.

We named our cat **Figaro**.
The jury found the defendant **guilty**.

See also **direct object** and **indirect object**.

complex sentence A sentence containing one independent clause and one or more subordinate clauses.

Although Stonehenge and other ancient stone structures may have been used as astronomical observatories (*subordinate clause*), no one can be sure (*independent clause*).

compound sentence A sentence composed of two or more independent clauses.

Thunder sounded faintly, so we turned the boat homeward. (two independent clauses joined by coordinating conjunction **so**)

compound-complex sentence A sentence containing two or more independent clauses and at least one subordinate clause.

While the customers fidgeted in their seats (*subordinate clause*), two violinists played their way through the restaurant (*independent clause*), and the manager went from table to table introducing himself (*independent clause*).

conjunction A word or word pair used to link elements within a sentence. See **coordinating conjunction, subordinating conjunction, conjunctive adverb,** and **correlative conjunction**.

conjunctive adverb An adverb that joins two independent clauses. Some conjunctive adverbs are **besides, consequently, however, nevertheless, therefore**.

There was a substantial amount of money in my account; **nevertheless**, the bank teller was reluctant to cash my check.

coordinating conjunction A word used to link words, phrases, and clauses of equivalent grammatical function. The coordinating conjunctions are **and, but, for, nor, or, so, yet**.

During the drought the crops wilted **and** died. (two verbs linked)
The book was a best seller, **but** the author did not want to make a movie of it. (two independent clauses linked)

correlative conjunction A pair of words or phrases used to link words, phrases, and clauses of equivalent grammatical function. Common correlative conjunctions are **both . . . and, either . . . or, not only . . . but also**.

Both the puppy **and** its mother had to be wormed.
Either they go **or** I go.

demonstrative pronoun A pronoun that points out. The demonstrative pronouns are **that, those; this, these**.

dependent clause See **subordinate clause**.

determiner A word that marks a noun. Determiners include articles, demonstrative pronouns, and possessive pronouns.

direct object The word or words naming what a transitive verb acts upon.

The children invented **a new game**.

elliptical constructions Clauses that omit words which can be understood from the context.

The retired pilot was convinced that he could still fly an airplane as well as any younger pilot (*could fly an airplane*).

expletive A construction in which a clause begins with **it** or **there** and a form of **be**.

It was a mistake to leave the car's motor running.
There are few if any ways to succeed in business without taking risks.

gender The classification of nouns and pronouns as *mascu-*

line (**workman, he**), *feminine* (**actress, she**), and *neuter* (**theater, it**).

gerund The present participle (**-ing**) form of the verb used as a noun.

Sally believes that **reading** is more important than **sleeping**.

A *gerund phrase* is a gerund, its object, and any modifiers:

Losing the game so quickly bothered the players.

helping verb A verb used to complete a main verb: **be, can, do, has, have, may, must, ought,** etc.

My sister **has** kept over twenty nameless dogs.

idiom A customary expression that is figurative or that does not follow conventional patterns.

The customer **caught the waiter's eye**.
Bear in mind that we have only an hour of daylight left.

imperative See **mood**.

indefinite pronoun A pronoun that does not refer to a definite person or thing: **any, each, everyone, neither,** etc.

independent clause A group of words comprising a subject and a predicate that can be punctuated as a sentence or can be combined with other clauses.

The young comedian laughed uproariously, but **the audience remained impassive**. (two independent clauses joined by the coordinating conjunction **but**)

indicative See **mood**.

indirect object The word or words that name what indirectly receives the action of a transitive verb, usually a verb indicating a transfer.

Donna gave **her spouse** (*indirect object*) a **quick kiss** (*direct object*).

infinitive The uninflected form of the verb (listed first in the dictionary) that takes the infinitive marker **to: to be, to help, to propose**.
An *infinitive phrase* is an infinitive, an object, and any modifiers.

Infinitive phrases serve as nouns, adjectives, and adverbs.

Congress voted **to adjourn early**. (noun phrase as direct object)

inflection An alteration to a word to communicate such ideas as time, case, or degree. The past tense inflection of **help** is **helped**. The objective case inflection of **he** is **him**. The comparative inflection of **happy** is **happier**.

intensifier A modifier that indicates the degree of an adjective or adverb (**so** foolish, **rather** indignant, **very** quickly).

interjection A grammatically independent word or phrase that expresses an exclamation or pure emotion: **Ah! Oh! Ouch! Please,** etc.

interrogative pronoun A pronoun used in asking a question.

Whose coat is this?
What is the answer to our question?

irregular verb See **verb**.

linking verb See **verb**.

modifier A word, phrase, or clause that describes another word, phrase, or clause. Adjectives, adverbs, and absolute phrases are modifiers, as are phrases and clauses used as adjectives and adverbs.

mood A form taken by a verb to indicate the writer's perspective on the subject matter. The *indicative mood* is the most common form and is used in statements expressing actual or very probable circumstances.

Our school **uses** several means to identify gifted students.

The *imperative mood* is the form of commands.

Use the stairs in case of fire in a hotel.

The *subjunctive mood* is the form used to express conditions that are hypothetical, recommended, or contrary to fact.

I wish that I **were** a year older!
A state law mandates that every driver **use** seat belts.

nominal A noun or any other word or word group that can serve as a noun.

To ask for help (*infinitive phrase*) is no disgrace.
Gaining the poet's permission (*gerund phrase*) to quote from her latest book was a long and frustrating task.
That he had bought a new suit did not mean **that he would dress up more often**. (two *subordinate clauses*)

nominative case Another term for *subjective case*; see **case**.

nonrestrictive modifier A word, phrase, or clause that does not limit the identity or meaning of what it modifies. Commas usually set off nonrestrictive modifiers. (Compare to **restrictive modifier**.)

Germaine, **who has no talent for drawing**, was given the task of designing the decorations.

noun A word that names. Most nouns can be made plural, usually by adding **-s** or **-es** (**parts, classes**). Nouns can also indicate possession, usually by adding **-'s** in the singular and **-s'** in the plural (the **day's** end, the **horses'** food). Nouns can serve as subjects, objects, and complements in sentences. A *proper noun* names a specific person or place: **Barry, Philadelphia**.

noun clause A clause that, like a noun, serves as a subject, object, or complement. See **clause, nominal**.

The detective discovered **that the murderer was a relatively tall person**. (subordinate clause as direct object)
What remained after the tornado interested no one. (relative clause as subject)

noun phrase A phrase that, like a noun, serves as a subject, object, or complement. See **phrase, nominal**.

Spending two weeks on duty in the Army Reserve (*gerund phrase as subject*) was not my idea of a vacation.

number The forms taken by nouns, pronouns, and verbs to indicate singular or plural meaning: **a record, several records; a man, several men; she swims, they swim; he is, they are**.

object A word or group of words naming what is affected by a verb, infinitive, or participle. See **direct object** and **indirect object**.

OBJECT OF VERB:	Contractors built **these houses**.
OBJECT OF INFINITIVE:	Allison wants to build **a house**.
OBJECT OF PARTICIPLE:	I had never heard of one person building **a house**.

A word or word group directly following a preposition is called an *object of a preposition:*

We swam for **a while**.
The Children hid in **the closet**.

participle A word made from a verb, usually by adding **-ing, -d,** or **-ed** to the form which the verb takes in the infinitive. Irregular verbs use inflections other than **-d** or **-ed**. Participles may serve as adjectives, adverbs, and, with helping verbs, as part of a predicate. A **participial phrase** serves as a modifier and is composed of a participle plus its own objects and modifiers: The joggers returned, **dripping** (participle) **sweat** (object) **on the floor** (modifier).

PRESENT PARTICIPLE: **acting, living, thinking, running**.
PAST PARTICIPLE: **acted, lived, thought, run**.
PERFECT PARTICIPLE: **having acted, having lived, having thought, having run** (or **having been acted**, etc.).
PRESENT PARTICIPLE AS ADVERB: The runner slept, **dreaming** of success in the next day's race.
PAST PARTICIPLE AS ADJECTIVE: The night guard found three **unlocked** doors.
PARTICIPLES AS PART OF PREDICATE: Mike is **running** in the race.

passive voice See **voice**.

person The forms taken by pronouns and verbs to indicate someone speaking, someone spoken to, or someone or something spoken about.

	Singular	Plural
FIRST PERSON	**I am** ready.	**We are** ready.
SECOND PERSON	**You are** ready.	**You are** ready.
THIRD PERSON	**She, he, it** is ready.	**They are** ready.

phrase A group of words that serves as a unit, such as an object, a complement, or a modifier. A phrase lacks a subject, predicate, or both. See **absolute phrase, adjective phrase, noun phrase, gerund, infinitive, participle, preposition**.

predicate The verb, its auxiliaries and modifiers, plus any objects or complements.
The wind and hail **had completely destroyed our garden.**

predicate adjective See **complement**.

predicate nominative Also called the *predicate noun*. See **complement**.

preposition A word that indicates a relationship between a following noun, noun phrase, or pronoun (called the *object of the preposition*) and another part of the sentence. Prepositions include **at, behind, for, in, over, to, upon, with,** etc.

The preposition and its object constitute a *prepositional phrase*. Prepositional phrases can serve as adjectives, adverbs, and nouns.

The fish **in this pond** (*adjective*) are not big enough to eat.
The moon shone **upon the fields** (*adverb*).
Toward the east (*noun*) was not the way we should have gone.

principal parts A verb's four basic forms: infinitive, present participle, past, past participle.

Infinitive	Present Participle	Past	Past Participle
(to) spill	spilling	spilled	spilled
(to) make	making	made	made
(to) see	seeing	saw	seen

pronoun A word that takes the place of a noun or noun phrase (the pronoun's antecedent). Pronouns are commonly classified in the following eight categories:
DEMONSTRATIVE: that, these
INDEFINITE: anybody, everyone
INTENSIVE: himself, yourself
INTERROGATIVE: what, which
PERSONAL: I, they
RECIPROCAL: each, other
REFLEXIVE: I myself, you yourself
RELATIVE: who, which
See **antecedent**.

proper noun See **noun**.

regular verb See **verb**.

relative clause A clause that has a relative pronoun as its subject. Relative clauses are a type of subordinate clause, and they usually serve as adjectives.

Houston is a city **that has no zoning codes**.

restrictive modifier A word, phrase, or clause that limits the identity or meaning of what it modifies. Restrictive modifiers are not set off by commas. (Compare to **nonrestrictive modifier**.)

A committee member **who has no talent for drawing** was given the task of designing the decorations.

sentence modifier A word or phrase that modifies the entire sentence.

Frankly, I am bored.

See **absolute phrase.**

simple sentence A sentence composed of one clause.

We should make some plans.
The flock of geese returned.

subject The noun or nominal about which the predicate makes a statement.

Horses canter.
The snow turned my car into a white hill.

The *simple subject* is the subject without its modifiers. The *complete subject* is the subject plus its modifiers.

The old broken broom leaning against the door is still useful. (**Broom** is the simple subject. **The old broken broom leaning against the door** is the complete subject.)

subordinate clause A clause that serves as an adjective, adverb, or noun. A clause is subordinated by an introductory subordinating conjunction.

Shimmering under the sun were a dozen large puddles **that the storm had left behind**. (adjective clause)
If erosion continues at this rate, nothing will grow in this ground three years from now. (adverb clause)
The twins did not believe **that they would ever live apart from each other**. (noun clause)

subordinating conjunction A conjunction that introduces a subordinate clause. Some subordinating conjunctions are **after, because, if, once, while**.

superlative degree See **adjective**.

tense The form of a verb that indicates the time of the verb's action or condition.

PRESENT	I think	PERFECT	I have thought
PAST	I thought	PAST PERFECT	I had thought
FUTURE	I will think	FUTURE PERFECT	I will have thought

transitive verb See **verb**.

verb A word or group of words indicating an action or condition. A *transitive verb* takes a direct object: Bees **spread** (verb) **pollen** (direct object). A *linking verb* connects a subject to a complement: He **became** (linking verb) **a star** (complement). An *intransitive verb* does not take an object or a complement: The professor **lectured** (intransitive verb). *Regular verbs* add **-d** or **-ed** to the infinitive form to make the past tense and the past participle. *Irregular verbs* form the past tense, the past participle, or both, in other ways.

	Present	Past	Past Participle
REGULAR VERBS	happen	happened	happened
	rule	ruled	ruled
	respond	responded	responded
IRREGULAR VERBS	fight	fought	fought
	make	made	made
	is	was	been

verb phrase A verb plus at least one helping verb.

The campers **will eat** three hearty meals each day.
We **had been accustomed** to a raucous environment.

Some grammarians use *verb phrase* to mean the same as *predicate*.

verbal A form of a verb used as a noun, adjective, or adverb. Gerunds, infinitives, and participles are verbals.

Swimming (*gerund*) gives me an appetite.
To hope (*infinitive*) sometimes requires courage.

voice The function of a transitive verb that indicates whether the subject of the verb acts or is acted upon.

ACTIVE VOICE: As usual, Al caught only tiny fish.
PASSIVE VOICE: As usual, only tiny fish were caught by Al.

Index

1 2 3 4 5 6 7 8 9 0